Hertfordshire
COUNTY COUNCIL
Community Information

1 3 FEB 2004
07/12

or
st
on
on
ch
ng
d.

Please renew/return this item by the last date shown.

So that your telephone call is charged at local rate, please call the numbers as set out below:

	From Area codes 01923 or 0208:	From the rest of Herts:
Renewals:	01923 471373	01438 737373
Enquiries:	01923 471333	01438 737333
Minicom:	01923 471599	01438 737599

L32

J. H. B. Peel

AN ENGLISHMAN'S HOME

Illustrated by
RONALD MADDOX

David & Charles
Newton Abbot   London   North Pomfret (Vt)   Vancouver

Library of Congress Catalog Card Number 78–52159

British Library Cataloguing in Publication Data
Peel, John Hugh Brignal
   An Englishman's home.
   1. England—Social life and customs
   I. Title
   942   DA110
   ISBN 0–7153–7637–3

First published by Cassell & Company Ltd 1972
First published by David & Charles Ltd 1978

© J. H. B. Peel 1972
Illustrations © Ronald Maddox 1972

The publishers are grateful to Mrs George Bambridge,
Macmillan & Co (London) and the Macmillan Co. of
Canada, for permission to quote extracts from *Something of
Myself* and *Puck of Pook's Hill* by Rudyard Kipling

Printed in Great Britain by
Redwood Burn Limited, Trowbridge & Esher
for David & Charles (Publishers) Limited
Brunel House Newton Abbot Devon

Published in the United States of America
by David & Charles Inc
North Pomfret Vermont 05053 USA

Published in Canada
by Douglas David & Charles Limited
1875 Welch Street North Vancouver BC

Contents

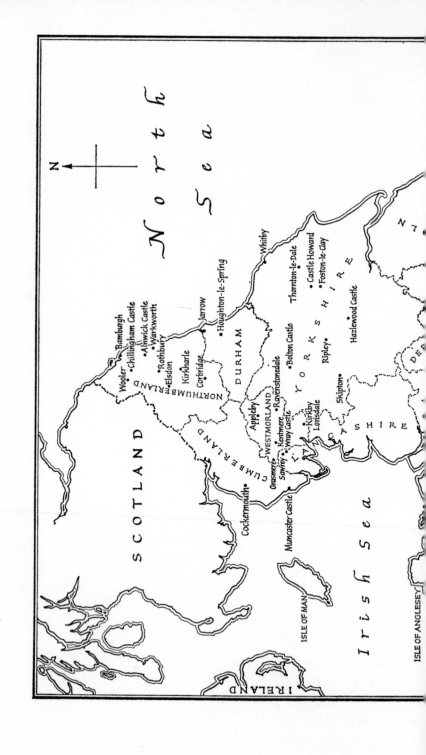

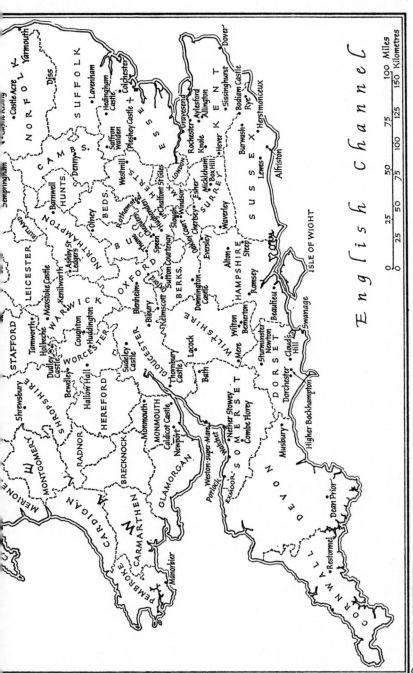

English Channel

NORFOL K · Yarmouth
· Castle Acre
· Diss
SUFFOLK
· Lavenham
· Hedingham Castle
· Saffron Walden · Colchester
· Pleshey Castle +
ESSEX

CAMBS.
· Denny
HUNTS.
· Barnwell
· Olney
BEDS.
· Westmill
HERTS.
· Rothamsted
BUCKS.
· Hampstead
LONDON · Gravesend
· Chalfont St Giles · Rochester
· Slough · Knole KENT · Dover
· Eton · Windsor · Hever · Aylesford · Allington
· Sutton Courtenay
OXFORD · Thame
· Oldon Court · Esher · Mickleham · Sissinghurst
· Chertsey · Box Hill · Bodiam Castle
· Eversley SURREY · Burwash · Rye
· Waverley · Hurstmonceux
· Alton SUSSEX · Lewes
· Romsey · Steep · Alfriston
HAMPSHIRE

LEICESTER
RUTLAND
· Ashby St Legers
NORTHAMPTON

STAFFORD
· Tamworth · Maxstoke Castle
· Holbeche · Kenilworth
WARWICK
· Dudley Castle · Coughton
· Bewdley · Huddington
WORCESTER
· Hallow Hall
SHROPSHIRE
· Shrewsbury

MONTGOMERY
MERIONETH
RADNOR
CARDIGAN
HEREFORD
· Monmouth
MONMOUTH
· Caldicot Castle
· Newport
GLAMORGAN
BRECKNOCK
CARMARTHEN
PEMBROKE
· Manorbier

· Sudeley Castle
GLOUCESTER
· Thornbury Castle
· Bath
· Blenheim · Bibury
· Kelmscott
· Lacock
BERKS.
· Speen
· Donnington Castle
WILTSHIRE
· Wilton · Bonterton
· Mere
· Sturminster Newton · Claud's Hill
DORSET
· Beaulieu
ISLE OF WIGHT
· Swanage

· Weston-super-Mare
· Porlock · Watchet
EXMOOR
SOMERSET
· Nether Stowey
· Combe Florey
· Musbury · Dorchester
· Higher Bockhampton
DEVON
CORNWALL
· Restormel · Dean Prior

0   25   50   75   100 Miles
0   25   50   75   100   125   150 Kilometres

© CASSELL & CO. LTD. 1972

A comfortable house is a great source of happiness. It ranks immediately after health and a good conscience.

REV. SYDNEY SMITH

Stanway / Manor House / Gateway

---

1 At Home

AN Englishman's home, it is said, is his castle; and the *Oxford
English Dictionary* confirms the saying: 'Home ... a place
where one finds rest, refuge.' Observe the defensive tone of
that definition, which clashes with the popular idea of castles.
But not every castle was rampant. Some lay couchant, like Bodiam
Castle, which was built to defend the upper reaches of the River
Rother in Sussex, presumably against invasion by the French. No
warlike knights ever rode from Bodiam, ravaging the land. No
warlike knights attacked Bodiam. The castle was a deterrent that
became a home. Those other and smaller castles—the peel towers
of the Border country—were even less aggressive. Indeed, they were
no more than stone houses, fortified against the marauding Scots.
Nevertheless, life and liberty were held more cheaply then than
they are now, so that home was often the place to which a man
retreated *pour mieux sauter*, the better to advance therefrom.
Even during the reign of Henry VII it was not unusual for a
great landowner to seek royal licence to fortify his home against

a peasants' revolt, or a covetous neighbour, or a foreign invasion, or the king himself (who therefore scrutinized every applicant). Something of that thrust-and-parry outlived the Middle Ages. A notable example is Oakley Court, a Victorian mansion beside the Thames near Windsor, so towered and turreted that its retainers —with the butler as sergeant-major—could have poured much boiling lead and many flaming arrows onto the head of any debt collector or other unwelcome caller.

Great landowners, however, were always a minority. To most people the word 'home' is best defined by another phrase from the dictionary: 'one's own house . . . a place in which one's affections centre.' Such affection must surely be as old as man himself. Dimly in their brief and brutish lives the prehistoric cave-dwellers felt more secure—more, as we say, at home—in their own accustomed cavern. The descendants of those cavemen—the nomadic food hunters—felt a similar fondness for the hides and pots that accompanied their travels and were visible signs of those spiritual intimations which the Romans personified as Lares and Penates, the household gods. Rome, indeed, gave classic utterance to sentiments which some people still express via a simple song, *Home, Sweet Home.* When Cicero's enemies destroyed his house, and tried to prevent him from rebuilding it, he appealed to the Roman people: 'Is there,' he cried, 'anything more hallowed, is there anything more closely hedged about with sanctity, than the home of each individual citizen?'

An Englishman's home resembles his climate; though it changes frequently, it maintains an immemorial constancy. Few homes a thousand years ago possessed a chimneypot, yet all burned a fire; few contained a transparent windowpane, yet all had windows; few received a written message, yet all shared the local gossip; few were owned by their occupants, yet all seemed dear because familiar. Home, then, is a house. Yet it is both more and less than a house; less, because it includes the contents of that house (a hearth, a chair, a bed); more, because it includes an adjunct of that house (a lawn, a lane, a view). Truly there is nothing more personal than a man's relationship with his home and his family and his friends; his garden, garage, fireside. And all those things are enhanced by being arrayed against a neighbourly background. To people who live in an industrial area or among the anonymity of a housing estate, the background may extend no farther than the nearest shop; but to countryfolk the background will seem more distant and at the same time more friendly.

Stone, mud, timber, thatch: those were the building materials when William won the battle of Hastings. To us they appear crude and limited; yet they would have seemed luxurious to the Celts who built their shacks on stakes of timber and clay beside a lake near Glastonbury in Somerset. And even those damp 'flats' would have astonished the food hunters who travelled so light that their home was often no better than a rook's, a hotch-potch of boughs with a leafy roof. Who, one wonders, invented the rafter whereon a sloping thatch was laid? Who invented the saw-pit wherein were sliced the trees which formed the framework of larger and warmer houses? When did the Englishman first cushion his buttocks against the bare boards of a chair? Did the wife of a Tudor merchant possess a looking-glass? Who devised our first clocks? When and why did the adze give way to the plane? Which poet described his home as 'an honest woman'? Which architect occupied the same house for sixty years? Which Victorian peer employed artillery to defend his home against the police? Has an Englishman's home become more, or less, vulnerable to unwelcome intruders? Those questions are the cruck or framework of this book.

Like wine, the old homes of England have improved with age. Their rafters, once brown, are ebony; their stonework has gathered the sun's gold; their bricks glow with the tan of many weathers. In a word, they are antiques. Yet some men saw them when they were modern. John Leland, for example, visited Bewdley in Worcestershire, which had lately been rebuilt, and was literally a new town, situated (he reported) 'on the side of a hill, so comely that a man cannot wish to see a town better. It ariseth from the Severne bank upon the hill by west, so that a man standing trans-pontem by east may discern almost every house, and att rising of the sunne the whole town glittereth, being all of new building, as it were of gold.' And yet, after all, an Englishman's home is not primarily a matter of aesthetics. If he is lucky enough to own a Georgian manor house, well and good; he will smile whenever he walks up the path or leans on his spade. But the majority of

homes were not built as show pieces. They were designed rather
to be lived in than looked at. It is therefore a tribute both to the
builders and to our own taste that many of those houses have
grown old with a gracefulness which pleases us. 'Be it never so
humble' ... the song was wise. Great beauty is not a condition of
true love. If it were, few of us could love the house we live in.
Beauty, like colour, lies partly in the eye of the beholder.

In his essay on books, Charles Lamb cited what he called *biblia
abiblia* or 'books that are not books', by which he meant 'Court
Calendars, Directories, Pocket Books, Scientific Treatises, Alma-
nacks, Statutes at Large ...'. Likewise we may dismiss homes that
are not homes, by which we mean caravans, barges, houseboats,
and those skyscraping human-hutches whose conspicuous unflat-
ness we describe as flats. Many people occupy such places, and
some people feel fond of them; but the places themselves lack
roots in the soil. They are not truly a home. They are not even a
house. They are merely premises.

Home, then, is a house and the contents thereof and the fields
and streets thereabouts. Some homes are mansions; others are
cottages; each is a biography of the people who dwelt there, and a
footnote to the story of England. But this book is neither an essay
in history nor a life story of people nor a treatise on architecture.
It is a tapestry of all those things, a picture of the Englishman
and his home during the past thousand years; homes stately,
homes humble; homes that are woven into the fabric of famous
lives; homes whose fame spread no wider than a brief obituary in
the parish magazine; all sharing that common factor which Emily
Brontë found at a moorland parsonage.

Brushwood Hall / nr. Henley-in Arden, Warwickshire

2 The Manor

FLANKED by stone cottages, the village street encircles a green and a pond with some ducks on it. Three shops supply many local needs. The inn stands a little apart, at a point where the circular lane unloops itself *en route* for the next village. Beyond the inn, on a knoll, is the church; and behind the church is the rectory, seven of whose twelve rooms are nowadays unfurnished and likely to remain so, at any rate during the tenure of the present incumbent, who is an elderly bachelor. If you follow the lane for another quarter-mile you reach a lodge beside a white gate which opens to a gravel drive between grass verges topped by rhododendrons. You pass a white-fenced paddock on your left, grazed by several hunters. Beyond the paddock, in a hollow, you sight the lichened roof of Home Farm. Then the drive bisects itself left and right around a lawn in front of the manor house.

Nobody knows for whom the house was built, for the deeds were lost when a party of Cromwellians looted the cellars, consumed the wine, and started a fire which destroyed the muniments chest in the library. However, there is evidence that the house belonged to the younger son of an Elizabethan yeoman who, having married a rich mercer's daughter, sent one of his boys to the Inner Temple, and the other into the Navy. The latter served with such distinction against the Dutch that his own son, likewise a sailor, attracted the notice of the Duke of York, under whose patronage he was knighted and then appointed as Gentleman to some privy part of the royal household. Neither before nor since was any member of the family so exalted; a fact which his descendant, the present squire, accepts with thankful resignation, being content to maintain the amphibious tradition of farming and navigation.

About the year 1788 the new squire, who was then twenty-two years old, decided that he would live like a lord, or, more precisely, like the sort of lord who stakes his birthright on a game of cards. The estate was actually sold to a creditor, but he never took possession, because the rake's uncle—a member of the East India Company—got wind of the sale, and promptly paid the young fool's gambling debt. The fool himself grew more stupid with age, and would have lost the estate for a second time, had it not been rescued by his younger brother, a Rear-Admiral, who had lately captured part of a French convoy, for which he received £10,000 in prize money. The lords of this manor have never been wealthy. Until the 1840s they lived solely on the produce and rents from their estate. Thereafter they gained a few extra thousands by investing in railway stock, but taxation long ago robbed them of anything more than a modest solvency. The present squire, a retired Commander R.N., maintains the tradition of service which his forebears practised as naval officers, Justices of the Peace, parliamentary private secretaries (once, an Under-Secretary of State) chairmen of hospital and school boards, and lords of a manor.

The squire's wife combines the best attributes of Martha and Mary. On Mondays, for example, she stoops elbow-deep over a washing machine. On Tuesdays she retires to her studio (formerly the coach-house) where she paints landscapes. Wednesdays are passed in the hunting field. Thursdays seem busiest of all, for then she delivers 'meals-on-wheels', spends an hour in the old people's ward, another in the children's ward, and the entire evening with her arrears of work as chairman of the parish council. Fridays are 'free', which means that she can do whatever she likes, which means that she either exercises the horses or polishes the oak floors, rafters, wainscotting, staircase, and furniture. Saturdays she calls her 'bits-and-pieces', when she tries to finish *War and Peace*, or to start *The Seven Pillars of Wisdom*, or to mend the household linen, or to 'baby-sit' for a visiting daughter, or to update the list of Christmas cards, birthdays, charities, household accounts, and so forth. On Sundays she attends Matins and Evensong, pausing *en route* to inspect the base of the tower (which is causing anxiety), the floor of the belfry (in similar condition), and the vestry curtains (the rector, a pipe-smoker, has a habit of setting them on fire). For the rest, she organizes fêtes, concerts, outings; she helps in the garden; she tends a house and family; and, as she once remarked to the postman, she occasionally has time to say 'Good morning' to her husband.

The manor house itself is relatively small because the Tudor yeoman felt no urge to adopt excessive airs and graces. Instead of building a fashionable E-shaped mansion, he bespoke what we would now call a comfortable farmhouse with spacious hall, floored and panelled in oak; an impressive staircase; and two upper storeys, the second of which contained attic bedrooms for the servants. Much of the furniture is antique, which leads some visitors to suppose that it must be valuable. They are therefore amazed when they learn that the Jacobean linen chest would fetch about £75. Like the 'Chippendale' chairs and the Regency dining table, the chest was made by a village carpenter for squires whose income it suited. In 1880 a water closet was installed, but the bathroom waited until 1906, and was not tiled until 1950. In 1931 a carillon of bells still hung above the kitchen door; but as the domestic staff then consisted of one old sailor and two young girls, the bells were dismantled and preserved as curios in the breakfast room, which served as a day nursery.

The squire has three married daughters and a son who is serving as midshipman. Grandchildren and their parents frequently visit the house. The permanent residents are the squire, his wife, the domestic staff (one widow), a retired petty officer who occupies the lodge, and an elderly kinswoman whom the villagers call 'The Miss'. Perhaps because the family could, if they wished, know everyone, their visiting list is amiably eclectic. They like the Earl, and they maintain what the midshipman calls 'a standing date' with the doctor and the schoolmistress in the next village. They do not like the colonel, nor the vet, nor the man who lately bought old Sir Timothy's place, and has already burdened it with two swimming pools and a golf course. Once every year a grandiloquent woman comes down from London, to arrange and cook for a large dinner party, thereby enabling the manor to feed many birds with one spree. When smaller dinner parties are held, a signal is sent to the lodge, and the petty officer comes alongside to impersonate a butler and to finish the washing up. Breakfast is often taken in the kitchen, except by 'The Miss', who carries her tray into the garden. Gossip says that she breakfasts *al fresco* whatever the weather, and was once seen in gumboots and oilskin, eating a boiled egg; and then for some moments was not seen at all, an avalanche of snow having slipped from the roof. The same source of information states that 'The Miss' was once engaged to a man who died before the wedding. When pressed to identify him, villagers box the compass by naming an Austrian archduke, a Scottish peer, and the eldest son of the Taj Mahal. On the whole, however, they approve 'The Miss': 'She's game, though. I'll say that for her. Reckon th'old gal would hunt eight days a week if she could.'

Despite its modest role in history, the manor does sometimes receive brief mention from guidebooks, chiefly because three of the kitchen rafters bear a joiner's mark that has been found on timbers which were taken from a Jacobean warship. Most of the guidebooks assume either that the house supplied the ship or that the ship supplied the house. But the books are mistaken. What happened was this: having helped to enlarge the kitchen, the village carpenter served with the squire in the Royal Navy, where he helped to repair the ship. There are, of course, larger estates and older lineages than those of our squire. An outstanding example in 1972 was Lieutenant-Colonel W. G. Luttrell of East Quantoxhead in Somerset; a descendant, through the female line, of the Luttrell to whom that manor was given by William the Conqueror, more than 900 years ago. Nevertheless, the Commander and his manor typify many others which once led this kingdom through thick and thin, and fair and foul.

The word 'manor' comes from the Latin *maneo*, meaning 'I remain' or 'I dwell'. It expresses the tempo of an age when roads were tracks, and all journeys so hazardous that travellers invoked a safe-conduct from their patron, Saint Christopher. The medieval manor was more than a homestead; it was a community of peasants and their fields, their livestock, their ploughs, mills, fisheries. It was, in short, the hub of the feudal system. Some knowledge of that system is a condition of understanding not only an Englishman's home but also his way of life, whether he were a swineherd or the king himself. For the sake of convenience, historians agree that the Middle Ages ended when Henry VII was crowned in 1485. The feudal system, however, outlived the Tudors. Indeed, it remains the basis of our unwritten Constitution. Named after the Old French *fieu* or wealth, feudalism was already established when William of Normandy conquered England in 1066, for it had taken shape during the so-called Dark Ages, when Rome withdrew from Britain, leaving the natives to their tribal wars and the invasions of pirates who brought with them a tradition which Tacitus recorded: 'it is a lifelong infamy and disgrace to survive the chief and run away from battle. To defend him, to protect him, even to ascribe to him their own exploits, is the essence of their sworn allegiance. The chief fights for victory, the followers for their chief.' During that traumatic birth of the English people, the peasants adhered to any lord who, by offering security, enabled them to earn their daily bread (the word 'lord' is an abbreviation of the Anglo-Saxon *hlaford*, meaning one who provides *hlaf* or a loaf of bread). The Normans imposed a new coherence on that pattern of life, though the pattern itself became a distribution of manorial land rather than a system of central government. In practice it was as simple as in theory. Thus, all land belonged to the king, who, in return for general allegiance and particular services, granted estates to his nobles. Byron equated William with 'Billy', and then made 'manor' to rhyme with 'banner':

> ... Eight and forty manors
> Were their reward for following Billy's banners.

William the Conqueror, however, was careful not to grant large areas *en bloc* to any one vassal, lest a subject became more power-

B

ful than the Sovereign. Large areas were indeed bestowed, but each holding was relatively small and at a distance from the rest. Only in a few regions, and only for military reasons, did William allow any subject to govern a quasi-kingdom of his own, as in the Marcher Country (a defence against the Welsh) and in the County Palatine of Durham (a defence against the Scots). In order to simplify the administration of his demesne, a great nobleman or tenant-in-chief would grant land to lesser vassals, from whom he received something of the service and allegiance which he himself owed directly to the king. By the end of the Middle Ages many of those sub-tenants had become the Tudor squirarchy.

A manor, then, was an estate. The first known use of the word to connote a single house occurred in 1426, as 'manor-place'. The name 'manor-house' did not appear until 1576. Insofar as the Middle Ages spanned five centuries, it is misleading to speak of a 'typical' medieval manor house, because the houses varied with the importance of their lord, the nature of their building materials, and the fashions of their time. The earliest manor house was basically a hall or communal living quarter, topped by a single storey which contained sleeping accommodation for the lord's family and a storehouse for his valuables. The retainers slept in the hall, on straw or pallets. Very likely the house was made of timber. England's first stone quarries were discovered near Bath, during the eighth century, by Saint Aldhelm, who imported Byzantine masons to work them. Slowly the foreign skill spread along the limestone belt that runs from the Cotswolds via Northamptonshire to Yorkshire, but timber ruled the domestic roost throughout the Middle Ages.

Nearly every building was designed by the men who made it; that is, by carpenters (if it were chiefly of wood) or by masons (if it were chiefly of stone). The earliest and simplest manor houses were mere shelters from the climate. The floor was bare earth, strewn with reeds or straw; the hearth was a fire in the middle of the hall; the chimney, a hole in the roof. Early medieval windows —aptly called 'wind-eyes'—were small (as a defence against arrows) and also draughty (because they lacked panes). Closing the window meant fastening the timber shutters. Such cold comfort explains why the medieval poets were oppressed by the prospect of winter:

> This winter's weather it waxeth cold,
> And frost it freezeth every hill,
> And Boreas blows his blast so bold
> That all our cattle are like to spill.

The lord of a medieval manor was a little king, and some of his servants were slaves (*servi*). Even the free men (churls) were in effect *glebae adscriptus* or bound to the manor, holding their land from the lord, as he held his from a tenant-in-chief, and the tenant-in-chief from the king. The lord or his reeve presided at the manorial court, where the rough-and-ready justice of Anglo-Saxon England was still practised, as in trial by combat or by fire. The baron and the customary courts heard civil disputes; the court leet dealt with minor crimes. Many years elapsed before the kings of England were able to despatch itinerant judges who imposed a less local rule of law. In due course the manorial assemblies were abolished, and the lords became Justices of the Peace. Throughout the Middle Ages all such men despised trade, and loved nothing better than to fight, joust, or hunt. But that does not mean they were a pack of boors. On the contrary, many were true gentle men, whose epitaph was written by Chaucer:

> A Knight there was, and that a worthy man,
> That fro the tyme that he first bigan
> To ryden out, he loved chivalrye,
> Trouthe and honour, fredom and courteisye. . . .
> He was a verray, parfit gentil knight.

In another book, *A Treatise on the Astrolabe*, Chaucer gave a more direct expression to the tenderness of home life, by dedicating the treatise to his young son, Lewis: 'Litel Lowis, my sone, I have perceived wel by certeyne evidences thyn abilitie to lerne sciencez touchinge noumbres and proporciouns....' That such tenderness and erudition could exist amid the brutality of the Middle Ages, was due largely to the influence of the Church; a fact which Chaucer acknowledged when he hoped that God and the Virgin Mary would allow his son to profit from the treatise: 'if God wol vouche-sauf and his modur the mayde....'

In the medieval world a man's life was held cheap. Weapons were nine-tenths of local law, and the manor house became a defended home. An outstanding example of such a place can be seen at Little Wenham Hall in Suffolk, which was built *c.* 1270 for Sir John de Vallibus and his successor, Petronilla of Nerford. This is the earliest known specimen of a brick manor house; flint having been used only in the base of the walls. The typical great hall led into a rib-vaulted chapel; the upper storey provided the lord's apartments; the walls were castellated against attack. The village church contains a sixteenth-century brass to a descendant of Sir Thomas Brews, lord of the manor of Topcroft in Norfolk, whose daughter, Margery, left a reminder that life at the medieval manor shared many of the problems of life at the modern manor. On or about Saint Valentine's Day, in the year 1477, Margery Brews wrote a letter to the man she wished to marry, John, son of Sir John Paston, lord of several Norfolk manors. Having greeted her lover with the beautiful courtesy of the period, Margery explains that her father refuses to increase the amount of her dowry, despite pleas by his wife. But, she adds, money is not all. If John Paston possessed only half of his present income, she would still love him. She ends by entreating him either to destroy her letter or to keep it to himself. Let us hear the voice of a medieval daughter of the manor, addressing the son of another: 'Right reverend and worshipful and my right well-beloved Valentine, I recommend me unto you full heartily, desiring to hear of your welfare, which I beseech Almighty God long for to preserve unto his pleasure and your heart's desire. And if it please you to hear of my welfare, I am not in good heal of body nor of heart, nor shall be till I hear from you. . . . And my lady my mother hath laboured the matter to my father full diligently, but she can no more get than ye know of, for which God knoweth I am full sorry. But if that ye love me, as I trust verily that ye do, ye will not leave me therefore; for if that ye had not half the livelode that ye have . . . I would not forsake you. . . . No more to you at this time, but the Holy Trinity have you in keeping. And I beseech you that this bill be not seen of none earthly save only yourself. And this letter was indite at Topcroft with full heavy heart, By your own M.B.' And what of the young man? He soon afterwards wrote to his mother, praising the mother whom he hoped to adopt by marriage: 'for I trow there is not a kinder woman than I shall have to my mother-in-law if the matter take....' The matter did take, chiefly because Lady Brews was coaxing as well as kind. So, in the end, Sir Thomas and the Pastons struck a bargain whereby Margery Brews married John Paston.

Although Thomas Brews and John Paston senior were lords of the manor, neither was a peer of the realm, for the lordship of a manor conferred no formal title, being simply a blend of privilege and obligation. As for Margery and her husband, they wore the same sort of clothes, ate the same sort of food, and played the same sort of games as their parents had done, and as their children would continue to do. Time had not yet become the slave of its own changeful momentum. A twelfth-century knight would soon have felt at ease in the home of a fourteenth-century knight. True, he would notice some alterations in the language, several new-fangled fashions, a higher standard of archery; but the food and the furniture and the routine would have altered scarcely at all. Assailed by the speed of change, the twentieth century needs to be reminded that domesticity is not a kaleidoscope of evanescent labour-saving. The love and the hate abide; the hope, the anxiety, the struggle. Here, for example, is a fifteenth-century widow, Agnes Paston, writing to her youngest son, a law student in London: 'To mine well beloved son, I greet you well, and advise you to think once of each day of your father's counsel to lern the law, for he said many times that whosoever should dwell at Paston should have need to con defend himself.' The student is then told to consult with his brother about 'the decorations': 'Weeteth of your brother John how many joists will serve the parlour and the chapel at Paston, and what length they must be and what brede and thickness ... for your father's will was, as I ween verily, that they should be 9 inches one way and 7 another way.' The mother ends her letter as some mothers now end theirs, even with the same apparent lack of leisure: 'God make you a right good man, and send God's blessing and mine. Written in haste at Norwich the Thursday after Candlemas Day....' At about the same time 'brother John' received a letter from his wife, reminding him that her father had bespoke a length of cloth 'to make a gown for me; and he told my mother and me, when he was come home, that he charged you to buy it. ... I pray you, if it be not bought that ye will vouchsafe to buy it and send it home as soon as ye may; for I have no gown to wear this winter but my black and green, and that is so cumbrous that I am weary to wear it.' A quarter of a century later, brother John's unruly heir begged his father's forgiveness: 'Right worshipful sir, in the most lowly wise I commend me to your good fatherhood, beseeching you of your blessing. Mote it please your fatherhood to remember and consider the pain and heaviness it hath been to me sin your departing out of this country, here abiding till the time it please you to show me grace, and till the time that by report my demeaning be to your pleasing. . . . Almighty God have you in keeping. Written the 5 day of March. By your older son, John Paston.'

Housekeeping was easier then than it is now; partly because shops and needs were simpler, and partly because the lady of the manor shopped as a rule by proxy. Here is Dame Paston's bailiff, exhorting her to do the Christmas shopping in a buyer's market: 'Mistress, it were good to remember your stuff of herring now this fishing time. I have got me a friend at Lowestoft to help buy me seven or eight barrel and they shall cost not more than 6s. 8d. a barrel. You shall do more now (in autumn) with 40s. than you shall do at Christmas with 66s. 8d.' The Pastons illustrate the flexibility of English society, even during the Middle Ages. They first appear as plain Norfolk farmers. Within a few generations they have become knights, lords of manors, judges. In 1459 they increase their estates by inheriting a moated manor house at Caistor, which Sir John Falstof had fortified. They end as Earls of Yarmouth. The famous *Paston Letters*, covering the period between 1422 and 1509, are a unique illumination of life at the medieval manor house. The second Earl of Yarmouth sold the letters to an antiquary, who sold them to a chemist at Diss, who sold them to an antiquary at Dereham, who printed a selection of them in 1787. The complete letters—about one thousand—were first published during the 1870s. They prove that Dame Margaret Paston was justified in advising her son 'to lern the law'. Sometimes, however, the law was powerless to redress a grievance, for the Pastons were only one among many families whose manor needed to be held by force. In the Norfolk hamlet of Gresham you can trace the foundations of a manor house which Chaucer's son sold to William Paston. When Dame Margaret had charge of

it, Gresham was coveted by a neighbour, Lord Moleyns, who became so aggressive that the Dame despatched an urgent message
to her husband in London: 'Right worshipful husband, I commend me to you, and pray you to get some crossbows....' Lord
Moleyns, however, was as ruthless as Ahab when he coveted
Naboth's vineyard, for while Dame Margaret was away he unlaw-
fully occupied the manor, filling it with his retainers, led by a
servant named Partridge. Dame Margaret continues the story:
'Partridge and his fellowship ... have made great ordinance
within the house, as it is told to me. They have made bars to bar
the doors cross-ways, and they han made wickets on every quarter
of the house to shoot out at, both with bows and with hand-
guns....' Nor were ignoble noblemen the only threat to a manor
house. Sir John Froissart was amazed by the stubborn independence of the English peasantry: 'No man,' he warned, 'may mock
them; the lord who governs them rises and lays down to rest in sore
peril of his life.... There is no people under the sun so perilous
in the matter of its common folk as they are in England.' Many a
mob made many a manor mend its ways.

The fate of Gresham was common throughout the Middle
Ages, which is why many lords fortified their home. The northern
counties of Westmorland, Cumberland and Northumberland
devised their own type of stronghold, the peel tower (Latin *palus*
or palisade of stakes). Timber, however, was no defence against
marauding Scottish bandits; therefore the English Borderers
built stone towers, into which the entire household retreated,
with some of its livestock. I have been a guest in one of those
manor houses, Kentmere Hall, at the foot of the mountains near
Staveley in Westmorland. The main body of the Hall is a fifteenth-century stone house, joined to a fourteenth-century peel
tower. Kentmere Hall was the birthplace of Bernard Gilpin,
whom the countrypeople still remember as 'The Apostle of the
North'. Born in 1517, Gilpin graduated at Oxford and then continued his studies on the Continent. He became Archdeacon of
Durham, and could have become Bishop of Carlisle, but preferred to work as parish priest at Houghton-le-Spring in County
Durham, whence he carried the Gospel into Tynedale and Tees-
dale, those wild haunts of brigands, wherein, said Gilpin, 'the
word of God was never heard to be preached'.

Historians have coined the phrase 'bastard feudalism' to describe the turbulence of the late fifteenth century, when the use of
artillery, and the decline of feudal obligations, began to curb the
power of the nobility in general, but not of some nobles in particular. Whenever a king was strong, he clipped the peers' claws;
whenever he was weak, the peers defied him; and all the while,
the Pastons of England continued to move from the yeomanry to
the gentry, from the farm to the manor house. It is a mistake
indeed to suppose that their houses were given a moat solely as an
ornament. Shakespeare likened England to a precious stone, set
in the English Channel,

> Which serves it in the office of a wall,
> Or as a moat defensive to a house. . . .

The point was underlined when Dame Paston described a fierce
encounter with Lord Moleyns, who had attacked Gresham manor
while she was staying there: 'the said Lord sent to the mansion a
riotous people, to the number of a thousand persons . . . arrayed
in manner of war with cuirasses, coats of mail, steel helmets, bows
and arrows, large shields, guns, pans with fire, long cromes to
draw down houses, ladders and picks with which they mined
down the walls, and long trees, with which they broke up gates
and doors.' Although she had only a dozen servants Dame Paston
defied the thousand invaders. When at last they forced their way
into the house, she refused to leave, and had to be carried out.

What has happened to those medieval manors? Some have disappeared without trace; others have been incorporated into
newer homes; a few survive and still are manor houses. It is fasci-
nating to trace the biography of an ancient manor and of the
families who owned it. Consider the manor of Scrivelsby near
Horncastle in Lincolnshire, which was granted by William of
Normandy to Roger de Marmion, descendant of the hereditary
champions to the Norman dukes. The king further honoured de
Marmion by appointing him to a new office, that of hereditary
Champion of England, whose privilege was to proclaim the
king's right to be crowned, and to challenge any who denied it.
Philip, the last of the male Marmions, died without leaving a son;
but in 1350 one of his great-grand-daughters married Sir John
Dymoke, who thereby inherited the manor and its office. And

from that day to this, both have been held by the Dymokes.

The role of the Champion was described by Celia Fiennes, a grand-daughter of Lord Saye and Sele, who witnessed the coronation of Queen Anne. After the ceremony, the second course of the banquet was 'ushered in by the Earle Marshall, Lord High Steward, and Lord High Chamberlain on horseback, their horses being finely dress'd and managed ... after which comes up the Lord High Steward again on horseback, with the two other Lords, and acquaints the King or Queen there is their Champion without, ready to encounter or combate with any that should pretend to dispute their legal title to the Crown of these Kingdomes, after which he is conducted in on horseback by the Earle Marshall and the Lord High Steward, and they come up to the stepps of the throne, and there the Champion (all dress'd in armour cap-a-pe) declares his readyness to combate with any that should oppose the Right of their Majestyes, and there upon throws down his gauntlet which is giving challenge, after which the King or Queen drinks to him in a gold cup with a cover, the same which is carried to the Champion, and he drinks, and then retires back and carrys it away, being his due, as is the best horse in the kings stable, the best suite of armour in the armory—this belongs to Sir John Dimmocks family....' The last display of medieval pageantry occurred at the coronation of King George IV in 1821, when the Champion's lance and shield were carried by two esquires. Mounted on 'a richly-caparisoned horse', the Champion cried: 'If any person of what degree soever, high or low, shall deny or gainsay our sovereign Lord George the Fourth ... to be the next heir ... here is his Champion, who saieth he lieth, and is a false traitor, being ready in person to combat with him, and in the quarrel will adventure his life against him on what day soever he shall be appointed.' The Champion then threw down his gauntlet, which the herald, after a moment of suspense, handed back to him. That done, a golden goblet of wine was passed to the King, who drank his Champion's health and then passed the goblet to the Cup-bearer, by whom it was presented to the Champion, for him to keep. The Dymokes preserve a number of those goblets at Scrivelsby. Their challenge, however, has been taken from them, together with the armour, the horses and the esquires. At the coronations of King Edward VII and King George V, Mr Frank

Dymoke merely carried the Standard of England in Westminster Abbey; at the coronation of King George VI he carried the Union Standard.

And what of the manor house, Scrivelsby Court? The medieval building has disappeared except for some brick fragments, a Tudor gateway and one fourteenth-century window. The present house was built during the eighteenth century, and the grounds laid out during the 1780s by Humphry Repton, who also designed the pair of octagonal lodges beside the Lion Gate at the western approach to the house. In or about 1833 a Louth architect, C. J. Carter, rebuilt the Lion Gate or arched entry, bearing a statue of a lion, which had been erected c. 1530 by Robert Dymoke, who lived through five reigns, and acted as Champion to Richard III, Henry VII, Henry VIII.

The medieval kings had co-opted and coerced a number of lesser manorial lords as unpaid jurors and coroners who, during the fourteenth century, became known as Justices of the Peace, and were empowered to fix maximum wages and to hold Quarter Sessions. By the end of the fifteenth century the manor house had either commuted or in some other way shed many of its feudal obligations to a tenant-in-chief. During the sixteenth century it supplanted the nobleman's castle, if not in power, then certainly as an influence closely in touch with local affairs. One instance, typical of many, is the FitzHerbert family, lords of the manor of Tissington in Derbyshire. About the year 1523, when Sir Anthony FitzHerbert was a Justice of Common Pleas, his younger brother, John, published a *New tract or treatyse ... for all husbande men*, based on forty years' experience as a country landowner, and written especially for 'poore fermers and tenauntes'. In it he described the latest methods of horse-breeding and cattle-raising; he discoursed on silviculture; he emphasized that bee-keeping requires little more than careful attention ('lyttell charge but good attendance'); and, like a fatherly squire, he appended some short essays on human health and happiness, including almsgiving and 'the Occupation of a Wife'. The FitzHerberts built their manor house four centuries ago. In 1972 the squire was Sir John Fitz-Herbert, a qualified surveyor and land agent. By way of postscript, we may mention another Tudor writer, Gervase Markham, younger son of the lord of several Nottinghamshire manors.

Among his books is *Country Contentments*, which contains a section for the lady of the manor, who, he says, 'must be cleanly both in body and garments, shee must have a quick eye, a curious nose, a perfect taste, and ready eare; (shee must not be butter-fingred, sweete-toothed, nor faint-hearted) for, the first will let every thing fall, the second will consume what it should increase, and the last will loose time with too much nicenesse.'

During the eighteenth century the manor house reached the zenith of its prestige, assisted by the fact that George I spoke no English, so that his chief adviser, Sir Robert Walpole, became in effect the senior or prime minister, acting as chairman of the Cabinet and leader of a House of Commons composed largely of squires. Moreover, the increasing complexity of local government had endowed the squires with the kind of knowledge and influence that were beyond the range of professional politicians in London. English literature contains many portraits of life at the manor. If you seek a boorish squire, you will find him in Goldsmith's Tony Lumpkin; if an overproud, in Dickens's Sir Leicester Dedlock; if a beneficent, in Steele's 'gentleman of Worcestershire, of antient descent, a baronet, his name Sir Roger de Coverley. . . . He is now in his fifty-sixth year, cheerful, gay, and hearty, keeps a good house both in town and country; a great lover of mankind . . . there is such a mirthful cast in his behaviour, that he is rather beloved than esteemed. His tenants grow rich, his servants look satisfied, all the young women profess to love him, and the young men are glad of his company.' Sir Roger understood his official duties: 'he fills the chair at a Quarter-Session with great abilities, and three months ago gain'd universal applause by explaining a passage in the Game-Act.' The character of Sir Roger de Coverley was drawn from life. It symbolizes many squires, both past and present. Steele, after all, wrote for the landowners of England, a sophisticated audience, who would have scorned to see themselves publicly canonized. Thackeray, a cynical townsman, created a different type of squire, Sir Pitt Crawley, lord of a slovenly manor, who 'spoke in the coarsest and vulgarest Hampshire accent' (the narrator, by the way, is Becky Sharp, a snobbish schemer). In appearance, she says, the squire is 'an old, stumpy, short, vulgar and very dirty old man, in old clothes and shabby old gaiters . . . and cooks his own

horrid supper in a saucepan'. R. S. Surtees depicted a comparable
clown—'stumpy, and clumsy, and ugly'—who lived in his steward's pantry, had a taste for tripe, and thought only of fox-hunting. Elizabeth Grant, author of *Memoirs of a Highland Lady*, met
a more amiable specimen when she visited Nottinghamshire at
the end of the Georgian era: 'A regular country squire,' she
found him, 'short, chubby, goodlooking, shooting, hunting, fishing, hospitable, kindly, a magistrate, and not an ounce of brains!'
Against those nonentities must be set such men as Arthur Young,
greatest of all English writers on farming; Coke of Holkham,
whose Norfolk estate became the most productive in Britain
(every one of his tenants, said Cobbett, 'made use of the expressions towards him which affectionate children use towards their
parents'); and Sir John Lawes, who converted his Hertfordshire
farm at Rothamsted into a research station which still enjoys
worldwide repute.

An objective portrait of the manor house was painted by
Richard Rush, an eighteenth-century American ambassador to
the Court of Saint James: 'Scarcely any persons who hold a leading place in the circles of their society live in London. They have
houses in London, in which they stay while Parliament sits, and
occasionally visit at other seasons; but their *homes* are in the
country.' As the ambassador emphasized, the best of those families
stood *in loco parentis* among the villagers: 'Those who live on
their estates through successive generations, not merely those who
have titles, but thousands besides, acquire, if they have the proper
qualities of character, an influence throughout the neighbourhood. It is not an influence always enlisted on the side of power
and privilege. On the contrary, there are numerous instances in
which it has for ages been strenuously used for the furtherance of
popular causes.' Arthur Young said the same thing in one sentence which explains why England suffered no French Revolution: 'Banishment alone will force the French to do what the
English do from pleasure—reside upon and adorn their estates.'

From the summit of an apparently impregnable *ancien régime*,
Madame de Pompadour foresaw the French Revolution: *Après
nous le déluge*. Few eighteenth-century squires foresaw the fall of
their own order, yet the signs were visible in the factories, the
mines, the harbours. Productivity was raising its sluice gates,

ready to unleash the prosperous desecration which Gerard Manley Hopkins found in Victorian England:

> ... all is seared with trade; bleared, smeared with toil,
> And wears man's smudge. ...

That lament was humanitarian and aesthetic. It shared little of the Augustan attitude toward trade, which to us appears laughably snobbish; as, for example, when the Home Secretary announced in 1813 that Justices of the Peace might, on occasion, be chosen from 'wealthy and respectable persons engaged in trade, but not in manufacture'. Money *qua* money, however, is useless. A shipwrecked sailor will gladly exchange his golden sovereign for a pork chop; a fact which the Romans recognized when they described money as *pecunia*, from *pecus* or a flock of sheep. Land was both the source and the symbol of wealth. By the end of the eighteenth century, when manufactured exports were enabling England to import much of her food, land began to lose something of its mercenary value, but the mystique persisted, especially among those 'wealthy and respectable persons' who craved the prestige which land bestowed. A notable specimen of the new commercial order was the Peel family, who throughout the Middle Ages had been yeomen and small squires. Having entered the cotton trade, one of the Georgian Peels acquired a fortune, a baronetcy, and a country mansion. His eldest son, Sir Robert Peel, went to Harrow and thence to Oxford, where he became the first man ever to achieve a Double First. From scholarship he lapsed into politics, and ended up as prime minister.

The best sort of parvenu was a blessing to rural England because he brought new ideas, new resources, new blood; his grandson lived as one to the manor born. The worst sort of parvenu was not a blessing. Cottagers despised him; squires snubbed him; literature lampooned him. Surtees, for instance, created Marmaduke Muleygrubs, who bought a yeoman's house and then converted it into a mansion, topped by 'massive stone towers, with loop-holed battlements'. Down in Berkshire another tycoon acquired an estate which he 'developed' after the style of Muleygrubs. Cobbett went livid when he saw it: 'Of all the ridiculous things I ever saw in my life,' he wrote, 'this place is the most

ridiculous.... I do not know who the gentleman is. I suppose he
is some honest person from the 'Change ... and that these *Gothic
arches* are to denote the *antiquity of his origins*.'

Not every manor house attracted the man in search of an
estate. Some were too remote; others, too small. England contains
many country homes which—although they resemble a manor
house, and may continue to style themselves a manor house—are
not and never were the seat of a seigneur. Such a one is William
Morris's old home beside the Thames at Kelmscott in Oxfordshire. Morris himself—founder of the Society for the Protection of
Ancient Buildings—bought the place from a family of farmers. It
had probably been designed by a Tudor yeoman, and enlarged
by his Jacobean descendants. To Morris it became a *raison d'être*.
'As others,' he confessed, 'love the race of man through their lover
or their children, so I love the earth through this small space of
it.' Morris's understanding of the past enabled him to avoid a
caricature of it. For the restoration of the house he used local
stone, local timber, and nails that were made by the local blacksmith. With his own hands he helped to restore the seventeenth-
century dove-cote. He used Kelmscott Manor as a set-piece for
News from Nowhere, in which one of the characters, Ellen, sets
her hand against the manor's lichened wall: 'How I love the
earth,' she cries, 'and the seasons and weather and all things that
deal with it and grow out of it.' Morris's daughter bequeathed the
house as a retreat for Oxford dons, but so few of them arrived
that she leased it to friends, on condition that they allowed visitors to inspect it. Among the contents of the house are some tapes-
tries woven by Morris, together with several of his wallpaper
designs, and a sketch of his wife by her too-fervent admirer,
Rossetti. During my last visit, in 1967, the house was being renovated, still under its assumed and erroneous name of Kelmscott
Manor.

Writing at the beginning of the nineteenth century, François
René de Chateaubriand, the French foreign minister, looked
back wistfully to the years when 'The gentleman farmers of England had not yet sold their patrimony in order to come and live
in London.' That was an overstatement because the majority of
squires never did come to live in London; they could not afford
to; and even had they been able, many would have remained

unwilling to acquire a house in Berkeley Square. Like Sir Jan Ridd of Plover's Barrow Farm on Exmoor, they regarded London as 'a very dirty sort of place'. If their womenfolk did coax or nag them into 'seeing the sights', they returned home as soon as possible. Adrift in the Mall, the Regency lord of a small Northumbrian manor in many ways resembled the Jacobean prototype whom Lord Macaulay described: 'When the lord of a Lincolnshire or a Shropshire manor appeared in Fleet Street he was as easily distinguished from the resident population as a Turk or a Lascar. His dress, his gait, his accent ... marked him out as an excellent subject for swindlers. . . .'

The manorial mystique was still so potent in 1848 that Benjamin Disraeli acquired the manor of Hughenden, hoping that it might help him to find favour—or at any rate less disfavour—in the House of Commons. The estate stands on the outskirts of High Wycombe in the Buckinghamshire Chilterns, and had belonged to Queen Edith *before* the Norman Conquest. Thereafter it passed to the Conqueror's half-brother, Odo, Bishop of Bayeux, who, having displeased the King, forfeit his estates, which were retained by the Crown until Henry I granted them to his Chamberlain, Geoffrey de Clinton, a pious man, who bequeathed Hughenden to the Priory he had founded at Kenilworth; the Priors whereof continued as lords until the Dissolution. In 1540 the manor was conveyed by Henry VIII to the Dormer family, who held it for 160 years, when it passed in marriage to the Earl of Chesterfield, whose descendant, Sir William Stanhope, sold it to Charles Savage in 1738. From Charles Savage the manor descended to his brother, Samuel, and thence to Samuel's nephew, John Norris, on whose death in 1786 it was inherited by Ellen Countess of Conyngham, niece of the aforesaid Charles and Samuel Savage. From the Countess it passed to her nephew, by whose executors it was sold to Isaac D'Israeli, an erudite Jew, who already owned the manor of Bradenham, a few miles away. A year or so later it became the seat of Isaac's eldest son, Benjamin, a politician and the object of much abuse. When he rose to make his maiden speech the House was repelled by his many-coloured clothes, his long and oily ringlets, his foppish mannerisms, his effeminate effusiveness. Members shouted him down, though never into defeat, for the landless Jew hit back:

'The time will come when you will hear me.' Yet Disraeli loved
the nation that had adopted him. He understood its past, its
people, its prospects. With some deceit and much daring he raised
it to the summit of prestige: *Rex et Imperator*. His domestic
policy was radical Toryism, as defined by Charles Kingsley: 'The
Church, the gentleman, and the workman should be ranged
against the shopkeepers and the Manchester School.'

Disraeli's new home was an eighteenth-century brick mansion
with thirteen bays, incorporating parts of a Tudor house. Half a
mile away stood the Manor Farm, a handsome example of new
building by Georgian squires. Disraeli held his manor for more
than thirty years; and although he never set cannons on the
battlements, he did arm the servants with revolvers as a pre-
caution against burglars. At the age of thirty-four he had married
a rich widow, twelve years older than himself, who acquired some
peacocks and a small boy to guard them. Known officially as the
peacock-herd, the child patrolled the park from dawn till dusk,
carrying a collapsible wooden chair because the Disraelis were
anxious lest he should catch cold by sitting on damp grass.

Despite Disraeli's preoccupation with politics, he wrote several
novels whose mission was to persuade what he called 'the two
nations'—the comfortably and the uncomfortably off—to co-
operate for the benefit of both rather than to clash for the self-
interest of one. In a novel called *Endymion* he depicted Hughenden Manor, calling it Hurstley, wherefrom hangs a tale. Many
visitors at Hughenden are puzzled when they discover that Disraeli's tomb in the churchyard is shared by that of a Mrs Willyams:
'In Memory' says the inscription, 'of Sarah Brydges Willyams, Re-
lict of James Brydges Willyams, Esqre., of Carnanton in the County
of Cornwall and Colonel of the Royal Militia. She died at Torquay, ii Nov., 1863, and was buried at her desire in this vault.' It
is easy to understand that a Victorian lady should have wished to
be buried beside Disraeli; but it is not easy to understand why
Disraeli should have wished it. The explanation is contained in
his own novels, which so delighted Mrs Willyams that, whenever
a new one appeared, she wrote to congratulate the author, who in
turn acknowledged each felicitation. And there the matter rested
until, finding themselves one day in Torquay, Disraeli and his
wife called on the unknown correspondent, with whom they

formed a lasting friendship, and from whom, when she died, they received a legacy. Disraeli's manorial pride is recorded by part of an inscription on the tombstone of his wife and himself: 'In Memory of Mary Anne Disraeli Viscountess Beaconsfield in her own right, for thirty-three years the wife of the Right Honourable Benjamin Disraeli Lord of this Manor....' From Queen Victoria the 'Lord of this Manor' received a mural in Hughenden church: 'To the dear and honoured memory of Benjamin Earl of Beaconsfield This memorial is placed by his grateful sovereign and friend Victoria R.I. Kings love Him that speaketh right, February 27, 1882.' When Disraeli died the manor passed to his nephew and heir, Major Coningsby Disraeli. During the 1930s the High Wycombe Council bought part of the estate as a memorial to King George V. The remainder was acquired by a Mr W. H. Abbey, who converted it into a trust. In 1972 the manor house and 169 acres of parkland belonged to the National Trust.

If you happen to know the beechwood footpaths, you can walk from Hughenden Manor to Chequers Court in not much above an hour. Of all our English manors, Chequers is the most widely known. Lipscomb, the nineteenth-century historian of Buckinghamshire, believed that King John built a palace near the site of Chequers Court; that a department of the Exchequer was established there; and that the medieval lords of the manor came to be known as de Scaccariis or of the Chequer. Certainly a Henry de Scaccariis held the land under Henry III. From the Chequers family it passed via an heiress to the Lincolnshire family of de Alta Ripa, who later spelt their name as D'Autry or Hawtry. From the Hawtrys it passed in marriage to Sir Henry Croke in 1616, and again by marriage to John Thurbane, Sergeant-at-Law. In 1741 the heir was Sir John Russell, eighth baronet, a descendant of the Thurbanes, Crokes and Hawtrys. In 1836 the manor was bequeathed to Sir John Frankland, a Yorkshire baronet. At the beginning of the twentieth century it was bought by Mr A. E. Lee (afterwards, Lord Lee of Fareham). When Lloyd George became premier he lacked a country house at which he could entertain distinguished foreign visitors. Lee therefore gave the Court and some of its parkland for the use of British premiers in perpetuity. The present Court stands on the site of several earlier houses, one of which was rebuilt by the Hawtrys in 1566, a noble

c

example of Tudor architecture, redbricked, many-chimneyed, over-looking a large park. On all sides the Chilterns rise up, dominating with Coombe Hill, not far short of a thousand feet high. The park is crossed by a public right of way which passes so close to the house that a bowman might knock on the door with his arrow. In 1972 Chequers Court had become so delapidated that the American ambassador gave a great sum of money toward the cost of repairs.

Chequers and Hughenden fared more fortunately than many other manor houses during the past century. On St Bartholomew's Day, 1871, having returned home from a walk along the Herefordshire border, the Rev. Francis Kilvert wrote a requiem: 'The old manor house has fallen into sad ruins since I used to come here to see old Mrs Buckland.... The great hall and the grand staircase both gone. All the back of the house tottering and the tall carved chimney stack trembling to its fall. From the huge oak beam which runs across and supports the vast ruined kitchen chimney, we stripped off large pieces of the bark which had never been removed and which looked as fresh as when the beam was placed there, perhaps hundreds of years ago.' Ichabod was the only inhabitant: 'The house seemed empty and deserted. Heaps of stones and rubbish lay round the yards. The orchards were tangled and over-grown, the garden run wild with weed, rank and neglected.... There was not a sound or sign of life or living thing about the ruinous deserted place. Nothing but silence and desolation.' Yet the ruin was not entirely deserted: 'A shepherd lives in a part of the house which still stands but as the staircase has fallen he is obliged to go out of doors and across a rude scaffolding stage before he can reach his bedroom.' And still the obituaries multiplied. W. H. Hudson, for example, described a visit to Knook manor house in Wiltshire: 'First a monks' house, it fell at the Reformation to some greedy gentleman who made it his dwelling, and doubtless in later times it was used as a farm-house. Now a house most desolate, dirty, and neglected, with cracks in the walls which threaten ruin, standing in a wilderness of weeds, tenanted by a poor working-man ... and his wife and eight small children. The rent is eighteen-pence a week—probably the lowest-rented manor-house in England, though it is not very rare to find such places tenanted by labourers.' When I visited Knook in 1969 the manor house had been restored.

Hudson and Kilvert cited two decaying manors. In *Lark Rise to Candleford* Flora Thompson described a thriving manor, the home of a squire who cared for his people, even when they stole his game: 'Two men were charged with poaching, and as this had taken place on Sir Timothy's estate he retired from the Bench while the case was tried. But not, it was said, before he had asked his fellow magistrates to deal lightly with the offenders. "For," he was suppose to have said, "who's going to stump up to keep their families while they are in gaol if I don't?" ' Miss Thompson detected an attitude which still exists among countrymen: 'For wealth without rank or birth they had small respect. When a rich retired hatter bought a neighbouring estate and set up as a country gentleman, the hamlet was scandalized. "Whoo's he?" they said. "Only a shopkeeper pretending to be gentry. I 'udn't work for him, no, not if he paid me in gold!" One man who had been sent to clean out a well in his stable-yard and had seen him, said: "I'd a good mind to ask him to sell me a hat...."' ' A manorial routine which Miss Thompson observed at the turn of the century was being observed during the 1920s: 'In summer the carriage was at the door at three o'clock in the afternoon to take the lady of the house and her grown-up daughters, if any, to pay calls. If they found no one in, they left cards, turned down at the corner, or not turned down, according to etiquette. Or they stayed at home to receive their own callers and played croquet and drank tea under the spreading cedars on exquisitely kept lawns.' The old pastimes pertained: 'In winter they hunted with the local pack. ... Summer and winter, they never failed to attend Sunday morning service at their parish church.' After service, some of them practised what had been preached: 'They had always a smile and nod for their poorer neighbours ... and more substantial favours for those who lived in the cottages on their estates.'

The plight of several mid-twentieth-century manor houses was portrayed by Gillie Potter via an imaginary manor, Hogsnorton Towers, seat of Lord Marshmallow, whose family had fallen on such hard times that their hearth rug was inscribed with what Mr Potter called a well-known Persian device: 'G.W.R.' (or Great Western Railway). The lodge gates were held together with string. Having collapsed, the west wing remained *in situ*, and was renamed the rock garden. In short, so far from being a *hlaford* or provider of bread, the squire of Hogsnorton would gladly have accepted half a loaf. Even now, however, there are many estates that have escaped from the frying-pan of penury without falling into the fire of commercial 'development'. It is my good fortune to spend many agreeable hours at Bushwood Hall, a Warwickshire home, whose history illustrates several aspects of the rise, fall, and renascence of English manors. More than 300 years old, the Hall stands alone, like an island among fields. The present owners took possession during the early 1960s when the place was being used as a farm. Indeed, at first glance you might suppose that it still is used as a farm, equipped with venerable redbrick barns at some distance from the house; but closer inspection suggests that Bushwood Hall was not built for a farmer. To begin with, the moat is long enough to invite skating, and wide enough to support the dinghy which I sometimes row between ducks and goldfish. But there is no need to speculate about the Hall's original role, for we know that it was indeed a manor house, birthplace of Robert Catesby, originator of the Gunpowder Plot, whose contemporary, Father Gerard, S.J., described him as 'a gentleman of ancient and great family in England, whose chief estate and dwelling was in Warwickshire, though his ancestors had much living in other shires also....' His father, Sir William Catesby, 'being a Catholic, and often in prison for his faith, suffered many losses, and much impaired his estate. This son of his, when he came to the living, was very wild, and as he kept company with the best noblemen in the land, so he spent much above his rate, and so wasted a good part of his living.'

The headquarters of the plot were at Lady Catesby's Northamptonshire home, Ashby St Ledgers, where the ringleaders met in an oak-panelled room above the gateway (it is still called 'the Plot Room'). Nevertheless, antiquarians assure me that, whenever I sit before the fire at Bushwood Hall, I am gazing at the hearth in whose flames the plot was conceived, for the room had been part of the house which Catesby knew; a stone house, designed by William Hoese in 1314 for Sir John Bishopden. The Catesbys acquired the house two centuries later, when one of them married into the Bishopden family, and begat the Cat (Sir

William Catesby), who with three other creatures—the Rat (Sir William Ratcliffe), the Dog (Lord Lovell) and the Hog (King Richard III)—formed a quartet whose power was enshrined in a medieval jingle:

> The cat, the rat, and Lovel the dog,
> Ruleth all England under a hog.

When the present owners dredged the moat they uncovered the timbers of a bridge with a central stone pier between two horizontal beams, and a footway of planks pegged to longitudinal cross-braced poles. The tenons of the original uprights were still tongued-in to the mortises of the base timbers. In his *Building in England down to 1540* L. F. Salzman states that the plans for the house specified 'a doorway to be so constructed that a drawbridge might be fitted'. It is therefore reasonable to assume that the remains of the bridge date from the fourteenth century.

As for Robert Catesby, we know that only his early years were spent at Bushwood Hall, yet he was old enough to understand that Roman Catholics were distrusted because the heir to Queen Elizabeth was a French-born Roman Catholic, Mary, Queen of Scots, who plotted against the person of the Sovereign and the safety of the State. Moreover, a Roman Catholic regarded all Protestants as infidels and therefore damned; a Protestant regarded all Roman Catholics as idolaters and therefore superstitious. So, mutual suspicion begat bilateral bigotry. Most people know that Catesby intended to blow up both Houses of Parliament; that one of the conspirators betrayed the plot by warning a Roman Catholic peer to stay away from Parliament; and that Guy Fawkes (erroneously rated as arch-plotter) was caught just in time. But the dissolution of Parliament, no matter how desirable it may have appeared, would not have eased the plight of Roman Catholics; and this the plotters knew. Their remedy was more ruthless, for they planned to blow up Parliament while the King, the Queen and the young Prince of Wales were attending the opening of it. That done, they would seize the Duke of York and his infant sister; proclaim one of them as a Roman Catholic monarch; raise a rebellion in the Midlands; and impose on Protestants a régime at least as bigoted as that which had persecuted Roman Catholics. The failure of the plot is famous; pagan Eng-

land still celebrates the triumph of the Protestant religion 'as by
law established'; but of the fate of the chief plotters it remains
contentedly ignorant. In fact, Catesby and his confederates
escaped and for several days wandered through the Midlands,
hoping to raise a rebellion. News of the débâcle, however, had
preceded them. Within forty-eight hours the Privy Council
printed and distributed a proclamation which not only named
the ringleaders but also warned all who might 'in any wise either
receive, abette, cherish, entertaine, or adhere unto them. ...' The
majority of Roman Catholics took the stern hint. With dwindling
hope the fugitives sought refuge among manor houses that were
already implicated. For a few hours they rested at Huddington
Court, Worcestershire, seat of the Wyntours, where a windowpane in a first-floor bedroom bears the *sauve qui peut* which
Robert Catesby and Thomas Wyntour scratched with a
diamond: 'Robert, Thom. Past cark. Past care.' At a second
manor—Holbeche House, four miles from Stourbridge—they
sheltered with another Roman Catholic family, the Lyttletons.
Next day the house was surrounded by a party of soldiers under
the Sheriff of Worcestershire, Sir Richard Walshe. The fugitives
thereupon resolved to make a stand, come what may. If they were
lucky, a bullet would rescue them from the fate of traitors, which
was to be disembowelled alive. But the men who had tried to
blow up Parliament were themselves the victims of an explosion,
for their powder had become damp, and while they were drying it
before the fire a live coal fell out, igniting the barrels. Smoke and
flames poured from the manor, damaging it so severely that only
a fragment now survives, incorporated into the rebuilt house.
Interpreting the disaster as an act of retribution, Robert Wyntour (Thomas's brother) escaped while he could, accompanied by
Catesby's servant, Thomas Bates. The rest prepared themselves
for death. At eleven o'clock on the morning of 8 November 1605,
Sir Richard Walshe led his men against the smouldering house.
As he advanced, some of the defenders opened fire; others
emerged to be captured. It was over in a few minutes. The origi-
nator of the Gunpowder Plot was shot by a trooper, named John
Streete, who received a pension for his marksmanship. So died
Robert Catesby, sometime of Bushwood Hall in the County of
Warwickshire. That is why my thoughts wander when I am at the

Hall; following its former inmate while he leads a misguided rabble from manor to manor; by few received, by many rejected, in one killed. Today his old home has been restored by the heirs of a tradition whose praise is set to the music of Wilfrid Scawen Blunt:

> I covet not a wider range
> Than these dear manors give;
> I take my pleasure without change,
> And as I lived I live.
>
> Nor has the world a better thing
> Though one should search it round,
> Than thus to live one's own sole King
> Upon one's own sole ground.

Milton's Cottage / Chalfont St. Giles, Bucks

3 The Cottage

UNTIL the Industrial Revolution compelled or bribed them to migrate to the towns, the majority of ordinary English-folk lived in cottages. Our Saxon forebears described such dwellings as a *cot*. Chaucer cited a poor widow who occupied a small cottage: 'A poure wydwe ... was whilom dwellynge in a narwe cotage.' The widow no doubt felt thankful for her home, though to us it would seem a one-storey hovel. Like the early medieval manor house, the cottage was built of whatever materials lay nearest to hand; very likely timber and mud. Remarking on the speed with which cottagers rebuilt their home when it had been destroyed by war or weather, Froissart observed that 'with three or four poles shortly they would make again their houses'.

The cottager himself was *glebae adscriptus* or bound to the soil of his village, either by service to the lord or by economic forces. He worked on the lord's land for several days each week; his own holding being divided into scattered strips, seldom more than twenty acres, sometimes less than ten. Corn for his daily bread was ground at the lord's mill. His crimes and his grievances were referred to the lord's court. He made his own furniture, which might consist of a bench, a table, a chest. The bed was probably a straw mattress alongside any cattle or sheep that had been invited to come in from the cold. It was said of the poet Edward Thomas, a twentieth-century cottager, that he regarded his home simply as a shelter from rough weather and the night hours; at most other times he was out of doors, either walking or gardening or reading. The medieval cottager likewise spent most of his waking life in the fields. Even the spacious home of a Tudor squire will cause some modern townsfolk to exclaim: 'How dark it is in here.' But neither the Tudor squire nor the medieval cottager found cause to complain on that score. What need had they of wide windows and bright lights? Few of them could read or write.

> When Adam delved, and Eve span,
> Who was then the gentleman?

A medieval Adam and Eve delved and span by daylight. Were their nights plunged therefore into utter darkness? By no means; even the poorest cottager could strike some sort of a light. In the fourteenth century Gower mentioned

> A pot of earth in which he hath
> A light brennyng in a cresset.

The cresset was a brazier containing pine needles, blubber, tarred oakum, or anything else that would smoulder brightly. Rush-lights, too, were a common feature of cottage life.

The cottager's diet was dull because men had not then learned to grow winter keep, so that their meat had to be slaughtered and salted during the autumn. His family lived chiefly on coarse bread, cold bacon, thick gruel, and whatever fruits and vegetables were produced from his land. Prince Henry, you remember, re-buked Sir John Falstaff for drinking so much sack or wine and for eating so little food with it: 'O monstrous! but one half-penny-worth of bread to this intolerable deal of sack!' Unlike Timothy, Sir John took wine for its own sake, never for the sake of his stomach, which had long ago sagged beneath a surfeit of susten-ance. Cottagers, by contrast, did take liquor for their stomach's sake ... for the sake, that is, of trying to make good a deficit of more solid fuel. Not Hilaire Belloc himself could have bettered the anonymous Englishman who spoke thus for his medieval fellows:

> Bryng vs in good ale, and bryng vs in good ale,
> For owr blyssyd lady sake, bryng vs in good ale.
> Bryng vs in no browne bred, fore that is mad of brane,
> Nor bryng vs in no whyt bred, fore there in is no game,
> But bryng vs in good ale.

Walter Map, the medieval chronicler, implied that village inns were common: 'quales Anglia,' he wrote, 'in singulis singulas habebunt diocesibus bibitoria', which may be translated as 'the kind of drinking houses that exist in every English parish'. Some scholars, however, deny that 'diocese' can be interpreted as 'parish'. Nevertheless, the drinking habits of Englishmen may be gauged by the fact that in 1347 the small Kentish town of Faversham contained eighty-four registered ale-wives or female brewers. Ale cost the cottager one farthing per four pints.

Some of the peasantry led itinerant lives as pedlars, carpenters, masons, and vagabonds. But they were exceptional. Few cottagers ventured beyond the parish; fewer still into another county; hardly any into foreign parts, unless as sailors, or soldiers, or servants. Even so, they enjoyed themselves when they could. After Mass on Sunday, or during the scores of holy days, they played a game which one Nottinghamshire chronicler detested: 'The game at which they met for common recreation was called by some the foot-ball game ... a game more common, undignified, and worthless than any other kind of game, rarely ending but with some loss, accident, or disadvantage to the players.' Then, as now, the womenfolk quarrelled with their neighbours. The Durham roll mentions a fine that was imposed on 'Agnes of Ingleby for transgression against William Sparrow and Gilian his wife, calling the said Gilian a harlot'.

Although he could neither read nor write, the cottager loved to sing and to hear others sing, especially when the tune was a folk-song, composed for the people and by the people. Unlike modern poetry, which is a cult for the few, medieval poetry echoed the life and thought of Everyman. Weary from lonely work in fields that winter has cast like iron, a peasant aches for rest and warmth and companionship:

> O western wind, when wilt thou blow
> That the small rain down can rain?
> Christ, that my love were in my arms
> And I in my bed again.

When the rain does come, borne on a warm west wind, the peasant perks up, and bids his small son do likewise:

> I have oxen that be fayre and brown,
> And they go a grassynge down by the town;
> With hay, with howe, with hay!
> Sawyste you not myn oxen, you litill prety boy?

Despite their harsh lives and superstitious religion, the cottagers achieved a gaiety which so passes our own understanding that we dismiss it as 'naïve'. Their songs and their dances differed indeed from our own. They thumped full-throated round the maypole or before a fire in the lord's hall. And always they waited for the death of winter and the birth of spring:

> Summer is icumen in,
> Lhude sing cuccu!
> Groweth sed, and bloweth med,
> And springth the wude nu—
> Sing cuccu!

It is doubtful whether any early medieval *cots* have survived. Mud walls and thatched roofs soon decay, a process that was hastened by the Black Death. Plagues were common during the Middle Ages, but the Black Death spread so widely and with such virulence that nearly one-half of the population perished. The dioceses of Exeter, Norwich and Winchester lost forty-eight per cent of their inhabitants; even the Archbishopric of York, with its scattered moorland parishes, lost thirty-eight per cent. The Bishop of Bath and Wells reported: 'The contagion of pestilence of this modern time, spreading everywhere, hath left many parish churches ... and the parishioners thereof, without curate and priest....' Labour being scarce, the cottagers demanded higher wages. More and more landowners forewent their feudal rights, and were content to pay cash. Fewer and fewer castles withstood the discovery of gunpowder. Rich merchants bought manors and knighthoods. By the end of the fourteenth century the feudal order showed signs of instability; by the middle of the fifteenth century it was falling. A gradual improvement in living conditions gave the better sort of cottage a hearth, a chimney and glass windowpanes; but many cottages continued to be built in ways that could not withstand the centuries. How, then, do we account for the thousands of Tudor 'cottages' that *have* withstood the centuries? The answer is simple: such places never were true *cots*. They were the homes of yeomen, parsons, merchants; men who would have been affronted had anyone suggested that they occupied the same sort of house as did their shepherd or their labourers. Consider Thomas Hardy's birthplace, the so-called 'cottage' at Higher Bockhampton near Dorchester in Dorset. Hardy's father was a self-employed mason with a comfortable income. His thatched 'cottage' had seven rooms and a large garden. To a Victorian farmhand it would have seemed a mansion; to a medieval peasant, a palace. The distinction between such places and a true *cot* is important. A famous instance may be seen in Milton's Cottage at Chalfont St Giles in Buckinghamshire. When I first visited Chalfont, more than forty years ago, it was a quiet backwater. When Nikolaus Pevsner arrived during the 1950s he reported that the village was a dormitory for commuters: 'nearly all now invaded by shops to cater for the London population. ...' Amid the car-crammed cacophony you can see traces of the old village, which was tree-lined, grass-verged, flanked by Tudor and Georgian houses. Milton's Cottage stands on the edge of the village, beyond the Babel. During the nineteenth century the cottage became a public house, *The Three Compasses*; in 1847 it was occupied by the village tailor and soon afterwards by the village policeman; in 1877, by way of celebrating Queen Victoria's Jubilee, a body of villagers bought the place, and converted part of the ground floor into a Milton museum, which is visited every year by thousands of pilgrims whose piety stops short at the fourth line of its *raison d'être*:

> Of Man's first Disobedience, and the Fruit
> Of that Forbidden Tree, whose mortal taste
> Brought Death into the World, and all our woe,
> With loss of Eden....

When Milton settled at Chalfont St Giles the world regarded him as a broken man. He had supported the rebels against Charles I, and had acted as Cromwell's secretary. Like Landor, he was that chameleonic creature, a patrician republican. But, as he often said, he was also *Johannes Milton Anglus*—John Milton, Englishman—and, as such, he became sickened by Cromwell's military dictatorship, and especially by the censorship of the press and the abolition of free speech. The rebels, he cried, revealed 'a besotted and degenerate baseness of spirit'. Only his former services saved him from imprisonment and perhaps death. He was allowed to sink into obscurity. Like many other republicans, he enjoyed a private income; but for how long would he continue to enjoy it? The dictatorship was crumbling; the people clamoured for the restoration of the King; yet Milton had approved the murder of that King's father. The outlook was made even more sombre by the Great Plague of 1665, from which Milton managed to escape, helped by a Chalfont man, Thomas Ellwood, whom he had tutored in Latin. Religious toleration having gone the way of free speech, the rebels imprisoned Ellwood because he was a Quaker; but not until he found a haven for Milton: 'some little time before I went to Aylesbury Prison,' he wrote, 'I was desired by my quondam Master Milton, to take an House for him in the Neighbourhood where I dwelt, that he might go out of the City for the safety of himself and his Family, the Pestilence then growing hot in London. I took a pretty box for him in Giles-Chalfont....' In that phrase—'a pretty box'—lay the genesis of the non-cottage which we now call a cottage; not a farmhand's home, but a weekend *pied-à-terre*, or at any rate the home of a man of means. Milton's new home was a sizeable redbricked residence, with dormer windows, sloping roof, gnarled beams; its bedrooms alone were more spacious than the whole of a true *cot*. Writing in 1862, J. J. Sheahan, the antiquary, knew nothing of Milton's Cottage. He called it—as everyone else then called it— Milton's House.

Milton never saw his new home. He was blind:

> When I consider how my light is spent,
> Ere half my days, in this dark world and wide,
> And that one Talent which is death to hide
> Lodg'd with me useless. . . .

John Milton was mistaken. His talent never did become useless, nor did he ever hide it. On the contrary, at Chalfont St Giles he completed *Paradise Lost*, the greatest poem in the English language. And with it he answered his own prayer:

> What in me is dark
> Illumin, what is low raise and support;
> That to the highth of this great Argument
> I may assert Eternal Providence,
> And justifie the wayes of God to men.

How did a blind poet find his way among more than 9,000 lines of verse so adroitly cadenced that even a sighted poet—supposing he could ever have achieved such mastery—would have needed keen eyes to pursue the nimble caesurae? Milton chose the only method open to him, which was dictation. The chief amanuensis was his nephew, Edward Phillips, helped sometimes by Milton's youngest daughter, Deborah, though she could not have been more than thirteen years old when the poem was finished. Milton's third wife stated that her husband 'used to compose his poetry chiefly in the winter'. Jonathan Richardson added some details: 'He frequently Compos'd lying in Bed in a Morning ('twas Winter Sure then). I have been Well inform'd that when he could not Sleep, but lay Awake whole Nights, he Try'd; not One Verse could he make; at Other times flow'd Easy his Unpremeditated Verse.... Then, at what Hour soever, he rung for his Daughter to Secure what Came.' On Edward Phillips fell the task of spelling aloud the many learned words, and repeating the punctuation, which in those years was used with correct amplitude, to guide both the ear and the eye. Milton received £10 for *Paradise Lost*. His widow sold the copyright for £8. Remarking that the book trade had not lost on the deal, Lord Camden added: 'Milton knew that the real price of his work was immortality, and that posterity would pay for it.'

Phillips and Deborah must have worked hard at Milton's cottage, for when Thomas Ellwood was released from prison, he visited the poet, who showed him a manuscript of *Paradise Lost*, whereupon Ellwood ventured a small jest: 'Thou hast said much about Paradise Lost; but what hast thou to say of Paradise

Found?' When Ellwood next called, he was shown the manuscript of a new poem, *Paradise Regain'd*:

> I who erewhile the happy Garden sung,
> By one man's disobedience lost, now sing
> Recover'd Paradise. . . .

Dr Johnson alleged that life at Milton's cottage was 'sour and
morose'. But Milton's friends thought otherwise. Twice made a
widower, he had married a woman thirty years younger than himself, whom he never saw. By all accounts the lady was kind,
capable, cultivated. Milton assured his brother that the third Mrs
Milton 'had been very kind and careful to him'. Despite those
nocturnal dictations, his daughter, Deborah, remembered him as
'delightful company . . . the life of the conversation. . . .' Jonathan
Richardson confirmed that remembrance: 'he play'd much upon
an Organ . . . and would be cheerful even in his gowt fitts and
sing.' He enjoyed a pipe of tobacco and a glass of wine. We may
therefore picture the English Homer sitting at the door of his
'pretty box', as his friends had often seen him do in London: 'he
Us'd to Sit in a Grey Coarse Cloath Coat at his Door . . . in Warm
Sunny Weather to Enjoy the Fresh Air.'

When the plague had passed, Milton returned to London,
survived the Restoration, and in 1674 died 'with so little pain
or Emotion', said Richardson, 'that the time of his expiring was
not perceiv'd by those in the room'. His widow survived him by
fifty-three years. His grand-daughter—Deborah's child—was hard-
pressed for money despite the sales of *Paradise Lost*. Dr Johnson
persuaded David Garrick to help the lady by giving a benefit
performance of Milton's *Comus* at Drury Lane; himself writing a
prologue to the masque, thereby assisting 'the grand-daughter of
the author of *Paradise Lost* . . . our incomparable Milton'.

Milton's grand-daughter lived to see the beginning of a process
which in our own time has converted the farmhand's cottage and
the yeoman's house into highly desirable residences, costing more
than the first occupants earned in a long and laborious life. The
process was so complex—varying from county to county, and from
one part of a county to another—that any generalization must
encumber itself with innumerable reservations. Nevertheless, the
main drift of events was as follows: the medieval *cot* gave way to

a larger and more comfortable dwelling, partly because the standard of living had risen, and partly because the risen standard enabled parsons and yeomen to move from their old homes into larger ones. Either way the true cottagers gained from the change. On the one hand, they received new homes; on the other, they entered vacated premises that were better than their former cottages.

In some respects the eighteenth century was as brutal as the fourteenth. For poaching the manorial pheasants a starving labourer might be hanged, transported, or imprisoned for many years. Mental illness was treated by means of thrashing, fetters, ridicule, neglect. Poverty and unemployment were accepted as part of the natural order. Yet that is only one aspect of truth. The eighteenth century abolished slavery through most of the British Empire, and sent the Royal Navy to capture any slave ship of any nation. Against bitter opposition a group of Tories persuaded Parliament to lessen the appalling hardship among factory-workers and to remove something of the shame of child labour. Without in any way denying the poverty, nor exaggerating the benevolence, it is correct to say that the average cottager fared better than the average factory-worker. Thomas de Quincey summed it up: 'Poverty—how different the face it wears looking with meagre eyes from a city dwelling ... and when it peeps out, with rosy cheeks, from amongst clustering roses and woodbines at a little lattice, from a one-storey cottage.' De Quincey knew both the slums of Manchester and the fells of Westmorland. He wrote for a wide audience, many of whom would have shouted him down had he tried to pull the wool over their eyes.

Every campanologist knows the story of the church whose six bells proudly pealed a challenge: 'Who-can-ring-like-we-can?' To which a neighbouring belfry replied: 'We-can ... we-can ... we-can.' So also with the cottages; they stand in their own right, as various and handsome as the manors and the castles and the farms. A travelled man can use them as maps. He sees the red sandstone cottages of Westmorland, squatly defying the Helm Wind that sweeps down from Cross Fell. He sees the Chiltern cottages of Buckinghamshire, built of local brick and flint. He sees the cob cottages of Devon; 'the poor cottager,' wrote Carew, 'contenteth himself with Cob for his Walls.' He sees the rubric cottages of Sussex; timber-faced reminders that the Weald was once woodland. He sees the Cheshire magpie; wood and white-wash gleaming throughout the year. He sees the stone cottages of Exmoor; made-to-measure for men who dwelt among high winds and a tang from the Severn Sea. He sees the incomparable Cots-wold cottages; when Odell Shephard saw them at Bibury, he found them unforgettable:

> I shall remember cottages
> Carved out of sunlight and gold,
> And how the great beech-darkened hills
> Tenderly enfold
> That little human island
> Washed round by meadow and wold.

A countryman lives among such homes. He takes them for granted, seldom pausing to enquire how they were built, or why the builders chose one material rather than another. When Cobbett rode through the Chiltern Hills he admired their cottages: 'All along the country which I have come, the labourers' dwellings are good. They are made of what they call *brick-nog* (that is to say, a frame of wood, and a single brick thick, filling up the vacancies between the timber).' The bricks were often interspersed with flint which had been chosen less for its appearance than for its proximity, because the Chilterns are chalk hills, studded with flint. Cobbett noticed that the cottage roofs were 'generally covered with tile'. But many of them were (and are still) covered with thatch.

Carew's cob—commonly called 'the poor man's masonry'—was probably introduced by Crusaders who had admired the cob-walled palaces of Islam. It became especially popular in the south-west of England, which remained remote until the coming of railways, and never did share the prosperity of East Anglia and the southern counties. The simplest cob is mud and chippings, bound together with straw and farmyard dung. A more refined cob can be obtained by mixing mud with sand, loam, clay, and chopped straw. Cob being highly porous, an old maxim declared that cob cottages require 'a wide hat and stout shoes' ... that is, thatched eaves and a rubble foundation. Even so, if a cob wall is well-maintained by scraping and refilling, it will last for centuries.

D

Most people agree that the largest number of most consistently handsome cottages is to be found in the 'Cotswold stone' areas of Warwickshire, Oxfordshire, Wiltshire, Gloucestershire and Worcestershire. The stone itself is called oolite (from two Greek words, meaning 'egg' and 'stone') because it is composed of egg-shaped particles of calcium carbonate resembling a fish's roe. Part of the charm of a Cotswold building lies in the variety of its hues. Some of the stone is dark grey; some is light grey; some is tawny. The Cotswold cottages were built by village masons and village carpenters who worked with something of the fervour which had raised York Minster, Durham Cathedral, Bath Abbey, Bolton Priory. John Drinkwater praised their achievement:

> I see the barns and comely manors planned
> By men who somehow moved in comely thought,
> Who, with a simple shippon on their hand
> As men upon some godlike business wrought....

Nearly 2,000 years ago the Roman poet Martial complained about the noise of town life: 'Do you imagine,' he asked, 'that I can write poetry in Rome?' From the eighteenth century onward many English poets discovered that they could not write poetry in London; and presently they were joined by novelists, essayists, playwrights, composers, painters. Most of the eighteenth- and early nineteenth-century escapists had no need of a cottage. Some of them (like Charles Lamb and Christopher Smart) rusticated as the guests or the protegés of a patron; others (like Dickens and Landor) acquired their own country house. A pioneer among literary cottagers was Coleridge, who received a home from Thomas Poole, a farmer and tannery merchant of Nether Stowey in the Quantock Hills. Coleridge described his benefactor as 'a stout, plain-looking farmer, leading a bachelor life in a rustic, old-fashioned house'. The house, however, belied its appearance, for it contained 'a good library, superbly mounted in all departments, bearing at all upon political philosophy....' The farmer, too, belied his appearance, for Coleridge found him 'a polished and liberal Englishman, who had travelled extensively and had so entirely dedicated himself to the service of his humble fellow-countrymen ... that for many miles round he was the general arbiter of their disputes; the guide and counsellor of their difficulties. . . .' Poole, at all events, presented Coleridge with a comfortable home and a large garden at Nether Stowey, a village which John Leland, the Tudor topographer, found wanting: 'Stowey,' he reported, 'a poore village, stondith yn a Botom, emong Hilles.' Thither in 1796 came Coleridge with his wife and infant son, the fruits of a disastrous marriage. He had already revealed his neurosis by enlisting as a trooper under the name of Silas Tompkins. Rescued from the army by his friends, he plunged deeper into unreality by taking opium. His new house—nowadays called Coleridge's Cottage—was a thatched building, containing six rooms and offices; in other words, it was not a *cot*.

The family moved from Bristol to Nether Stowey shortly before Christmas, in bitter weather. Mrs and Master Coleridge went ahead with the poet's 'boxes of books, chests of drawers, kitchen furniture and chairs, bed and bed-linen etc. . . .' As there was no room for Coleridge in the waggon, he decided to save money by walking from Bristol despite neuralgia and a swollen face. On his back he carried twelve yards of green baize with which to plug the doors and windows of the new home: 'I can endure cold,' he wrote, 'but not a cold room.' The new tenants were greeted by a plague of mice: 'They play the very Devil with us,' Coleridge complained, 'but it irks me to set a trap.' The man who was soon to write

> He prayeth best who loveth best
> All creatures great and small. . . .

flinched from destroying his non-paying guests. ''Tis as if you said, "Here is a bit of toasted cheese: come, little mice! I invite you!" when (O foul breach of hospitality!) I mean to assassinate my too credulous guests. No! I cannot set a trap.' It is doubtful that Mrs Coleridge shared her husband's 'reverence for life'.

Although Coleridge described the cottage as 'the old hovel', he soon settled down: 'Our house is better than we expected. There is a comfortable bedroom ... another room for us, a room for Nanny; a kitchen and out-house. Before our door a clean brook runs of very soft water ... T. Poole has made a gate which leads into his garden.' Alas, Coleridge continued his flight from reality. Less than a month after moving in he assured a friend that the garden and orchard would provide an adequate source of income: 'I raise potatoes and all manner of vegetables; I have an orchard and shall raise corn (with a spade) enough for my family.' But his attitude to weeds resembled his attitude to mice: 'The weeds,' he confessed, 'have taken the liberty to grow, and I thought it unfair in me to prejudice the soil towards roses and strawberries.' From time to time, however, the clouds of fantasy cleared, and through them poured the harsh light of reality: 'At Stowey I provided for my scanty maintenance by writing verses for a London morning paper. I saw plainly that literature was not a profession by which I could expect to live. . . .'

It is possible that Coleridge's cottage overheard the most brilliant talk ever uttered in an Englishman's home, especially when Wordsworth and Hazlitt arrived to share it. Hartley Coleridge remembered his father's conversation as 'an exhibition of intellectual power in living discourse . . . unique and transcendent. . . .' Metaphysics, optics, theology, ethics, history, painting, poetry, sculpture, fiction, drama, education, philology, psychology, medicine, law: all were themes on which he improvised so sublimely that Hazlitt reeled beneath 'such mystical sounds'. Madame de Staël, not herself a taciturn woman, was stunned into silence: 'Monsieur Coleridge,' she gasped, 'c'est un monologue.' But when the guests had departed, the talk at Coleridge's cottage became trivial because his wife was an amiable *hausfrau*, and the sum of their conversation was discord, exacerbated by the fact that Dorothy Wordsworth was half in love with Coleridge. Between February 5 and February 13, 1798, while staying in the Quantocks, she visited Nether Stowey six times: 'Walked to Stowey with Coleridge,' said her *Journal*. Next day: 'Walked to Stowey over the hills, returned to tea, a cold and clear evening, the roads in some parts frozen hard.' Four days later: 'Walked with Coleridge to Stowey.' Next day: 'Walked alone to Stowey. Returned in the evening with Coleridge.' Next day: 'Walked with Coleridge through the wood.' March 23 was a rubric in the calendar of English poetry: 'Coleridge dined with us. He brought with him his ballad finished.' The ballad was *The Rime of the Ancient Mariner*, a by-product of the two poets' decision to co-operate in writing *Lyrical Ballads*, a book of poems that would eschew the Augustan manner of Pope and Thomson. It was on a walk with

Wordsworth, when they had reached Watchet, that Coleridge
chose to launch his *Ancient Mariner* from the quay there:

> The ship was cheered, the harbour cleared,
> Merrily did we drop
> Below the kirk, below the hill,
> Below the lighthouse top.

Another walk from Nether Stowey, this time taken alone, produced what Coleridge himself described as 'a Vision in a Dream.
... A Fragment'. It seems that he had wandered as far as Porlock,
in a mood of despair, oppressed by his broken marriage and by
the opium with which he tried to escape from it. Porlock is several
hours' walk from Nether Stowey, so Coleridge rested at a farm,
where he slept and dreamed:

> In Xanadu did Kubla Khan
> A stately pleasure-dome decree:
> Where Alph, the sacred river, ran
> Through caverns measureless to man
> Down to a sunless sea.

We know that Coleridge had been reading certain travel books
which stirred his imagination:

> A damsel with a dulcimer
> In a vision once I saw:
> It was an Abyssinian maid,
> And on her dulcimer she played....

The rest of the story is famous. Having awakened, Coleridge
began to weave his dream into a poem, but was interrupted by a
visitor, a person from Porlock; and when he resumed work, he
found that the vision had faded.

'Whatever my talents might or might not be,' he once wrote,
'they were not of the sort that could enable me to become a
popular writer.' Nevertheless, he did become a popular writer—at
any rate among Somerset seamen—for he remarked to his son: 'I
was told by Longmans that the greater part of the *Lyrical Ballads*
has been sold to seafaring men, who having heard of the *Ancient
Mariner*, concluded that it was a naval book....' One wonders
what the bo'sun really did say when, on perusing the Ballads, he
found this:

With other ministrations, thou O Nature!
Healest thy wandering and distempered child:
Thou pourest on him thy soft influences,
The sunny hues, fair forms, and breathing sweets,
Thy melodies of woods, and winds, and waters.

In all the heartache of English literature, few pangs were more poignant than those of Coleridge, a good man gone wrong. The average drug addict is (in the vulgar phrase) a drop-out from society. He derides the loyalties and restraints that have supported morality since men became civilized. Coleridge, by contrast, was a patriot, a Christian, a defender of established *mores*. At Nether Stowey he waged war against the weak and ineffectual part of himself. In a letter to Thomas Poole he cried: 'O my God! my God! where am I to find rest! Disappointment follows disappointment, and Hope seems given me merely to prevent my becoming callous to Misery!' He knew that he was not fitted to be a family man, because he was not fitted for what we call a steady job, nor able to make full use of the literary genius which might have supplied an adequate income: 'I have,' his letter continued, 'been poring into a book as a show for not looking at my wife and the baby. By God, I dare not look at them....'

Could Coleridge return to Nether Stowey he would recognize parts of his cottage home; the two rooms beside the front door, for example, and the two rooms above. But the thatched roof has gone, and with it the footpath to Thomas Poole's house; gone, too, the 'clear brook of very soft water'. Despite his opium, Coleridge remained what he called 'a water drinker'. He must therefore have disapproved when, within a few years of his leaving it, the cottage not only became an ale-house but also co-opted his fame, calling itself Coleridge Cottage Inn. Many of his poems were not published until the end of the nineteenth century, when their appearance prompted several admirers to place a memorial on the wall of his old home. In 1908 a number of other admirers bought the house, as a monument to his genius; in 1972 Coleridge's Cottage was a museum, owned by the National Trust.

We have already noted that some manor houses became farmhouses. Others slid more steeply, and became cottages. Thomas Hardy described such a come-down in *The Trumpet-Major*, a tale of Dorset during the Napoleonic Wars. The heroine, Anne Garland, 'lived with her widowed mother in a portion of an ancient building formerly a manor-house, but now a mill, which, being too large for his own requirements, the miller had found it convenient to divide and appropriate in part to these highly respectable tenants'. More than one Englishman has made his home in a similar cottage, there to enjoy the sounds which enchanted Hardy's heroine and her mother: 'In this dwelling Mrs Garland's and Anne's ears were soothed morning, noon, and night, by the music of the mill, the wheels and cogs of which, being of wood, produced notes that might have borne in their minds a remote resemblance to the wooden tones of the stopped diapason in an organ.' Mrs Garland, we learn, 'first moved thither after her husband's death from a larger house at the other end of the village'. Like several modern cottagers, she discovered that 'those who have lived in remote places where there is what is called no society will comprehend the gradual levelling of distinctions that went on in this case at some sacrifice of gentility....' In short, she 'was sometimes sorry to find with what readiness Anne caught up some dialect-word or accent from the miller and his friends....' Fortunately, the lady from the large house came to terms with her small one because its landlord 'was so good and true-hearted a man, and she so easy-minded, unambitious a woman, that she would not make life a solitude for fastidious reasons'.

Country life changed scarcely at all during the first half of the nineteenth century. Railways were few and very far between. The words 'motor car' and 'aircraft' had not yet been coined. Stage coaches ruled the roads, as sails ruled the waves. Richard Jefferies, who was born into that era, became its most graphic rural historian: 'Such old-fashioned cottages,' he wrote, 'are practically built around the chimney; the chimney is the firm nucleus of solid masonry or brickwork around which the low walls of rubble are clustered. When such a cottage is burned down the chimney is nearly always the only thing that remains, and against the chimney it is built up again. Next in importance is the roof, which, rising from very low walls, really encloses half of the habitable space.' Although many Victorian squires built comfortable homes for their tenants, some of those homes were found wanting: 'The one great desire of the cottager's heart—after his garden—is plenty of sheds and outhouses in which to store wood, vegetables, and lumber of all kinds. This trait is quite forgotten as a rule by those who design "improved" cottages for gentlemen anxious to see the labourers on their estates well lodged; and consequently the new buildings do not give so much satisfaction as might be expected.' Antique dealers long ago discovered the truth of Jefferies's next remarks: 'A cottage attached to a farmstead, which has been occupied by a steady man who has worked on the tenancy for the best part of his life ... sometimes contains furniture of a superior kind. This has been purchased piece by piece in the course of years, some representing a little legacy—cottagers who have a trifle of property are very proud of making wills—and some perhaps the last remaining relics of former prosperity.' Jefferies emphasized the flexibility of a society that moved both up and down the ladder: 'It is not at all uncommon to find men like this, whose forefathers no great while since held the farms, and even owned them, but fell by degrees in the social scale, till at last their grand-children work in the fields for wages.' The classic Victorian example is *Tess of the D'Urbervilles*, whose heroine's family were poor farmfolk, though their ancestors had been lords of the manor of Wool in Dorset.

Some cottages still display a feature which Jefferies noted in mid-Victorian cottages: 'Upon the shelf may be found a few books—a Bible, of course; hardly a cottager who can read is without his Bible—and among the rest an ancient volume of polemical theology, bound in leather.... This book has evidently been handed down for many generations as a kind of heirloom, for on the blank leaves one may see the names of the owners. ...' In my own childhood I saw and sometimes heard the same breed of dissenter whom Jefferies likened to a Roundhead: 'I have known men,' he wrote, 'who seemed to reproduce in themselves the character of the close-cropped soldiery who prayed and fought by turns with such energy.... His congregation approve his discourse with groans and various ejaculations.' Jefferies insisted that the best of such preachers 'are not agitators in the current sense of the term. ...' The Socialist agitators, he explained, were 'chosen from quite a different class'. The cottager's nonconformity was not primarily theological. He lacked the ability to sift

Calvin from Melanchthon. His reason for not going to church was secular; it enabled him to vex the squire.

In 1967, at the little town of Wooler in Northumberland, I met a shepherd who, eighty years earlier, had worn the same kind of clothes which Jefferies remembered from the 1850s: 'Some of the old shepherds still wear the ancient blue smockfrock, crossed with white facings like coarse lace; but the rising generation use the greatcoat of modern make, at which their forefathers would have laughed as utterly useless in the rain-storms that blow across the open hills.' Some cottagers still thumb their stick as they stride; and that, too, Jefferies saw: 'it is,' he wrote, 'a staff rather than a stick, the upper end projecting six or eight inches above the hand.' In deep country, such as Lakeland and Exmoor, a few cottage wives still bake their own bread, brew their own cider, kill their own pig, and sell their own produce at the weekly market. Their homes contain the sort of furniture which Jefferies described, the oak chest and Welsh dresser of their great-great-grandfathers.

What has happened to the old cottages which Jefferies knew, and those older ones which his grandfather remembered? Some of them were so neglected that not even their seasoned timber could withstand the years; others were burned to the ground. Writing of an old Wiltshire woman, Jefferies stated: 'A great part of the village had twice been destroyed by fire since she could remember. These fires are, or were, singularly destructive in villages— the flames running from thatch to thatch, and, as they express it, "wrastling" across the intervening spaces.... Such fires are often caused by wood ashes from the hearth thrown on the dustheap while yet some embers contain sufficient heat to fire straw or rubbish.' The woman herself was 'reputed to be over a hundred; a tidy cottager, well tended, feeble in body, but brisk of tongue. She reckoned her own age by the thatch on the roof. It had been completely new thatched five times since she could recollect. The first time she was a great girl, grown up; her father had it thatched twice afterwards; her husband had it done the fourth time; and the fifth was three years ago. That made about a hundred years altogether.' The Wiltshire centenarian had witnessed the beginning of the cult of the literary cottage. Indeed, she was already middle-aged when Jane Austen's family acquired

Chawton Cottage near Alton in Hampshire. Miss Mitford, who called there in 1812, noted a 'total absence of the vulgar hurry of business or the chilling apathy of fashion'. Jane Austen's study was also the family sitting room. According to her nephew, 'she was careful that her occupation should not be suspected by servants, or visitors, or any persons beyond her own family.... She wrote upon small sheets of paper which could easily be put away, or covered with a piece of blotting paper.' Defective joinery gave the alarm: 'There was, between the front door and the offices, a swing door which creaked when it was opened; but she objected to having this little inconvenience remedied, because it gave her notice when anyone was coming.' In 1972 Chawton Cottage belonged to the National Trust.

In 1812 Charles Lamb inherited from his godfather a seventeenth-century cottage, called Button Snap, at Westmill near Buntingford in Hertfordshire. Three years later he sold it for £50, having waived the tenant's last payment of rent because, as he put it, 'you may have been at some expenses in repairs'. In 1972 the cottage belonged to the Charles Lamb Society. Another early weekender was Fanny Burney, who, after the publication of her novel *Camilla* in 1796, had Camilla Cottage built near Mickleham in Surrey; the cottage was destroyed by fire in 1919. Honeymoon Cottage was rented by Dickens for his honeymoon at Chalk, formerly a village, but now part of Gravesend. The cottage long ago disappeared; a fact which has not deterred the occupants of a nearby cottage from displaying a notice that theirs is 'the one and only genuine Dickens Honeymoon Cottage'. Long after that honeymoon—when he was an elderly man—Dickens rented Elizabeth Cottage at Slough in Buckinghamshire, where he installed his mistress, a young actress named Ellen Ternan, who later married a Bournemouth clergyman. Elizabeth Cottage was destroyed by fire in 1889.

George Meredith spent the last forty-two years of his life at Flint Cottage on Box Hill in Surrey, on whose steep garden he built a chalet to serve as study-bedroom. Mrs Meredith had made it her business to deter the inquisitive sightseers who prowled around the novelist's home, but when she died, in 1885, Meredith gave up the struggle, and allowed the cottage to become a place of pilgrimage. Among his visitors were James Barrie and Robert

Louis Stevenson. In *The Amazing Marriage*, one of his lesser tales, Meredith depicted Stevenson as Woodseer, a young man with a notebook, in which it was his custom to scribble 'a verse, hints for more, and some sentences which he thought profound'. In 1946 Flint cottage was given to the National Trust by Mr M. E. Ruffer.

On the outskirts of Petersfield in Hampshire lies the well-named village of Steep, dominated by Stoner Hill, where you may see the semi-detached cottage that became the last home of Edward Thomas, who was born in 1878, at a time when a man might still hope to support himself by writing what Sainte-Beuve called 'quiet books', distilling the life of the English countryside. Thomas, however, had to support not only himself but also a wife and three children. With courage and stamina he pot-boiled many topographical and biographical books, none of which did more than maintain his family while he went in search of the next book. Shortly before he died he wrote an epitaph to his right hand,

> Crawling crablike over the clean white page,
> Resting awhile each morning on the pillow,
> Then once more starting to crawl on towards age.

In 1912 Thomas met Robert Frost, who had come to England because America refused to recognize him as a poet. Most people at that time regarded Edward Thomas as a journalist, but Frost saw beneath the surface: 'Edward Thomas,' he wrote, 'had about lost patience with the minor poetry it was his business to review. He was suffering from a life of subordination to his inferiors. Right at that moment he was writing as good poetry as anyone alive, but in prose form where it did not declare itself and gain him recognition.' At the age of thirty-five, under Frost's benign influence, Thomas amazed himself by starting to write poetry in verse. No other English poet has ever flowered so late. But the battle had scarcely begun. In 1913 Thomas was so poor that he was obliged to rent the very cheapest cottage he could find; Yew Tree Cottage at Steep, a drab home, without privacy or charm. There he continued his true vocation, poetry, while earning his living as a journalist. To W. H. Hudson he wrote: 'The nature of my work means nothing except food and drink for five or six people. Journalism is as tedious and meaningless as a clerk's work, and, unlike that, cannot be escaped from. It fills my normal day from 10 a.m. to 12 p.m., and haunts me all the other days.' He never lived to see his poems published under his own name. Editors would have nothing to do with them. When at last a magazine did accept one, it had been submitted under an assumed name, Edward Eastaway, because Thomas feared that his real name would prove a poor advertisement.

To cut a sad story short, Thomas went to the War, declined to accept a safe berth, served as an Artillery officer, and was killed in action, at the age of thirty-nine. Walter de la Mare summed up the man's courage and the poet's achievement: 'When it is considered how many books he wrote; how much of his best writing is practically buried in the newspapers ... then it is little less than tragic to think how comparatively unheeded in any public sense was his coming and going. When Edward Thomas was killed in France, a mirror of England was shattered, of so pure and true a crystal that a clearer and tenderer reflection of it can be found no other where than in these poems. ...' The years have answered 'Yes' to the question which Edward Thomas just had time to ask before he died:

> Out of us all
> That make rhymes,
> Will you choose
> Sometimes—
> As the winds use
> A crack in the wall
> Or a drain,
> Their joy or their pain
> To whistle through—
> Choose me,
> You English words?

One might compile a litany of famous men and women who made their home in a cottage. Mary Webb and her husband built a sandstone cottage on Lyth Hill near Meole Brace in Shropshire. Edmund Rubbra, the composer, lived in a brick-and-flint cottage near Speen in the Buckinghamshire Chilterns. An English premier, the first Earl of Oxford and Asquith, bought a riverside cottage, called The Wharf, at Sutton Courtenay in Berkshire. For a weekly rent of 9*s* 6*d* W. H. Davies acquired a cottage at Newport in Monmouthshire; it stood, he said, 'at the top of a hilly road, from where one could see, on a clear and mistless day, the meeting of the Severn and the Bristol Channel'. T. E. Lawrence, illegitimate and psychopathic son of Sir Thomas Robert Chapman, won fame as Colonel Lawrence of Arabia, and then tried to lose it as Private Shaw, Royal Tank Corps, before moving to Cloud's Hill Cottage in Dorset, where he received letters and visits from Bernard Shaw, Robert Graves and Noël Coward. On the door of his cottage he carved a foolish tag from Herodotus, *anglice* 'I couldn't care less'. The only other occupant was his male secretary, a rare luxury among private soldiers. The two men occupied sleeping bags, marked respectively *Meum* and *Tuum*. Women were not admitted, except for Lawrence's mother. Lawrence was inordinately proud of a Brough Superior motorcycle which had several times nearly killed either himself or someone else. In 1935 he was gratified to learn that the Press was naming 'Lawrence of Arabia' as the one man who might profitably try to reason with Hitler. On May 13 of that year a friend wrote to Lawrence, suggesting that they met to discuss the Hitler parley. Greatly excited, Lawrence mounted his machine, raced to the nearest Post Office and despatched a telegram accepting the offer. Returning at speed over the blind brow of a steep hill, he met two children on bicycles. The children survived, but Lawrence died. In 1937 his brother gave Cloud's Hill Cottage and some of its relics to the National Trust.

Men who are still relatively young can remember the death of Lawrence; yet Lawrence himself could remember cottages that were little better than those of Chaucer's 'poure wydwe'. In 1874, for example, F. G. Heath found an old labourer living alone near Weston-super-Mare: 'Unless I had seen it,' wrote Heath, 'I could not have believed that such a place existed in England.' The floor of the one-room hovel 'was irregularly paved with stones, with earth between them ... the walls were made of hardened mud'. The ceiling was so low that Heath could scarcely stand upright. The occupant—a man of seventy-seven—worked from six in the morning until six at night, for seven shillings a week. Mrs Hemans painted a too-rosy picture when she likened the English cottages to thousands of miniature Edens:

> The cottage homes of England!
> By thousands on her plains.

Which is the most-visited English cottage? Statistics suggest
that the prize goes to Dove Cottage at Grasmere in Westmorland,
the home of William Wordsworth and his sister Dorothy, a Mecca
for thousands of pilgrims every year. How potent is poetry, to
attract so many people, of whom not one in a thousand has read a
book of poems since last at school he yawned over *Marmion*.
Wordsworth himself, son of an attorney, was born in 1770 at
Cockermouth in Cumberland. His sister arrived twenty months
later, on Christmas Day, 1771. Their father and mother died
while the children were still at school. Wordsworth went from
Hawkshead Grammar School to St John's College, Cambridge,
where he became conscious of his destiny, hoping

> that I might leave
> Some monument behind me which pure hearts
> Should reverence.

The two children received only a nominal legacy from their
father, and some of that was long withheld. Not until middle age
did Wordsworth achieve a modest financial security, thanks
chiefly to a rich friend and a government sinecure. As a youth he
tramped through Europe, acquiring a knowledge of people and
places which he afterward wove into poetry. During those travels
he fell in love with a French girl, a royalist, by whom he had a
daughter. The couple wished to marry, but were unable to do so
because the revolutionaries would have murdered any royalist
who tried to escape to freedom, and any Englishman who tried to
marry a royalist. Disappointed in love, and disillusioned by revolution, Wordsworth revealed a latent neurosis. In the end he
triumphed by using the neurosis in order to write poetry, and by
writing poetry in order to resolve the neurosis. Throughout the
malaise he was sustained by his sister:

> thy breath,
> Dear sister, was a kind of gentler spring,
> That went before my steps.

In December 1799 Dorothy and William set up home together
at Dove Cottage, formerly an inn, the Dove and Olive-Bough.

Like his friend Coleridge, Wordsworth was a water-drinker. Indeed, he wrote a long poem, *The Waggoner*, about a local waggoner whose inebriate footsteps from the Dove and Olive-Bough led both himself and his vehicle into the waters of oblivion:

> There, where the Dove and Olive-Bough
> Once hung, a poet harbours now,
> A simple water-drinking Bard. . . .

Dove Cottage stands in a cul-de-sac under the lee of a hill, confirming Wordsworth's description of a typical Lakeland cottage: 'such places,' he observed, 'may rather be said to have grown than to have been erected—to have arisen by an instinct of their own, out of the native rock—so little is there in them of formality, such is their wildness and beauty.' The four small rooms—dark and low—were designed for farmfolk who had no wish either to admire the view or to read a book. Against that, the cottage overlooks the most dramatic corner of Westmorland, within easy walk of Windermere; less than a mile from Rydal water; and only a few hundred yards from Grasmere, a lesser lake.

On Christmas Eve, 1799, Wordsworth wrote to Coleridge: 'We arrived here last Friday, and have now been four days in our new abode. . . .' Remembering his own move to Nether Stowey, Coleridge must have expected the worst. Wordsworth certainly reported it: 'Our first two days,' he continued, 'were days of fear as one of the rooms upstairs smoked like a furnace; we have since learned that it is uninhabitable as a sitting room on this account. . . .' Fortunately, Dorothy perceived the bright side of that smoky cloud: 'D is much pleased with the house and *appurtenances*, the orchard especially . . . in imagination she has already built a seat with a summer shed on the highest platform in this our little domestic slip of a mountain.' At least there was no servant problem: 'We have agreed to give a woman, who lives in one of the adjoining cottages, two shillings a week for attending two or three hours a day. . . .' Despite their straitened means, the newcomers were generous: 'We could have had this service for eighteen pence a week, but we added the sixpence for the sake of the poor woman, who is made happy by it.' The neighbours were true Westmorland farmfolk: 'The manners of the neighbouring cottagers have far exceeded our expectations ... kindhearted, frank, and manly, prompt to serve without servility.' Like many other householders of modest means, the Wordsworths did-it-them-selves: 'We have been overhead,' Coleridge was informed, 'in confusion, painting the rooms, mending the doors, and heaven knows what!' The effect upon the Bard was unfavourable: 'Composition,' he complained, 'I find invariably pernicious to me, and even penmanship, if continued for any length of time at one sitting....' And with that he ended his house-warming: 'I am afraid half of what I have written is illegible, farewell.'

For two years the brother and sister lived at Dove Cottage, much visited by Coleridge, who was disintegrating among drugs and domestic discord. The household, in fact, resembled a Strind-berg drama because of Dorothy's involvement with both men. Yet she maintained an apparently equable blend of Martha and Mary. Her *Journal* for 19 May 1800, says: 'Bound carpets, mended old clothes, read *Timon of Athens*.' A year later it mentions an important guest: 'Baked bread and giblet pie—put books in order—mended stockings. Put aside dearest C [Cole-ridge's] letters, and now at about 7 o'clock we are all sitting by a nice fire. Wm. with his books and a candle, and Mary writing to Sara.' Mary was Wordsworth's fiancée, a childhood friend, whom he married in 1802. The extent to which he had conquered his neurosis is proven by a long and happy married life.

But Dorothy's role at Dove Cottage ventured far beqond giblet pie and homemade bread. On 2 October 1800 she becomes a poet: 'The moonlight lay upon the hills like snow.' Three weeks later she sights a new simile: 'The moon shone like herrings in the water.' On St George's Day in the following year she evokes the spirit of Lakeland before it became a playground: 'not Man's hills, but all for themselves, the sky and the clouds and a few wild creatures.' Six months later the season of unmarried bliss came to an end: 'On Monday, 4th October, 1802, my Brother William was married to Mary Hutchinson.' Dorothy could not bear to attend the service: 'William had parted from me upstairs. I gave him the wedding ring....' Modern insight understands the sig-nificance of her next words: 'I took it from my forefinger where I had worn it the whole of the night before.' But there was no self-pity: 'My tooth broke today. They will soon be gone. Let that pass, I shall be beloved—I want no more.'

The new *ménage à trois* achieved a miraculous harmony. Dove Cottage, indeed, brought Wordsworth to the peak of his power, for in it he completed his masterpiece, *The Prelude: or, Growth of a Poet's Mind*:

> How strange that all
> The terrors, pains, and early miseries,
> Regrets, vexations, lassitudes interfused
> Within my mind, should e'er have borne a part,
> And that a needful part, in making up
> The calm existence that is mine when I
> Am worthy of myself!

Dorothy's *Journal* adds chapter and verse: 'In the afternoon we sate by the fire: I read Chaucer aloud, and Mary read the first canto of *The Faerie Queene*. After tea Mary and I walked to Ambleside for letters ... a sweet walk. It was a sober starlight evening, the stars ... sometimes hiding themselves behind small greyish clouds ... so we came happily homewards....' Thus did the Wordsworths practise their own gospel of 'plain living and high thinking'. Like every other home, Dove Cottage suffered the interplay of light and shade. In 1803 the Wordsworths' first child was born, a son, John. In 1804 Coleridge sailed to Malta, more than ever a source of disappointment and anxiety to the woman whom he called 'Wordsworth's divine Sister'. In 1805 Wordsworth's brother, a sea captain, went down with most of the crew and passengers when his ship struck a rock off Weymouth. The news numbed Dove Cottage. 'Never again,' wrote Dorothy, 'can I have a perfect joy in this world.' Wordsworth weighed himself in the balance, and was not found wanting:

> I have submitted to a new control ...
> A deep distress hath humanised my soul.

Despite his achievement as a poet, he continued to be under-rated by many of the book reviewers. Even the neighbours remained unimpressed. If news of another poem did reach them, it was received coolly: 'I hear owd Wudsworth's brok loose agin.'

E

Nevertheless, the years at Dove Cottage were the richest and most rewarding of his long life. They prepared the way for the renown which he enjoyed when he moved to a larger house, Rydal Mount, and was appointed Poet Laureate. Then at last Coleridge could felicitate his friend: 'he has won the battle now, ay! and will wear the crown, whilst English is English.' If, in the end, the happiness of human affections are rated above the *Sturm und Drang* of artistic creation, then Wordsworth's old age may be likened to Job's: 'So the Lord blessed the latter end of Job more than his beginning. . . .'

And what of Dorothy? Her supreme achievement was the one which gave her the greatest satisfaction, and was acknowledged with a single line by its beneficiary:

She gave me eyes, she gave me ears.

Wordsworth himself had withstood neurosis by achieving great poetry and a happy married life. Dorothy was denied those defences. In her forty-seventh year she collapsed, and for nearly another forty years the once-blithe spirit inhabited a nether-world of dementia, outliving her brother. During a moment of lucidity she wrote a letter to her cousin Edward, which, although it referred to Charles Lamb's sister, was a portrait of herself: 'His sister still survives, a solitary twig patiently enduring the storms of life. In losing her Brother, she lost her all—all but the remembrance of him, which cheers her the day through.' Dorothy Wordsworth wrote many memorable passages, but none excels her description of Dove Cottage: 'It calls home the heart to quietness.'

The state of English cottage life during the second half of the twentieth century may justly be described as schizophrenic. On the one hand, farm workers despise a 'period' home, and prefer a council house with garage; on the other hand, businessmen and retired townspeople will pay more for a Georgian shepherd's hovel than the shepherd himself earned in a long and arduous life. Within forty miles of any industrial town the demand for old cottages has outstripped even the pretence of sanity. Homes which in 1920 might have fetched £50 now fetch £5,000 even though their 'spare bedroom' is an attic landing, and the 'spacious garden' is a small paddock. So, while old cottagers seek new houses, the urban immigrants outbid one another for the privilege of dining in the very room where their grandfather's coachman chewed cabbage and bacon. *Quantum mutatus ab illo*: what a topsy-turvy prospect.

Maxstoke Castle / Warwickshire

4 *The Castle*

THE castle was so much a home that I caught sight of my host in the courtyard, waiting to receive me. A golden retriever sat beside him, as though to safeguard the present; and in the background a small grandson appeared, as though to maintain the future of a heritage which his family had held for four centuries. This was Maxstoke Castle in Warwickshire, truly an Englishman's home, and not a public museum. The castle doors were six centuries old, studded with their original ironwork, and blazoned with armorial devices. The hinges, too, were six centuries old; and on them the oak doors swung smoothly. But before we enter a particular castle, let us remind ourselves of castles in general, their role and evolution.

The word 'castle' is derived from the Latin *castellum*, a diminutive of *castra* or fortified camp. The majority of English castles were defensive rather than aggressive. Only along the Scottish and Welsh borders, and near the English Channel, were they designed primarily for war; and only the king or a trusted vice-regent built them. The earliest medieval castles were made of

earth and timber, like the one in the Bayeux Tapestry, where a
wooden tower and log palisades are set on a mound or *motte*
surrounded by a ditch. The lesser manorial buildings were sheltered by an adjacent bailey and courtyard, likewise with ditch
and palisades. Nearly every Norman baron erected a castle on his
English estates as a defence against rival Normans and rebellious
Saxons. In it he built a chapel for the use of his family and his
retainers. Sometimes he appointed a kinsman as the priest. If the
manor itself became a parish, the chapel served as the church
thereof. Most of our counties retain several examples of a castle
and a church and a manor house, each within a short distance of
the others. Many castles which began as timbered buildings were
enlarged as stone castles. Pleshey Castle, for example, was built
near Colchester *c.* 1180 by William de Mandeville, on the *motte*
and bailey pattern. In 1397 the castle was forfeit to Richard II,
who contrived the murder of its owner, the Duke of Gloucester,
and then looted the place; in Shakespeare's *Richard II* the be-
reaved Duchess laments because nothing remains

> But empty lodgings and unfurnished walls,
> Unpeopled offices, untrodden stones.

Another timbered castle was built by the Normans at Restormel
in Cornwall; a third, at Lewes in Sussex; a fourth, at Warkworth
in Northumberland.

Those early timber homes were replaced by the stone fortresses
which conform most closely with the popular concept of a castle.
Gerald of Wales, the twelfth-century historian, described his
family's castle at Manorbier in Pembrokeshire, typical of many
British castles: 'It is excellently well defended by turrets and
bulwarks, and is set on the summit of a hill, extending on the
western side toward the seaport, having on its northern and
southern flanks a splendid fish-pond under its wall, conspicuous
as much for its grandeur as for its depth. There is also a beautiful
orchard on the same side of the castle, enclosed on one part by a
vineyard, and on the other by a wood, remarkable for its projecting rocks and for the height of its hazel trees. On the right of the
promontory, between the castle and the church, and not far from
a large lake and a mill, a never-failing brook flows through a
valley.' The larger medieval castle was not a single building; it

included a medley of premises, surrounded by a wall. The inner courtyard contained timber huts that served as kitchen, dairy, forge, pigeon-loft, and sometimes as a servants' chapel. The hub of home life was the great hall, with dais, fireplace, and screens against the draught. Above it lay the lord's bed chamber, the only private apartment. The wardrobe served as a strong room, where jewels, spices, cloth, and plate could be locked in oak chests. In 1290 the Bishop of Hereford fitted one glass windowpane at his manor of Bosbury; but only a rich man was able to afford the current cost of fourpence per square yard of plain glass. Most windows had wooden shutters, and all were small.

Castles today look grey, but during the Middle Ages they were white-washed within and without. Bishop Grosseteste declared that his ideal castle, Le Chateau d'Amour, would be painted red, blue, and green. Kenilworth Castle contained privies on every floor of its keep, some of which emptied into the moat; others, into a pit; all being potentially infectious. Nevertheless, the medieval upper classes were relatively well-washed. Henry III not only built a conduit to carry kitchen waste into the Thames but also installed a piped bathroom at Windsor Castle. Every noble household kept wooden bath tubs; daily ablutions in a basin were taken for granted; washing of hands before and after meals was part of the meal itself. A medieval peer would have been shocked by the behaviour of Jacobean courtiers who, according to Anthony à Wood, used the corridors of an Oxford college as public lavatories.

Throughout the Middle Ages every large castle maintained a *curia* or council of servants, headed by the estates steward, who was always of gentle birth, and often a nobleman's son. He presided at the *curia*; he deputized for his lord in the manorial court; he appointed bailiffs and reeves. The household steward was a lesser figure (one thinks of Malvolio, household steward to Olivia). A lawbook of the late-thirteenth century describes his duties: 'It is the steward's responsibility to account every night in person or through a deputy appointed by the lord ... for the expenses of the household, and to ascertain the total of the day's expenditures. It is his duty to take delivery by tally from the larder, at the hands of the reeve, of flesh and fish of every kind as may be necessary, and this he shall have cut up into portions in his presence and counted as they are delivered to the cook and for these he shall hear a reasonable account. It is also his task to know exactly how many farthing loaves can be made from a quarter of wheat.... Further, he should know how many loaves and how many portions are needed for the normal household on ordinary days. And all the serjeants are answerable, jointly and severally, to the steward for their offices. And he is bound to witness to what they do.' The household steward supervised a retinue of butlers, cooks, poulterers, almoners, chandlers, porters, brewers, bakers, tailors, farriers, clerks, domestic servants, and armed retainers.

Domestic life was ruled by the lady of the castle, for it is quite untrue to suppose that medieval Englishwomen were the slaves of the male. In private law the woman ranked with the male. She could dispose of her own chattels as she wished, if necessary by making a will. Should her husband die, she could become the sole guardian of her children by him. She could act as his attorney in a lawsuit. She could become a lady of the manor in her own right. She could even hold that manor by military tenure. One of the most detailed accounts of medieval domesticity was compiled on the instructions of Eleanor, Countess of Leicester, widow of Simon de Montfort, and sister to King Henry III. Her household diary covers about seven months of the year 1265, most of which she spent as the defender of Dover Castle during civil war. The entries were written in Latin: *Computandum cum Roberto de Westmol' die sabbati post pascham pro c.xix lb cere*; which means: 'Bargained with Robert of Westmol' on the Saturday after Easter for 119 lbs of wax.' No item escaped the scrutinizing Countess; not even the cost of the kitchenmaids' stockings.

Like the modern French, a Norman castle eschewed bacon-and-eggs. The first meal of the day consisted of a slice of bread with some ale or watered wine. The principal meals were dinner (which was taken between ten and eleven in the morning) and supper (between four and six in the afternoon). The chief ingredients of both meals were bread, meat, fish, eggs, fruit. Meat was banned on Wednesdays, Fridays and Saturdays, and throughout Lent also, at which season the Countess's household consumed one thousand herrings a day. Their throats must have been as parched as that of the medieval schoolboy who wrote to his mother: 'Thou wyll not beleve how wery I am off fyshe, and how moch I desir that flesh wer cum in ageyn, for I have ate non other but salt fysh this Lent, and it hath engendyrde so moch flewme within me that it stoppith my pyps that I can unneth speke nother brethe.' The Countess herself observed the rules of etiquette, which required that the lord or his lady 'both see and be seen of their people in Hall'. Only twice during those seven months was she absent from dinner. The household diary recorded every one of her attendances at high table; each time setting her name at the head of the list of those present. Dinner at the castle was taken with simple ceremony. On sitting down, and again at rising, guests washed their hands from ewers carried by servants. Silver spoons and forks were provided, but each diner used his own knife, which he kept in a sheath slung from his girdle. One bowl of food was shared among two guests; the younger serving the elder; the man serving the woman. Each portion was eaten from trenchers or hunks of stale bread which were afterwards dipped in gravy and then given to the poor. A contemporary cookery book described the course of the meal: 'Guests be set with their lord in the chief place of the board, and they sit not down at the board before the guests wash their hands. Children be set in their place, and servants at a table by themselves. . . . Household servants busily help one another to do everything diligently, and talk merrily together. The guests are gladded with lutes and harps. At the last cometh fruit and spices, and when they have eaten, cloths and relief [trestles] are borne away, and guests wash and wipe their hands again. The grace is said, and guests thank their lord. Then, for gladness and comfort, drink is brought yet again.' The reference to boards or trestle tables is a reminder that fixed or 'dormant' dining tables were rare. Chaucer regarded a table as a sign of wealth:

> His table dormant in his halle alway
> Stood redy covered all the longe day.

The Countess of Leicester's household diary shows that every castle was as self-sufficient as its situation allowed. Meat, bread, fruit, vegetables and cheese, together with wool and leather for clothes and shoes, were supplied by the adjacent fields. Fish came from the nearest river. Corn was ground at the castle mill. Meat was chiefly mutton, beef and pork; with venison as a luxury. Most of the cattle and sheep were slaughtered in autumn, and the carcasses salted as winter fare. The medieval Assize of Bread mentions six sorts of loaf; the best being wastel or white bread, which was made from the finest flour; the worst, a mixture of coarse wheat and edible chaff. For Yarmouth herrings the Countess paid tenpence per hundred. Sturgeon and porpoise were fishes royal, eaten only by the King and his guests. Whale was not uncommon, but the head had to be sent to the King, and the tail to the Queen. Eggs during the thirteenth century cost fourpence per hundred. Cheese became a common item of food, much chewed by mariners and besieged garrisons. Spices, on the other hand, were so expensive that the Countess's steward kept a separate account of them. Pepper cost sevenpence per pound; ginger, about tenpence; cinnamon, about one shilling. The price of sugar ranged between one and two shillings per pound. Wine was plentiful because Burgundy, Gascony and Bordeaux were parts of the kingdom of England, a dowry reaped by Henry II when he married Eleanor of Aquitaine.

A nobleman's children were taught to be hardy and self-reliant. A newborn baby was handed to a nurse who suckled and reared it; and each child had its own nurse. The girls either married, or entered a nunnery, or stayed at home. Boys were sent to learn manners in the household of another nobleman. Having served as pages, they became esquires to a knight. The Middle Ages always revered and sometimes practised chivalry, the conduct of a *chevalier* or horseman, epitomized in Chaucer's 'parfit gentil knight'. At its highest, chivalry was Christianity *à la mode*; at its lowest, the romantical pose of *trouvères* and troubadours. A medieval knight kept his soul for God; his heart, for women; his life, for the king; his honour, for himself:

> *A dieu mon âme,*
> *Mon cœur aux dames,*
> *Ma vie au roi,*
> *L'honneur pour moi.*

A feudal magnate owned several castles, partly because one alone could not have fed his retainers indefinitely. He therefore went the round of his manors, accompanied by those retainers; so also did the medieval kings and their chief courtiers. The Court was often invited—and sometimes invited itself—to lodge with a nobleman. Queen Elizabeth I was especially fond of such hospitable economy. When she visited the Habingtons' home at Hallow Hall near Worcester she brought with her *inter alios* fifteen hundred horses, which had to be pastured at Pitchcroft beside the Severn.

Whenever the medieval kings were weak, the barons became aggressive. Therefore Henry II decreed that no man might fortify his home without royal licence to crenellate or erect battlements. Such fortifications, often transformed an Englishman's home. Thus, in 1272 Sir Stephen de Penchester received licence to fortify his house at Hever in Kent; seventy years later the family received a second licence, which enabled them to enlarge their house into the present moated castle. By the middle of the fifteenth century, however, the role of the castle was waning, partly because of the discovery of gunpowder, and partly because the nobility had decimated itself by civil war and attainder. Yet the peerage continued to trouble the monarchy. Ten years after he had been crowned, Henry VII was still so insecure that he persuaded Parliament to pass an Act exonerating anyone who should help him if ever he were dethroned, attainted or impeached. Several times during the preceding century the kings had tried to curb the barons' private armies. Henry VII struck the final blow. Any subject, he said, who fortified his home without licence, or kept too many armed retainers, must appear before the Court of the Star Chamber, so-called because of its interior decorations. Some historians have implied that the Court was created in order to curb the baronage; in fact, however, it was the King's Council sitting in judicial capacity, as it had done for many decades. Bacon's *Historie of the Raigne of King Henry the Seventh* recalls a dramatic encounter between the King and the Earl of Oxford at Hedingham Castle in Essex: 'At the King's going away, the Earl's servants stood ... in their livery coats, with cognisances, ranged on both sides, and made the King a lane.' Although he enjoyed the Earl's hospitality, the King did not approve his private army: 'The King started a little and said "By my faith (my lord) I thank you for your good cheer, but I may not endure to have my laws broken in my sight. My attorney must speak to you." ' The attorney did speak, very sharply indeed, for Bacon adds that the Earl was fined 'no less than fifteen thousand marks'. Nor was the Earl the only offender. Lord Hastings, for instance, became High Chamberlain of the Royal Household, Master of the Mint, Receiver of the Duchy of Cornwall, Chamberlain of North Wales, Lieutenant of Calais, Ambassador to France, Scotland, Brittany, Burgundy. Puffed with the pride of his power, he made a compact with two lords, nine knights, and forty-eight esquires, that they should fight for him against anyone in England, and, if required, raise an army at his own charge. He transformed his Leicestershire manor house into the castle of Ashby-de-la-Zouch, with a tower ninety feet high, and walls nine feet thick. Like Wolsey, such men set themselves above their king: *Ego et Rex Meus.*

The last overtly military castle was built (though never completed) at Thornbury in Gloucestershire, during the reign of Henry VIII, by the High Constable of England, Edward Stafford, Duke of Buckingham, who may have designed it rather to defend himself than to attack others, for he had incurred the jealousy of Wolsey, and might therefore expect the displeasure of the King. The castle walls were studded with crosslets and gunloops; the towered gatehouse contained a portcullis; the retainers' quarters and stables resembled a barracks, 300 feet long and nearly 200 feet wide. But nothing could save the Duke from Wolsey's venom. According to Lord Herbert of Cherbury, the Duke had remarked to Lord Abergavenny 'that, if the king died, he would have the rule of the realm. . . .' Arrested on a charge of treason, he was tried by his peers: 'They condemning him,' wrote Lord Herbert, 'the Duke of Norfolk deliver'd his sentence, not without tears.' The owner of Thornbury Castle was then beheaded.

With the nobility tamed at last, and their castles outdated by artillery, Queen Elizabeth I would have smiled had she been told that those castles would once again fire their guns and muster their garrisons. Yet that is what happened when Colchester Castle withstood a three months' siege by Cromwellians. Having expended their food and powder, the castle commanders, Sir Charles Lucas and Sir George Lisle, parleyed with the rebels, who granted an honourable surrender; but when they marched in, their first act was to shoot the two commanders. On the site of the Norman bailey an obelisk confirms the prophecy of a contemporary historian that the victims' valour would be long remembered, and with it the evil fame of their murderers: 'the names of those blood-thirsty men that perpetrated and counselled it, shall rot and stink.'

Perhaps the most dramatic siege of an Englishman's home occurred when the rebels attacked Donnington Castle in Berkshire, whose garrison possessed only 4 guns, 25 horsemen, and less than 200 infantry. Although greatly outnumbered, the royalists repulsed direct assault and twelve days of bombardment by heavy artillery. When the shelling ceased, the commander, Colonel John Boys, led a sortie which captured a large quantity of arms and ammunition. For his gallantry he was knighted by the King, who, in an effort to relieve the pressure, had engaged the enemy under the castle walls. During that brief respite, the King lodged at the castle, leaving the State Crown and the Great Seal of England with Sir John. The royal party then eluded the rebels, and made toward Oxford. The attackers, however, soon returned, this time declaring that, unless the garrison surrendered, they would raze every stone of the castle. Once more the Colonel refused; once more the bombardment began; once more the King relieved the pressure. But neither side could force an issue. Fearing to lose face against such a small force, the rebels invited Cromwell himself to launch an attack; which he declined to do, saying that it was 'such a knotty business'. The mock-Parliament thereupon voted a huge sum of money to reinforce the besiegers with men and artillery, including a fifteen-inch mortar. Again Sir John led his dwindling band in a counter-attack, but was driven back by weight of numbers. With only twenty barrels of powder left, and less than 150 able-bodied men, he sent a messenger to the King, seeking permission to surrender. The King concurred. On 30 March 1644 Sir John and his garrison laid down their arms in honourable surrender; and this time the rebels refrained from shooting them. The inscription on the Colonel's tomb says truly that the ruins of Donnington Castle are 'a noble monument to his fame'.

By the end of the seventeenth century the castles had become an Englishman's home and nothing more. Never again did they lower their portcullis against an invader, nor raise it to unleash an attack. Most of them were in ruins; many were grassy tumps.

When Celia Fiennes rode through Newark-on-Trent the castle was a husk: 'only the ruinated walls remaine....' When Daniel Defoe visited Tintagel the castle was scarcely visible: 'little or nothing, that I could hear, is to be seen at it.' Yet some castles survived for many centuries; among them is Dudley Castle, Worcestershire, which continued as an Englishman's home until 1750, when it was gutted by fire. In 1972 the Norman earthwork was the site of a zoo.

Caldicot Castle in Monmouthshire was built by the Norman Earls of Hereford. Having been enlarged during the thirteenth and fourteenth centuries, it decayed until the twentieth century, when the walls and towers were patched up, and the gatehouse converted into an impressive residence.

Lewes Castle in Sussex was built by William de Warrenne, first Earl of Surrey, son-in-law to William the Conqueror. In 1382 the castle was damaged by riotous townsfolk. Two centuries later it became a quarry. In 1774 the ruins were rented by a local wool merchant who renovated the keep. In 1972 the castle belonged to the Sussex Archaeological Society.

Tamworth Castle in Staffordshire began as a *motte* and bailey edifice, and was enlarged during the twelfth century. From the sixteenth to the eighteenth century it served as a private residence. In 1972 it belonged to the local corporation, which used part of it as a museum.

Restormel Castle in Cornwall was several times visited by a fourteenth-century Duke of Cornwall, alias the Black Prince. In 1649 the Cromwellians reported that the royalist stronghold was 'utterly ruined, nothing but the out walls thereof remaining, which are not ... worth taking down'. In 1925 the Duchy of Cornwall placed the ruins in the care of the Office of Works.

A few castles have either survived more or less intact or have been so skilfully restored that they appear to be intact. Bodiam Castle, for example, was built in 1386 by Sir Edward Dalyngruge to protect that part of Kent and Sussex from a French invasion. Like the men in Sir Walter Scott's poem, the defenders of Bodiam stood always at action stations:

> They quitted not their harness bright,
> Neither by day nor yet by night....

So far as I can discover, the garrison never went into action. An eighteenth-century antiquary described the derelict castle: 'This venerable structure, whose mouldering towers and walls ... afford at once a picturesque subject for the pencil. ...' Bodiam was bought and repaired by Lord Curzon in 1925, who then presented it to the National Trust.

Richmond Castle in Yorkshire was built c. 1071 by Alan the Red, a kinsman of the Duke of Brittany. Set dizzily above the river, and several times enlarged, it appeared so formidable that neither the English barons nor the Scottish raiders dared to attack it. Time was the only enemy, and not even the years have done overmuch damage.

Allington Castle in Kent began as a Norman manor house on the site of a Roman villa which the Saxons fortified. During the thirteenth century the house was converted into a castle; during the sixteenth century the ruins of that castle were converted into a Tudor residence by the Wyatt family; and in it was born Sir Thomas Wyatt, first master of the English sonnet:

> My love is like unto th'eternal fire;
> And I as those which therein do remain,
> Whose grievous pain is but their great desire
> To see the sight which they may not attain.

Tennyson, who lived close to Allington, set the scene in one of his plays, *Queen Mary*, where Wyatt's son undertakes to collect his father's manuscripts:

> ... it were a pious work
> To string my father's sonnets, left about
> Like scattered jewels. ...

Henry VIII and Cardinal Wolsey stayed at Allington Castle, holding Court in its Great Hall, and watching jousts in the tilting-yard. Thereafter the place decayed, and at the beginning of the twentieth century was roofless. Sir William Martin-Conway then restored it, refilled the moat, and uncovered the tilting-yard. In 1972 the castle was a Carmelite nunnery.

The fifteenth-century castle at Herstmonceux in Sussex was built on the site of a manor house by a family from Herstmonceux in Normandy. In 1441 Sir Roger Fiennes received licence to 'enclose, crenellate and furnish with towers his manor of Herst Monceux', which became the largest brick residence in England, surrounded by a moat, and topped by towers nearly ninety feet high. The Fiennes family held Herstmonceux until 1708, when it was bought by Bishop Francis Hare (grandfather of Augustus, the diarist) who died in 1740. Thirty-four years later the interior of the castle was demolished, and its materials were used to build Herstmonceux Place. In 1911 Sir Claude Lowther, lord of the manor, began to restore the castle. During the 1930s a later owner, Sir Paul Latham, completed the work. In 1972 the castle was the seat of the Royal Observatory.

Strange indeed were the destinies of some of our castles. Rochester Castle in Kent became a temporary coastguard station, and in 1914 was bombarded by German warships in the Channel. Bamburgh Castle in Northumberland converted part of itself into private flats. Holy Island Castle, in the same county, was captured in 1715 by the Pretender, who invited the garrison to dine on board a rebel ship, and there made them drunk; during the twentieth century the castle was renovated as an Englishman's home by Sir Edwin Lutyens, and is now administered by the National Trust. Appleby Castle in Westmorland reappeared as a neo-classical Renaissance residence. Kenilworth Castle in Warwickshire was presented to the Office of Works by its owner, Lord Kenilworth, who contributed toward the cost of repairs. In 1972 the interior of the ruined Norman castle at Barnwell in Northamptonshire was used as a tennis court by T.R.H. the Duke and Duchess of Gloucester, who lived at the Elizabethan mansion nearby. Castle Rising in Norfolk occupies the site of a sea fort which the Romans built as part of their defence system against Saxon pirates. When the Romans left Britain, the Saxons invaded it. An uncouth people, they possessed nothing of the Romans'' skill as builders, but they did patch-up the fort. Their successors, the Normans—who inherited something of the Roman genius—demolished the fort, and on the site erected a castle which justifies its name, rising 112 feet on a mound, guarding an important harbour. Then the sea receded, leaving the castle high and dry. A seventeenth-century lord of Castle Rising, Henry Howard, Earl of Northampton, built a Bede House or Trinity Hospital for eleven old ladies and their governess, each with her own chair and bedstead. In 1972 the bedeswomen on their way to church still wore the livery of their Jacobean predecessors ... steeple hats, red cloaks and the Howard badge. Bolton Castle in Yorkshire—home of the powerful Scrope family—received Mary Queen of Scots as a prisoner of Queen Elizabeth I. Forty servants attended the French-born captive, under the keen eye of Sir Francis Knollys, who taught his prisoner to speak English, or at any rate to speak it less Frenchly; a service which she rewarded by calling him 'my good schoolmaster'. Sir Francis, however, was no Rizzio to be suborned by winning ways. When, therefore, he observed that one of the sentries *was* being suborned, he ordered the man to be removed from his post: 'Let Kit Norton watch no more.'

Hazlewood Castle in Yorkshire was for centuries the seat of the Vavasours, who gave material for the building of several famous churches: 'Out of a little pece of a Quarry, within ye Mannor of Haslewood hath been taken ye Cathedrall churche of Yorke, ye Minsters of Howden, Selby and Beverley ... and divers other churches.' In 1829, when York Minster was set on fire by a mad-man, the Vavasours gave stone for the repairs; a truly generous gesture, for the family were Roman Catholics. Despite his re-ligion, Sir Thomas Vavasour was given command of the *Foresight* against the Armada. Even more remarkable, the family were allowed to hear Mass openly and without penalty, at a time when almost every other Roman Catholic in England did so at peril of his life or of his lands. At another Yorkshire castle—Ripley, seat of the Ingilbys—a hiding place was discovered by Sir Joslan Ingilby when the timbers of the King's Chamber were being treated for worm in 1936. The cavity was five feet high and only three feet wide; the seat or ledge being six inches wide. Venti-lation was provided via a small breathing-hole in the wall.

Bamburgh Castle, on the Northumbrian coast, is haunted. I was told so by Miss Calmady-Hamlyn, who in 1899 stayed at the castle, which belonged to her cousins. As the clock struck mid-night she saw the ghost and heard his chains. Both for size and situation, Bamburgh is the most impressive of all the Border castles, perched like a red eagle above a grey eyrie. Sir Walter Scott called it

King Ida's castle, large and square....

The Anglo-Saxon Chronicle stated that in the year 597 'King Ida began his reign, from which the royal stock of Northumbria draws its origins. He built Bamburgh which was surrounded first by a hedge and then by a wall.' The stockade became one of the most important towns in the far north, covering five acres of rocky promontory above the sea; but in 1066 its glory had departed: 'She who was once the mistress of cities,' sighed the chronicler, 'has been humbled to the lowness of a handmaiden.' William the Conqueror built a new fortress on the rock, allowing some of his tenants to hold their land by the service of carrying firewood to the castle. After a siege by the rebellious Earl of Northumberland, Bamburgh was enlarged to withstand the Scots. Hither in 1346 they carried the King of Scotland, a prisoner-of-war, so gravely wounded that surgeons were summoned from York, to extract the embedded arrow. Twice during the Wars of the Roses the castle withstood siege and bombardment, for medieval artillery could not destroy a fortress whose sandstone walls, ten feet thick, were made of blocks that had been pack-horsed from North Sunderland. In 1644 Sir Ralph Grey captured it for the King. During the eighteenth century it was bought by Lord Crewe, Bishop of Durham, who founded the Crewe Charities or Bamburgh Trust whereby a part of the castle became a free boarding school for thirty-four prospective maidservants. A free surgery and dispensary were added; one of the castle towers served as a granary; and a windmill was built to grind corn for the poor. The Trust further provided that a beacon should burn every night, to guide ships; that signal-contact with Holy Island should be maintained; that mounted coastguards should patrol the coast in stormy weather; and that shipwrecked sailors should be accommodated at the castle. During the second half of the nineteenth century Bamburgh was bought and renovated by the first Lord Armstrong, a civil engineer, who at the age of thirty became a Fellow of the Royal Society. In 1972 the castle belonged to the National Trust, as also did the parish church and a museum to the memory of Grace Darling and her father.

When warfare ceased to be a part of domestic politics, the aristocracy were able to build rather for comfort than for carnage; the more so because they ignored the medieval taboo on trade, at least to the extent of enriching themselves as speculators.

F

An Elizabethan Secretary of State, Sir Thomas White, visited the stately homes of Devonshire, urging them to subsidize an export drive, and 'giving them books and maps, showing them how in six months the most of those ships had made their voyage'. Few of our stately homes are larger or more beautiful than Audley End, a mansion near Saffron Walden in Essex, whose story begins during the Middle Ages, when Geoffrey de Mandeville endowed at Saffron Walden a Benedictine priory which became a rich abbey, owning lands beside the River Cam. At the dissolution of the monasteries the abbey was granted to Sir Thomas Audley (afterwards Baron Audley of Walden, Lord High Chancellor of England) who, as Speaker of the 'Reformation' Commons, had assisted Henry VIII to loot the Church. Sir Thomas demolished the abbey, and in its place raised a large house which, however, was not large enough for his grandson, Thomas Howard of Walden, first Earl of Suffolk, soon to become Lord Treasurer of England. His lordship therefore demolished the old home in order to build the biggest house in Britain; so big that when King James I saw it he exclaimed: 'Too much for a King, but it might do very well for a Lord Treasurer.' When Celia Fiennes saw it, in 1697, she was so amazed that she mis-named the owners: 'Thence we went to Audlyend 10 miles a house of the Earle of Sussex which makes a noble appearance like a town, so many towers and buildings off stone within a parke which is walled round, a good River runs through it, we pass over the bridge; its built round 3 Courts, there are 30 great and little towers on the top and a great Cupilow in the middle, the roomes are large and lofty with good rich furniture tapistry etc, but noe beds in that part we saw, there are 750 rooms in the house; the Cannall in the midst of the parke look'd very fine its altogether a stately palace and was built for one of the kings.' The regal reference is probably a misunderstanding of an event which Pepys had recorded on 8 March 1665: 'The King and Duke are to go to-morrow to Audley End, in order to the seeing and buying of it of my Lord Suffolk.' Although the King took possession of the mansion in the following autumn, the conveyance was not completed for another three years, and less than one-half of the price was paid. In 1701, when the Crown cancelled its debt, the fifth Earl of Suffolk recovered his ancestral seat (but not the forty-one years' interest on a debt of £20,000).

Pepys's friend, John Evelyn, remarked that the house itself was 'twixt antiq and modern'. The gardens, unfortunately, were 'not in order'.

In 1721 even the wealthy Suffolks decided that they could no longer afford to maintain such a vast home. They therefore sought the advice of Sir John Vanbrugh, who prescribed some pruning, starting with the demolition of an enormous courtyard. But pruning was not enough. So, thirty years later, other parts of the house were demolished, which left the rest much as it is today. Within a few years of that second subtraction the house passed to the future Lord Braybrooke, who spent a large fortune on restoring and enhancing it. 'Capability' Brown was employed to ensure that the gardens were no longer 'not in order'; Robert Adam designed the graceful bridge on the approach road, as well as a suite of apartments which include an alcove room and a dining parlour. Like many other Georgian landowners, Lord Braybrooke combined beauty with benevolence; notably in the cottages he built, just outside the Lion Gate. As though to atone for receiving stolen property, the founder of Audley End, Sir Thomas Audley, had endowed a group of almshouses nearby—the College of St Mark—which in 1972 served as a home for retired Anglican clergy (one of whom told me that the inmates are unofficially classified either as 'Prots' or as 'Cats'; that is, as Low Churchmen or as Anglo-Catholics).

If I were asked to choose the most impressive castle that is still an Englishman's home, I would name Castle Blenheim, commonly called Blenheim Palace. As at Audley End, the story begins before the digging of the foundations. On 13 August 1704, an English General, much pressed for time, borrowed a scrap of paper—it happened to be a Colonel's wine bill—and on the back of it pencilled a message to his wife: 'I have not time to say more but to beg you will give my duty to the Queen, and let her know her army has had a glorious victory. . . .' It had indeed, over Louis XIV of France, the European dictator. Tens of thousands of his troops were captured. Hundreds of French Generals and noblemen were soon to reach the Channel ports, to be detained at castles and manors throughout England. The man who had planned and led the victory—the scribbler of the message—was John Churchill, Duke of Marlborough; and the site of his victory was a village in Germany named Blenheim. When Queen Anne received the message, and afterwards the formal despatches, she rose royally to the occasion. As a token of gratitude she appointed him Colonel of the First Foot Guards, the regiment in which he had begun his career. As something more substantial than a token, she granted him a pension, which Parliament approved by reminding the nation that the Duke, 'after a Bloody battle, at or near Blenheim (altho' the Enemies had the Advantage of Number and Situation) did gain as Absolute and Glorious a Victory, as is Recorded in the History of any Age. . . .' The Queen further granted to Marlborough and his heirs the Royal Manor and Park of Woodstock, covering 15,000 acres. Finally, she announced that, at her own expense and to her own plans, she would build for the Duke a new home, to be called the Castle of Blenheim; for which purpose she engaged Sir John Vanbrugh as architect, and with her own hands constructed a model of the castle.

Like King James I when he first saw Audley End, the Duke must have been amazed when he saw the foundations of his castle, so different from his early home, Ashe House near Musbury in Devon, the seat of plain country squires. During Marlborough's childhood the King was in exile. Many loyal families were ejected from their homes by the rebels; others were fined, harassed or imprisoned. Marlborough's father, Sir Winston Churchill, had been compelled to seek shelter with his widowed mother-in-law, Lady Eleanor Drake, at whose house John Churchill was born. From such inauspicious beginnings arose the greatest of all English soldiers. When the King came into his own again, John Churchill obtained a commission in the First Foot Guards. After distinguished service abroad, he was promoted Captain. After another six years, being then Colonel, he married Sarah Jennings, Maid of Honour to the Princess Anne. A quarter of a century later, while sailing to the wars, he wrote to his wife: 'I did for a great while have a perspective glass looking upon the cliffs in hopes I might have had one sight of you.' His wife had already confirmed that theirs was among the great love stories of history: 'Wherever you are whilst I have life my soul shall follow you, my ever dear Lord Marlborough, and wherever I am I shall only kill the time, and wish for night, that I may sleep, and hope next day to hear from you.' It has been said that the hour breeds the man, and that without the hour no man can reach the summit of his potentiality. Of John Churchill it may be said that he surmounted his era by defeating the tyranny which Louis XIV had imposed upon it. In return he was created an Earl by William III, and a Duke by Queen Anne. Neither as a soldier nor as a civilian could he rise higher. And all this he achieved despite the irresolution of allies abroad, and the treachery of politicians at home. At last, it seemed, the English people had recognized their debt to him.

But the master of Castle Blenheim was required to remain on active service overseas, and could follow the building of his new home only by hearsay. A day or so before his victory at Oudenarde he wrote to the Duchess: 'pray let mr Travers know that I shall be glad to hear sometime from him how the Building goes on at Woodstock. . . .' Like many modern householders, he loved his garden: 'for the Gardening and Plantations I am at ease, being very sure that Mr Wise will bee diligent.' Shortly after another victory—the battle of Ramillies—his letter to the Duchess began hopefully: 'Every day gives us fresh marks of the great victory. . . .' But it ended anxiously: 'I beg of you to do all you can that the house at Woodstock may be carried up as much as possible, that I may have a prospect of living in it.' The prospect seemed uncertain because the Duke had passed the prime of life, and was a soldier on active service, constantly within range of enemy gunfire. After yet another victory, when Castle Blenheim was sufficiently advanced for the Duchess to take up residence, the Duke expressed an optimism which he may have affected rather than felt: 'I hope Mr Hacksmore will be able to mend those faults you find in the house.' A year later, still with his troops abroad, he reminded the Duchess that envious politicians were already belittling his victories: 'It is true what you say of Woodstock, that it is very much at my heart, especially when we are in prosperity, for then my whole thoughts are of retiring with you to that place. But if everything does not go to our own desire, we must not set our hearts too much upon that place, for I see very plainly that whilst I live, if there be troubles, I must have my share of them.' He ended his letter by confronting the calendar: 'This day makes your humble servant fifty-seven. On all accounts I could wish myself younger; but for none so much as that I might have it more in my power to make myself more agreeable to you, whom I love with all my soul.' Marlborough's fears were justified. One of his friends, the Duke of Shrewsbury, who had made a habit of riding over to Castle Blenheim, to enquire how the work was progressing, ceased to call, because he wished to unhitch himself from a waning star. Marlborough received the news calmly: 'I do by no means approve of the behaviour of the Duke of Shrewsbury.' But worse was to follow. Forgetful of its recent gratitude, Parliament withheld payment from the contractors and workpeople who were building the castle. The Duke, in short, was forced, either to pay them himself or to watch them suffer. Writing from Oxford, William Stratford described the effect of Parliament's cynical ruse: 'It will go hard with many in this town and the country.... Their creditors begin to call on them, and they can get no money at Blenheim.' When the Duke sent funds to be distributed among the needy, one of the contractors, who was being pressed for £600, received something on account: 'The fellow thanked him with tears, and said that the money for the present would save him from gaol.'

Yet Castle Blenheim was only one of the humiliations that were heaped on Marlborough, for the Queen turned against him and against the Duchess who had been her closest friend. The Duke was dismissed the Service; the Duchess was deprived of her offices at Court. When at last the Duke did take up residence at his new home, he entered a kind of exile; and when he died, at the age of seventy-two, the castle was still unfinished. That it was ever completed is due to the zeal of his widow, who survived him by twenty-two years. Unlike Marlborough, the Duchess never had cared for Castle Blenheim, but she had cared for the Duke, and would continue to do so until she died. Meanwhile, as a widow of sixty-two—witty, capable, handsome—she declined proposals of marriage from Lord Coningsby and from the Duke of Somerset. Her task was to complete her husband's monument. She began by using the £50,000 which he had bequeathed for that purpose; and when the legacy was spent, she used her private fortune. At the Woodstock entrance to the park she erected a triumphal arch. On a mound facing the castle she erected a pillar, 130 feet high, bearing a statue of the Duke, 25 feet high; on one side of the pillar's base she inscribed an account of his ten campaigns; on the other three sides, the Statutes whereby the Queen and the nation had presented the castle as a gift. In her will she decreed that the Duke's body be removed from King Henry VII's Chapel in Westminster Abbey, to rest beside her own, in the tomb which she had built at Castle Blenheim.

The last home of the first Duke of Marlborough justifies its newer name of palace. The building alone covers three acres; its wings or blocks are joined by arcades which form courtyards; the north and the south fronts are 350 feet long. 'Capability' Brown is said to have planted the avenues and trees as a plan of the Battle of Blenheim (one of his avenues is two miles long). By damming the River Glyne he enlarged the natural lake. Sir James Thornhill painted the ceiling in the great hall; Rysbrack designed the Duke's monument in the chapel; Grinling Gibbons graced·many of the apartments; Sir John Vanbrugh bridged the lake. This stateliest of homes is sometimes open to the public. Visitors are especially eager to see the room in which was born a second 'saviour of Europe', Sir Winston Churchill K.G., and also the nearby churchyard where he was buried. The first Duke of Marlborough, we have said, was insulted and injured by the nation whose liberty he had defended. Both he and his wife were expelled from Court. Having been promised a home, they received a liability. More than any other woman in England, the Dowager Duchess had cause to feel bitter against the nation in general and the Queen in particular. Yet when she added the finishing touches to the Long Gallery, she set there a statue of that Queen, and on it she inscribed these words: 'To the memory of Queen Anne, under whose auspices John, Duke of Marlborough, conquered, and to whose munificence he and his posterity with gratitude owe the possession of Blenheim.'

Even during the late twentieth century the castle was still a home for some Englishmen. The outstanding example is Windsor, which was converted from a fortress into a palace by King Henry I, and thereafter either enlarged or adorned by almost every English sovereign. Henry III extended the walls, and built three towers. Edward III added the Round Tower (which is less round than its name suggests). St George's Chapel was the work of Edward IV, Henry VII, Henry VIII. Queen Elizabeth I built the north terrace and a gallery overlooking it; Charles II renovated the State Apartments; George IV made many changes, both within and without. Among the architects were William of Wykeham during the fourteenth and Sir Jeffry Wyatville during the nineteenth century.

Castle Ashby in Northamptonshire has been held by the same family for 400 years. In 1512 Sir William Compton bought the manor of Ashby David, so-called in memory of David de Ashby, who had founded a local chantry chapel during the fourteenth century. In 1574 the first Lord Compton began to build a new castle on the site of a ruined one, using the Tudor E design. In 1618 Lord Compton was created Earl of Northampton; his successor died fighting for King Charles I against the rebels, who set fire to his castle, damaging one side of it. In 1624 the stone parapet was added, inscribed with a Latin version of: 'Except the Lord keep the house the watchman waketh but in vain: Except the Lord build the house they labour but in vain that build it....' About ten years later the two arms of the E were joined by means of a screen (Inigo Jones is said to have been the architect). Besides its valuable pictures and furniture, Castle Ashby contains a collection of Greek vases and a pair of bellows by Benvenuto Cellini. In 1972 the castle belonged to the Marquess of Northampton.

'A palace, a town, a fortified city': so said Horace Walpole when he first saw Castle Howard, the largest home in Yorkshire, seat of the Earl of Carlisle. Nor were the fortifications a mere ornament, because north Yorkshire was still troubled by the Scots, who, nineteen years after the castle had been completed, raided as far south as Derby, reinforced by the French, and led by the Young Pretender. The castle itself was built for the third Earl of Carlisle, between 1699 and 1726, to a design by Sir John Vanbrugh, who made the north front more than 600 feet long. The Great Hall is thirty-five feet square, paved with marble lit by the windows of a dome. In the park a circular mausoleum was designed by Nicholas Hawksmoor, assistant to Sir Christopher Wren. The west wing, containing the chapel, was built by Sir Thomas Robinson during the middle of the eighteenth century. Among the castle's treasures are works by Van Dyck, Holbein, Rubens, Gainsborough; and Britain's largest private collection of costumes from the seventeenth to the twentieth century.

Chillingham Castle in Northumberland was fortified by Sir

Thomas de Heton in 1344, whereafter it passed to the Greys of Wark-on-Tweed and thence by marriage to the Earls of Tankerville. During the seventeenth century it received some graceful additions from Inigo Jones. The park supports the remnants of the Chillingham herd of white cattle, which have grazed the district for seven centuries, and are said to be descended from *Bos taurus* or the wild ox of prehistory. The king bull is chosen by the herd, and he rules it until old age or infirmity compel him to abdicate. Thomas Bewick, the eighteenth-century engraver, made a drawing of the Chillingham Bull, which so displeased its subject that the artist was compelled to finish his sketch from the safety of a tree. A comparable reception was accorded when Sir Edwin Landseer, arriving to take sketches for his 'Dying Bull', found the animal so full of life that he had to run for his own. In 1972 Chillingham Castle still belonged to the Earl of Tankerville, but he could neither afford to reside there nor find anyone who wished to. Some of his herd was sent to Whipsnade Zoo in Bedfordshire; the remainder is tended by volunteers from the Chillingham Wild Cattle Association.

Northumberland contains England's outstanding example of a long-occupied home: Alnwick Castle, seat of Hugh Algernon Percy, tenth Duke of Northumberland, Lord Lieutenant of that County, Knight of the Most Noble Order of the Garter, Earl of Northumberland, Baron Warkworth, Earl Percy, Earl of Beverly, Lord Lovaine, Baron of Alnwick. The castle was built during the twelfth century by a Norman named de Vesci. Since 1309 it has been the home of the Percies, who enlarged and strengthened it. Sir Henry de Percy, the first lord of Alnwick, rebuilt the keep and then added the postern and the Constable's Tower. Alnwick Castle is surrounded by a wall ten miles long, enclosing 3,000 acres of woods, moors, farms, and a park that is open to the public. The history of this home is a précis of the history of England. Of its seven centuries of life, only two have passed without an attack. For nearly five centuries it stood within the No Man's Land of border feuds, when the Scottish Douglases and the English Percies glared like Ghibelline and Guelph:

> It fell about the Lammas tide,
> When the muir men win their hay,

> That doughty Douglas bound him to ride
> Into England, to drive a prey.

Shakespeare dramatized Henry IV's warning to the overproud Percies:

> My blood hath been too cold and temperate,
> Unapt to stir at these indignities,
> And you have found me; for accordingly
> You tread upon my patience: but be sure
> I will from henceforth rather be myself,
> Mighty and to be feared....

War or peace, the life of the castle went its own way. In 1569 it supported 166 servants, excluding pages, esquires and attendant knights. Enough food for fifty-seven visitors was prepared every day, together with four gallons of wine and forty gallons of beer.

The castle dominates the town paternally and also maternally, for the boys' school is named The Duke's School, and the girls' school is named The Duchess's School. The Drill Hall was built for a local troop of the Northumberland Hussars, with whom the tenth Duke served during the Second World War; here, too, are the headquarters of the seventh battalion of the Royal Northumberland Fusiliers, named after the second Duke, who commanded them during the American War of Independence; their Honorary Colonel is the tenth Duke. A tall plinth, crowned with the Percy Lion, was erected by tenants who enlisted in the Percy Tenantry Volunteers, a local defence force, founded by the Duke during the Napoleonic wars; the inscription says: 'To Hugh, Duke of Northumberland, K.G. This column is erected, dedicated, and inscribed by a grateful and united tenantry. Anno Domini MDCCCXVI.' Three ancient customs are observed at Alnwick: a Shrove Tuesday football game is played in the pastures, and the first man to retrieve the ball from the River Aln receives a prize from the Duke; the season's first salmon is presented to the Duke; and he yearly receives a red rose in lieu of rent for his lands at Newburn on the River Tyne. The castle stables contain a state coach that was used by the third Duke when he served as ambassador to King Charles X of France. At the coronation of Queen Elizabeth II the Duke carried the Sword of Mercy, and the Duchess was Mistress of the Robes to the Queen Mother. In the castle the old Border tunes are played by the Duke's piper. Of the many heirlooms, two seem especially evocative because they suggest a visitor's immemorial habit of leaving something behind; in this instance, King Edward VI's gloves and Oliver Cromwell's nightcap. Few English homes enjoy a prospect wider than Alnwick's, a fact that was appreciated by the first Duke, who in 1781 commissioned Robert Adam to design the Brislee Tower on a nearby hilltop. The candid type of suburban gardener will not scorn the self-appreciation which the Duke inscribed on the tower, in Latin: 'Look around! I myself measured out all these things; they are of my own ordering, my own design. Many of these trees were planted with my own hands.' From the top of that tower seven castles are visible: Alnwick, Warkworth, Bamburgh, Holy Island, Ros, Chillingham, Dunstanburgh.

By the mid-twentieth century the castles of England had become and seemed certain to remain either ruins or museums or residences. No other role appeared possible. Yet in 1940 many of them once again served as wartime strongholds. The Tate Gallery hid some of its treasures at Muncaster Castle in Cumberland and at Sudeley Castle in Gloucestershire; specimens from the Natural History Museum went to Tattershall Castle in Lincolnshire and to Wray Castle in Westmorland; heirlooms from the Public Record Office went to Belvoir Castle in Leicestershire; the British Museum sent many exhibits to Skipton Castle in Yorkshire.

Though each is rooted in its native county, the castles are so widely scattered and so richly endowed that they create a grapevine of English history. More resoundingly than any other kind of home, they recite their own roll-call: Barnard Castle, Bishop's Castle, Blaise Castle, Corfe Castle, Hanley Castle, Hazlewood Castle, Hopton Castle, Peckforth Castle; and others beyond counting: Castle Acre, Castle Ashby, Castle Bromwich, Castle Bytham, Castle Carrock, Castle Cary, Castle Combe, Castle Donington, Castle Eaton, Castle Ford, Castle Frome, Castle Gresley, Castle Hedingham, Castle Howard, Castle Rising, Castle Side, Castle Town.

And to the sound of that resonant fanfare we reach the place whence we started, which was Maxstoke Castle, built by Sir William de Clinton, later the first Earl of Huntingdon, who in 1346 received King Edward III's licence to crenellate (the licence is still preserved among the castle archives). As you enter the main door, you see—framed on the wall—some of the documents whereby Maxstoke was conveyed to the Comptons, the Egertons, and—400 years ago—to the family of the present owner, Captain C. B. Fetherston-Dilke, R.N. The ground floor apartments include a spacious sitting room; a snug little dining room alongside the modernized kitchen; and the Captain's office, with his name and rank inscribed above the door, on a board made by shipwrights of one of the ships he commanded. When you open another door, you notice the work-bench and tools that are a part of his ceaseless war against delapidation. But Maxstoke Castle is now divided into compartments, the home and the museum, a living present and a mummified past. The timbered banqueting-hall, for example, is still the scene of parties and charitable events. In it dined King Richard III, on his way to Bosworth Field:

> I shall despair. There is no creature loves me;
> And if I die, no soul shall pity me....

In it (they say), when the battle was over, dined the dead king's successor, Henry VII, first of the Tudor monarchs:

> God and your arms be praised, victorious friends,
> The day is ours....

The door from the banqueting-hall to the Tudor drawing-room forms a wooden alcove which is thought to have come from Kenilworth Castle, and to have been carved in Nürnberg. It is called the Whispering Door because it served as a foyer where guests and servants could rehearse *sotto voce* their news, or their greeting, or their private opinion of the castle and everyone in it. The drawing-room, which overlooks the courtyard, is part of a timbered addition of 1598, whose façade was uncovered during the late twentieth century. Far below, a grass walk encircles the red sandstone walls, and beyond it stand some of the oak trees of Shakespeare's Arden Forest.

The castle library is both old and new. You may take up either a modern novel or—if you are strong-armed—an early edition of *The Antiquities of Warwickshire* by Sir William Dugdale of Blyth Hall, which caused such a stir in learned circles that

Anthony à Wood, himself an Oxford scholar, felt impelled to write: 'This summer [1656] came to Oxon "The Antiquities of Warwickshire" etc. written by William Dugdale, and adorn'd with many cuts. This being accounted the best book of its kind that hitherto was made extant, my pen cannot enough describe how A. Wood's tender affections and insatiable desire of knowledge were ravish'd and melted down by the reading of that book.' Blyth Hall, nearby, is still the Dugdale family home. Of the many other heirlooms at Maxstoke, I remember most vividly a four-poster bed that belonged to Amy Robsart, unhappy wife of Robert Dudley, Earl of Leicester, the man whom Queen Elizabeth loved. I remember, too, a portrait of Tom Grainger, last of the castle jesters, dated 1681; he is shown smoking a clay pipe, with an owl on his shoulder. Alongside the portrait are his bauble and his ale-pot.

Maxstoke Castle is a home where history comes alive in the loving hands of those whose forebears made it. Francis Bacon gave thanks for all such places: 'It is a reverent thing to see a Castle or other ancient Building that is not in decay.'

Hampton Court Palace / Gardens

5 In the Garden

WRITING in 1822, William Cobbett expressed his admiration for a unique feature of the Englishman's home: 'You see, in almost every part of England, that most interesting of all objects, that which is an honour to England, and distinguishes it from the rest of the world, namely those neatly kept and productive little gardens round the labourers' houses, which are seldom unornamented by more or less of flowers.' A medieval Englishman would have read those words with as much amazement as he would have stared at the gardens which they describe. His own life was too brief and too laborious ever to persuade him that weeding a lawn is a pleasant pastime. England, however, never became a flowerless kingdom. Even in places where no man exists to pick them, the apple abounds, the snowdrop multiplies, the primrose propagates. The true gardens of medieval England were the hedgerow, the river bank, the heather-honeyed moor. If a man did cultivate the land beside his house, it was in order to produce healing herbs and nourishing vegetables. An exception to that utilitarian rule was the Church, whose sons were the chief gardeners. On major feast days the priest wore a garland of flowers, colour being then an important part of worship. In 1405, when Roger de Walden was consecrated Bishop at St Paul's Cathedral, he and the canons wore a necklace of red roses. Many large churches maintained their own garden, usually called the Sacristan's Garden. Some cathedrals maintained also a Prior's Garden and a Canon's Garden. All kept a kitchen garden and an orchard. It was a churchman, Alexander Neckham, Abbot of Cirencester, who wrote what is said to be the first book on English gardening. Another of his achievements was to share his nursery meals with a future King, Richard Coeur-de-Lion: 'In the month of September, 1157,' said a chronicler, 'there was born to the King at Windsor a son named Richard, and the same night was born Alexander Neckham at St Alban's, whose mother gave suck to Richard with her right breast, and to Alexander with her left breast.' Neckham's book—which discussed learnedly the barrenness of mules and the magical property of rubies—described a typical monastery garden: 'The garden should be decorated with roses and lilies, the tumsole or heliotrope, violets, and mandrake ... parsley, cost, fennel, southernwood, coriander, sage, savory, hysop, mint, rue, ditanny, smallage, pellitory, lettuce, garden cress and peonies. There should also be beds planted with onions, leeks, garlic, pumpkins and shalots. The cucumber, the poppy, the daffodil, and the brank-ursine ought to be in a good garden.' The orchard must contain 'medlers, quinces, warden-trees, peaches, pears of St Riole, pomegranates, lemons, oranges, almonds, dates and figs'.

Gardens being a prerogative of eminence, privacy was imposed thereon, as recommended by a medieval poem, *The Flower and the Leaf*:

> The hedge as thick as is a castle wall,
> That who that list without to stand or go,
> Though he would all day pryen to and fro,
> He should not see if there were any wighte
> Within or no. ...

King Henry III had already set the fashion by ordering his bailiff at Woodstock Palace 'To make round the garden of our Queen two walls, good and high, so that no one may be able to enter, with a fitting and honourable herbary near our fish pond, in which the same Queen may be able to amuse herself....' When Henry VIII received Hampton Court as a gift from Cardinal Wolsey he became so proud of its gardens that he insisted on showing them to every new visitor, even if the visitor arrived at dusk. Among the King's favourite flowers were violets, sweet-williams, and roses (at fourpence per hundred). The royal paths and flower beds were flanked by railings, painted with green and white stripes. The Pond Garden was tended by labourers who carried 'water out of ye Temmes to fyll the pondes in the night tymes'. Another of the gardens contained twenty brass sundials, each on a grassy mound. Greenhouses, however, were unknown, so that the King had to be content with what Parkinson's *Earthly Paradise* described as 'flowers which our English ayre will permitt to be noursed up'.

Everyone knows the introit to Bacon's essay *Of Gardens*: 'God Almighty first planted a garden. And indeed it is the purest of all human pleasures.' Few people, however, seem to have read beyond that paragraph, to discover that Bacon was writing a technical treatise for Jacobean landowners: 'There ought,' he continued, 'to be gardens for all months of the year.... For December and January and the latter part of November, you must take such things as are green all winter: Holly; ivy; bays; juniper; cypress trees; yew; pine-apple trees; rosemary; lavender.' For May and June he suggested 'honeysuckles; strawberries; bugloss; columbine; the French marygold; flos Africanus; cherry tree in fruit.' Had a literate cottager chanced on Bacon's essay he would have learned that an Englishman's garden 'ought not to be well under thirty acres of ground'. Given such acreage, the gardener must surround it 'with a stately hedge. The arches to be upon pillars of carpenter's work, of some ten foot high and six feet broad.' Bacon did not approve those labourers who had carried 'water out of ye Temmes to fyll the pondes in the night tymes'. On the contrary: 'ponds,' he declared, 'mar all, and make the garden unwholesome and full of flies and frogs.'

By the middle of the seventeenth century every gentleman kept a garden, as also did many merchants and other prosperous townsfolk. Samuel Pepys, for example, who lived next door to his office in Seething Lane, where he enjoyed his garden: 'It being a very fine moonshine,' said his diary, 'my wife and Mercer come into the garden, and my business being done, we sang till about twelve at night....' So far from objecting to his serenade, the neighbours got out of bed to hear it, for Pepys added that the singing brought 'pleasure to ourselves and neighbours by their casements opening....' Another eminent townsman—Sir Thomas Browne of Norwich—found a comparable delight in his own garden: 'The most pleasant and delectable thing for recreation,' he believed, 'is our Flower Garden, to behold at a window faire and comely Proportions, handsome and pleasant Arbors, and, as it were, Closets, delightfull borders of lavender, Rosemarie, Boxe, and other such like.' Nor were scent and colour the only pleasures, for the good Doctor loved to 'heare the ravishing music of an infinite number of pretie Small Birds, which continually, day and night, doe chatter and chant their proper and naturall branch-songs upon the Hedges and Trees of the garden....'

The day of the garden had dawned at last, and Eden came down to Earth, to be greeted by the book trade: *Arte of Grafting and Planting Trees* (1572), *England's Happiness Increased: Potatoes* (1664), *Flower Garden and Complete Vineyard* (1683). It was indeed an age of gardens. In 1682 the Earl of Danby gave to Oxford University five acres of land, on what had been a Jewish cemetery; and there the famous Botanical Gardens were built, enclosed by walls twice as high as a tall man. Celia Fiennes enjoyed the entrée to many mansions when she explored England on horseback. At Wilton she admired the Earl of Pembroke's estate: 'The gardens are very fine, with many gravel walks with grass squaires set with fine brass and stone statues, with fish ponds and basons that easily conveys by pipes water to all parts. Grottoe is at the end of the garden garnished with many fine figures of Goddesses....' The Earl, it seems, had devised a booby trap: 'about 2 yards off the doors in severall parts pipes in a line that with sluce spoutts water up to wett the Strangers.' Wilton was altogether an amphibious home: 'on each side is two little roomes which by turning their wires the water runnes in the rockes you see and hear it, and also it is so contrived in one room that it makes the melody of Nightingerlls and all sorts of birds....'; after which, another douche: 'but at the entrance off each room, is a line of pipes that appear not till by a sluce moved it

G

washes the spectators, designed for diversion.' One hopes that Wilton House contained an airing cupboard. But those informalities were balanced by formal precision. Thus, when William of Orange became King of England, tulips accompanied him from Holland, together with directions for planting. Beds, said the catalogue, must be two-and-a-half feet wide, and the bulbs set exactly five inches apart (gardeners were provided with a wooden ruler).

Kings, cardinals, earls, knights; they could afford a staff of gardeners. But what of lesser men? Already they were beginning to acquire and cultivate their own patch of Paradise. Abraham Cowley, a poet and therefore poor, lived at Porch House in Chertsey, where he fulfilled a lifelong ambition: 'I would never have had,' he confessed, 'any other desire so strong, and so like to covetousness, as that one which I have always had, that I might be master at last of a small house and large garden....' Like most modern gardeners, Cowley plucked his own weeds, planted his own seeds, burned his own bonfires: 'that pleasantest of human industry,' he said, 'the improvement of something which we call our own.' Another poet, Wordsworth, used his garden as something more than a garden, a fact which Kilvert noted in his *Diary*: 'When William Howitt was at Rydal Mount looking about after Wordsworth's death he fell in with old James the gardener and asked him which was the poet's study. "This," said James, pointing to the arbour and grass mound from which Rydal Mount takes its name.'

The eighteenth century denied Bacon's belief that 'God Almighty first planted a garden'. According to Horace Walpole, God had created an ungentlemanly eyesore: 'Open country,' he complained, 'is but a canvas on which a landscape ought to be designed.' In Walpole's opinion, which he shared with all landowners, the bad workmanship of God must be amended by the good taste of Man: 'Any tract of land whose characteristic expressions have been strengthened by art, and in which the spontaneous arrangements of nature have been improved by the hand of taste, ought to be considered as a Garden.' The outstanding example of an Augustan gardener was Lancelot Brown, whose eye for the potentialities or capabilities of an estate was so sharp that men dubbed him 'Capability'. He was born in the Northumberland hamlet of Kirkharle, where the cottagers still cherish their own small gardens. As a youth he worked for the Loraines at Kirkharle Park, which in 1972 was a farm. Promoted, he prospered and set up as landscape gardener. The landowners were soon competing for his services. He designed the gardens at Kew, at Blenheim Palace and at scores of other stately homes. For nine years he worked in partnership with William Kent, the architect. Having begun life as garden-boy, he ended it as High Sheriff of Huntingdonshire and Cambridgeshire, and father-in-law to Lord Holland. Brown's speciality was to beat Nature at her own game. He pumped rivers uphill, creating a waterfall. He designed bridges, concealing the fact that no river ran beneath them. As Dr Gilpin remarked: 'Mr Brown was often very happy in creating these artificial obstructions.' But nothing must seem too real, too wild. The Augustans had no head for heights. When Daniel Defoe, a hard-bitten journalist, returned from the summit of Hampstead Heath, he uttered a warning: "tis so near heaven, I dare not say it can be a proper situation, for any but a race of mountaineers, whose lungs have been used to a rarify'd air. . . .'

But again we have strayed into high society. Again, therefore, let us join the poets, this time William Cowper, living modestly at Olney in Buckinghamshire. Although he had no non-existent river to bridge, Cowper consoled himself by applying to language the artificial pattern which Brown imposed on Nature; thus, instead of stating that dung does well in a compost heap, he wrote:

> The stable yields with stercoraceous heap,
> Impregnated with quick fermenting salts.

Cowper's timid temperament would have prevented him from following the advice which Miller's *Dictionary* offered: 'it would be well to try whether the firing of Guns near such Trees as are infected with Caterpillars would not destroy those Insects.'

Despite his good opinion of English gardens, Cobbett thought little of English gardeners: 'The far greater part of persons who possess gardens really know very little about the matter.' Many rural householders were still preoccupied with what Sir Thomas Browne called 'the elegant co-ordination of vegetables'. Even so, one feels that Cobbett was wide of the mark. Dorothy Wordsworth's *Journal* records the loving skill with which she and her brother created their own garden on a slope above Dove Cottage (Wordsworth, you remember, called it 'our little domestic slip of a mountain'). On 16 May 1800, only a few months after they had moved in, Dorothy was at work: 'hoed the first row of peas, weeded etc....' Next day she was at it again: 'Transplanted radishes after breakfast. ...' William lent a willing hand: 'In the morning W. cut down the wintry cherry tree.' At other times his patience was tested, as on the day when he dug a path to the snowbound lavatory or 'necessary'. Dorothy recorded the incident: 'he cleared a path to the necessary, called me out to see it, but before we got there the whole housefull of snow had fallen from the roof upon the path....' When spring returned they could hardly control their eagerness to discover how the plants were doing: 'We went by candle light into the garden, and were astonished at the growth of the Brooms, Portugal, Laurels etc ...' Knowing that all work and no play makes Jack a dull gardener, the Wordsworths enjoyed the fruit of their labour, which was leisure: 'Sate out of doors reading the whole afternoon. ...' Having moved to a larger house with a rambling garden, the Wordsworths were compelled to employ a gardener, yet they never ceased to combine busyness and leisure among the flowers.

Most homes contain children, and some children tend 'their own' garden. Elizabeth Barrett Browning not only tended but also remembered her garden at Hope End in Herefordshire. At the age of nine, having read the story of Hector in the original Greek, she composed a portrait of that hero in flowers, using gentian for his eyes, scented grass for his hair, and daffodils for his helmet. Six years later she went one day to saddle her pony, but failed to secure the girth, which slipped and caused her to fall, so injuring the spine that for the rest of her life she was an invalid. In middle age, while living in Italy with her husband and young son, she suddenly remembered the garden at Hope End, and the portrait she had made:

> In the garden lay supinely
> A huge giant, wrought of spade,
> Arms and legs were stretched at length,
> In a passive giant strength,
> And the meadow turf, cut finely,
> Bound them laid and interlaid.

Another Victorian personage, Mrs Nickleby—mother to Nicholas —encountered a different type of Hector; not one who skulked in his tent, but an eccentric neighbour who expressed his affection for Mrs Nickleby via a spate of unsolicited testimonials: 'The bottom of his garden,' Mrs Nickleby told her son, 'joins the bottom of ours, and of course I had several times seen him among the scarlet-beans in his little arbour, or working at his little hot-beds. I used to think he stared rather, but I didn't take any particular notice of that as we were new-comers, and he might be curious to see what we were like. But when he began to throw his cucumbers over our wall ... and vegetable marrow likewise. ...'

Photography has revealed that the gardens of some English homes were much the same in 1972 as they had been in 1872. One such garden belonged to William Barnes, the poet, philologist, schoolmaster, historian, walker, parish priest, who was born in 1801, at what he described as 'a little farmling' near Sturminster Newton in Dorset. He became a village schoolmaster; married happily for life; contrived (by overworking and under-eating) to start a school of his own at Mere in Wiltshire; sent himself up to Cambridge at the age of thirty-seven; took Holy Orders; was appointed Rector of Winterborne Came in Dorset; and—when it was too late to do much good—received a Civil List pension (about three shillings a day) in recognition of his achievement as a poet (whose books earned about fourpence a day). Barnes's rectory was and still is a two-storey thatched house with three roofs forming a verandah above the ground floor. His daughter, Miss Laura Barnes, left an endearing picture of the white-bearded parson-poet: 'And how he enjoyed his garden and tended his shrubs! Sometimes he took a fancy to mow his own lawn, in memory of early days at Mere, but the use of a little mowing machine, the invention of later times, useful though it was, never gave him the same feeling as did the scythe of his earlier years, making its graceful curves.' William Barnes wrote several poems in the Dorset dialect, but his fame rests on a mastery of standard English:

> Leaves of the summer, lovely summer's pride,
> Sweet is the shade below your silent tree,
> Whether in waving copses where ye hide

> My roamings, or in fields that let me see
> The open sky....

Cobbett's 'productive little gardens round the labourers' houses' are neither so numerous nor so well-tended as they were in my childhood. Young labourers would rather buy than grow vegetables. Allotments have almost disappeared from England. The cottage garden reached its zenith during the early years of the twentieth century. Flora Thompson remembered the Edwardian villages: 'The women never worked in the vegetable gardens or on the allotments, even when they had their children off hand and had plenty of time, for there was a strict division of labour and that was "men's work" ... any work outside the home was considered unwomanly.' Cottage women were content to 'cultivate a flower garden, and most of the houses had at least a narrow border beside the pathway ... they grew all the old-fashioned cottage garden flowers, pinks and sweet williams and love-in-a-mist, wallflowers and forget-me-not in spring and hollyhocks and Michaelmas daisies in autumn. Then there were lavender and sweetbriar bushes and southernwood, sometimes called "lad's love", but known there as "old man".' The men were tireless: 'The energy,' wrote Miss Thompson, 'they brought to their gardening after a hard day's work in the fields was marvellous. They grudged no effort and seemed never to tire. Often, on moonlight nights in late spring, the solitary fork of some one who had not been able to tear himself away would be heard and the scent of his switch fire would float in at the windows.'

Some Englishmen live for their garden. A cynic might say that they died for it. Their money, their leisure, their energy ... all are invested in the garden. So rich seem the dividends—or so acute the fear of losing them—that the gardener will not forsake his home even for a weekend, lest the moths corrupt, or the rust stain, or the strawberries overpass their prime. Other gardeners allow the land to lie fallow, and all creation to feed thereon. Such a one was Captain Frederick Marryat, C.B.E., F.R.S., R.N., an officer so daringly outspoken that he fell foul of their Lordships, and beached himself prematurely at the age of thirty-eight, thereafter to win fame as the author of *Peter Simple, Mr Midshipman Easy* and *The Children of the New Forest*. Some of the Captain's characters were as outspoken as their creator. Coleridge, indeed, said of *Peter Simple* 'this novel would have lost nothing in energy if the author had been more frugal in his *swearing*'. In 1843 the Captain bought a small estate at Langham in Norfolk, not far from Nelson's birthplace at Burnham Thorpe, and only ten miles from North Creake, whose rector—brother to Admiral Sir Henry Keppel—had retired from the sea in order to enter the Church (and unwittingly to become the original of Mr Easy).

Theodore Hook once visited Marryat's many-childrened home, a thatched house, called Manor Cottage, since demolished. His first impressions were of the garden, which seems to have been zoological rather than botanical. As he approached the front door a brace of tame partridge got up. His host then explained that Manor Cottage was also Liberty Hall: 'I open my bedroom window,' Marryat remarked, 'and jump out when I am dressed, which saves the trouble of unbarring doors.' Hook had no need to avoid walking on the grass. 'There were,' he recollected, 'animals everywhere: calves feeding on the lawn; ponies and a donkey under a clump of larches; a colt and its mama. There were coops of fowls standing on the gravel path in front of the dining room....' The children shared their father's love of animals: 'A jackdaw sat on the shoulder of one of the little girls, and as the party neared the lawn, it was joined by a number of pigeons.' But that was only part of the zoo: 'there were also an aviary, rabbits, pheasant, partridges, cats, dogs, and donkeys.' The Captain moreover had seasoned his crew with a nautical tang: 'In the walled garden a tame sea-gull and a heron followed them around.' Each member of the household appeared to get on well with the others, for Hook noticed that one of the Captain's daughters 'seized and held a large rodent in her bare hands, so fierce that it had killed a ferret'. Captain Marryat would have shared Joseph Addison's admission: 'I value my garden more for being full of blackbirds than of cherries.'

The twentieth century has produced many eminent gardeners. Were I asked to choose the most eminent, I would name the late Vita Sackville-West, known more formally as the Hon. Lady Nicolson, who was born at her ancestral home, Knole House, a mansion built in 1456 by Thomas Bourchier, Archbishop of Canterbury, and enlarged by Thomas Sackville, first Earl of

Dorset, in 1603. The house, the gardens, and much of the eighty acres of parkland were given to the National Trust by the fourth Earl of Sackville in 1946. Having learned the craft at Knole, Lady Nicolson—helped by her husband, Sir Harold—created the famous gardens at their castle of Sissinghurst in Kent. But Vita Sackville-West was something more than a gardener; she was the author of two long poems, *The Land* and *The Garden*. Milton, you remember, began *Paradise Regain'd* by saluting *Paradise Lost*:

> I who erewhile the happy Garden sung,
> By one man's disobedience lost, now sing
> Recover'd Paradise....

Miss Sackville-West began *The Garden* by saluting *The Land*:

> Once of the noble land
> I dared to pull the organ-stops, the deep
> Notes of the bass, the diapason's range
> Of rich rotation, yielding crop by crop ...
> But now of agriculture's little brother
> I touch the pretty treble, pluck the string,
> Making the necklace of a gardener's year,
> A gardener's job, for better or for worse....

'A gardener's job' indeed, since the poet preached her own practice:

> Delicate are the tools of gardener's craft,
> Like a fine woman next a ploughboy set,
> But none more delicate than gloveless hand. ...

Because she was a major poet, not simply a cult for the annotated *avant-garde*, she put a feminine gloss on Wordsworth's maxim, that a poet is 'a man speaking to men' in words which they can understand:

> Keep the too eager bulbs from ardent light;
> Store in a gloomy cupboard, not too chill;
> Give grateful moisture to the roots unseen,
> And wait until the nose of bleached shoot
> Pushes its inches up....

But again we have wandered into high society, and for a third time we must return whither most of us belong, to homelier houses and smaller gardens. Nor need our return be downcast; on the contrary, never before were the best of those homes so comfortable, the best of their gardeners so skilled. Never before have so many Englishfolk shared William Cowper's fragrant ease: 'Now I sit with all the windows and the doors wide open, and am regaled with the scent of every flower in a garden as full of flowers as I have known how to make it.' Never before have so many Englishfolk shared Dickens's sylvan suburbia: 'If the regular City man, who leaves Lloyd's at five o'clock, and drives home to Hackney, Clapton, Stamford Hill, or elsewhere, can be said to have any daily recreation beyond his dinner, it is his garden.... He always takes a walk around it, before he starts for town in the morning, and is particularly anxious that the fish-pond should be kept specially clean.' Could William Cobbett ride through England in 1972, he would withdraw his assertion that the 'greater part of persons who possess gardens really know very little about the matter'. If moreover he could have been persuaded to exchange his seat on a horse for a seat in a train, he might have agreed that the gardens which move us most deeply are not, after all, the great gardens, but the fume-filthy square yards backing onto a railway line at the approaches to an industrial town. Some of those gardens are wilderness, reflecting the people who neglect them; but others are as a light that shineth in the darkness of mechanized Mammonland. You may perhaps regret the gnomes which sometimes haunt such gardens; you may, like Francis Bacon, feel that a pond is out of place there; but, if you have eyes to see, and a heart that beats, you will give thanks to the men and women who, with a packet of seeds and a trowel and a spade, have restored to the earth its natural role, so that scent and colour prevail above concrete and cacophony, as though the householders had interpreted the Bible literally: 'And the Lord God took the man, and put him into the garden of Eden to dress it and to keep it.'

Castle Acre Priory / Norfolk

6 God's House

FOR more than a thousand years the principal creators and custodians of English culture lived in a monastery (Greek *monazein*, meaning to dwell alone). The earliest monks were called anchorites (Greek *anachoresis*, departure) because they had moved from the cities to the Egyptian deserts, prompted by a literal interpretation of Christ's eschatology which believed that the world would soon end, and that asceticism was the surest passport to Paradise. Such men were concerned chiefly to save their own souls. In the Egyptian deserts—and later among the wilds of Syria—they eschewed all save the bare necessities for survival. Some of them eschewed even those, and presently died. The anchorites followed no set pattern of domesticity. Many lived alone; others joined a *laura* or informal community. When, however, the world showed no sign of ending; when, on the contrary, the brotherhood of Jesus became the Church of Rome, then the anchorites were outnumbered by men who rejected the desert life, preferring to live in more hospitable places, as a community of monks.

When John Milton declared 'I cannot praise a fugitive and cloistered virtue,' he supposed that he was confuting monasticism; in fact, he was merely revealing the extent to which his temperamental bias had blinded him. Different men become monks for different reasons, not all of which are consciously perceived by them. A true monk does not enter a monastery in order to escape from the trials and temptations of the world; he enters in order (as he believes) to serve the world by interceding and working for it as farmer, doctor, missionary, scholar, artist, craftsman, friend. Long before the end of the Middle Ages many monks had become idle and worldly. In every civilized nation their secular mission—caring for the poor, the sick, the old—has been assumed either by the state or by private charity. At their best, however, the medieval monks achieved a noble form of domesticity. Before we examine that life, it will be helpful to consider the principal types or orders of monasticism, each with its own discipline and dress.

The most abiding influence on English monasticism was exerted by the Benedictine order, which had been founded by an Italian nobleman, St Benedict, who imposed obedience, poverty, celibacy, and at least seven hours' manual labour each day. After twenty-five years as Abbot of a remote monastery in the Apennines, Benedict moved to a mountain-top, eighty miles from Rome, where, in the year 509, he founded the monastery of Monte Cassino. Barbarians destroyed it during the Dark Ages, and it was destroyed again in 1943 when the Germans used it as a fortress; but the ruins were rebuilt, and are still the headquarters of Benedict's *Regula Monachorum* or Rule of Monks. During the tenth century St Dunstan compelled every English monastery to follow the basic Benedictine rules, but when Duke William conquered England, the monastic ideal had already lost something of its early fervour. There were, in fact, only thirty-five English monasteries; all of them Benedictine, and only one of them north of the Trent. Five centuries later England contained more than 2,000 religious houses.

Although the Benedictines continued to set the pattern, they relaxed the rigours of their rule and thereby caused other monks to found new orders. The outstanding example was an Englishman, Stephen Harding, who became Sub-Prior of a Benedictine monastery at Molesme. In 1098, being dissatisfied with the rules of that monastery, Harding led a party of monks to a remote valley in Cîteaux, where they built a new monastery, still closely associated with the mother house, yet observing its own variant rules. For ten years Harding served as Prior. In 1112 St Bernard arrived with thirty recruits. Known as Cistercians, from the Latin form of Cîteaux, the monks ultimately formed a separate order. They re-imposed the rule of prolonged manual labour, and became successful sheep breeders. In order to emphasize humility, they built their homes in low-lying places. They forbade lofty towers and all images except a wooden crucifix. Their candlesticks were of iron; their chasubles, of fustian; their napkins, of coarse cloth. Within the monastery they wore the Benedictine black habit; without, a white hooded gown over a white cassock. The first English Cistercian house was founded (1128) near the Thames at Waverley in Surrey.

The Cluniac order was founded at Cluny in Burgundy. Since I cannot shorten it, I quote the brief description of that order which I gave in *Along the Roman Roads of Britain*: 'the monks of Cluny dedicated their days to the *opus Dei* or worship of God. By the number of their prayers, the perfection of their chanting, the precision of their ceremonies, the holiness of their lives . . . by these the Cluniac monks endued their corporate worship with a beauty and dignity never before attempted. So renowned was their austerity, so evident their piety, that William the Conqueror begged the Abbot of Cluny to send twelve monks whom he might set as bishops and abbots over his Saxon subjects. In return, he offered to pay a large sum of money. The Abbot declined without thanks: "The monks of Cluny," he said, "are not for sale." The Abbot of Cluny acknowledged no ecclesiastical superior except the Pope; all Cluniac houses were exempt from episcopal jurisdiction; all were supervised by their Priors, subject only to the Abbot himself and *in extremis* to the Pope. Once a year every Prior attended the Chapter at Cluny. After 1301 the English Priors were allowed, if they so wished, to attend every second year; a concession to the pains of travel in general and of seasickness in particular.' The first English Cluniac monastery was founded (1077) at Lewes in Sussex by William de Warenne, first Earl of Surrey, and his wife Gundrada, daughter of William

I, to mark the admiration and gratitude which they had felt when, as pilgrims to Rome, they were given shelter by the Abbot of Cluny.

The most austere of the reformed Benedictines were the Carthusians, so-named because their order was founded (1086) at Chartreuse near Grenoble in France. Unlike the members of other orders, who shared a common dormitory and refectory, each Carthusian lived in his own cell, and observed an almost perpetual silence. Meat was forbidden, even to the sick; the one daily meal consisted of vegetables, bread, water. Because of their frugality, only nine Carthusian houses were founded in England, led by the Charterhouse in London, which became successively the site of two public schools, Charterhouse and Merchant Taylors'. It was my good fortune to have been educated at the latter while it was still in Charterhouse Square. There I rough-and-tumbled in cloisters that were nearly 1,000 years old. We called our dark den 'The Clois', and regarded it as the property of the Lower School. On reaching the venerable age of thirteen, we passed by, not deigning to share the antics of juveniles.

The Augustinians claim St Augustine of Hippo as their founder. His writings prove that he did indeed encourage the anchorites in Africa, but there is no evidence that he ever founded an order. Certainly no order adopted his name during his lifetime nor for centuries after. The Augustinians included secular canons and regular canons. The former lived in monastic fashion as priests of a cathedral or of a collegiate church; the latter lived very much in the world, and were the least ascetic of any order. Enyol de Provins, a minstrel who became a regular canon, said of the brothers: 'Among them one is well shod, well fed, well clothed. They go out as they like, talk at table, and mix with the world.' Several orders modelled themselves on the Augustinians, notably the Premonstratensians, founded during the twelfth century by a German nobleman, St Norbert, in a barren Picardy valley called Prémontré; the Bonhommes or Good Men, who had only two English houses, in Buckinghamshire and in Wiltshire; and the Gilbertines, the only order of purely English origins, which was founded *c.* 1130 by a knight's son, Gilbert, who, being a cripple, could not follow a knightly calling, and chose instead to serve as parish priest at Sempringham in

Lincolnshire. When he died, at the age of 100, St Gilbert had founded fourteen houses, most of them in Lincolnshire and York-shire.

How, then, did the monks live? What were their quarters like? What their food, clothes, work, recreations? A typical monastery was governed by its abbot, who had been chosen either by the monks themselves or by the king or by a patron. Abbots of impor-tant houses—the mitred abbots—ranked as peers of the realm, and sat therefore in the House of Lords. Under Henry VIII no less than twenty-four abbots (and the Prior of Coventry) attended Parliament. An abbot wore the same habit as the monks, but on high occasions he carried a crozier, and, if so entitled, wore his mitre. Under him came the prior, who either ruled a lesser house or served as second-in-command of an abbey. The prior occupied his own house (a notable example may be seen at Castle Acre, a Norfolk priory) in which he entertained the less important guests. His deputy, the sub-prior, said grace at meals, ensured that all doors were locked at 5 p.m., kept the keys until 5 a.m., and slept in a bed nearest the dormitory door (to detect vagrant delin-quents). Next in rank was the chantor or precentor, who acted as choirmaster, librarian, and keeper of the seals and archives. His deputy, the succentor, led the left-hand half of the choir. A cellarer resembled somewhat the bursar of a college at Oxford or Cambridge, being concerned chiefly with food and wine. A sacri-stan tended the furniture and fittings of the church. An in-firmarian supervised the sick bay, which nursed both laity and clergy. An almoner distributed gifts of fuel, clothing, money. A master of the novices taught local children in the monastery school, and selected the youths who seemed suitable as candidates for the Church. The porter, who was chosen for his age and gravity, lodged at the gates, with two assistants to carry messages. The cook not only prepared but also purchased the food. The seneschal was often a layman of noble birth, acting as land agent for the monastic estates; Chaucer depicted him:

> This noble monk, of which I you devise,
> Hath of his abbot, as him list, licence
> (Because he was a man of high prudence
> And eke an officer) out for to ride
> To see their granges and the barnes wide.

The monks were their own millers, tailors, bakers, physicians, smiths, shoemakers, scribes, carpenters, masons, gardeners, bee keepers, fishermen; all symbolized in the person of the hospitaller, for every monastery was a hospice or guest house offering free board and lodging for a night and a day. For longer sojourns a small charge was sometimes made, according to each guest's means. Even so, the monks entertained at a loss to themselves because some of the guests contrived to leave without paying, while others went one worse by absconding with other guests' money and the monastic plate. When Isabella, Queen to Edward II, was entertained by the monks at Canterbury, she left behind a pack of hounds which the brothers were obliged to feed until she claimed them two years later. Some houses became so poor that they tried to cover their deficit by opening a tavern.

Except for the Carthusians, who slept in their own cells, almost every English monastery followed the Benedictine ground plan, whose nucleus was the cloister court or quadrangular lawn, around which were set the church, chapter house, refectory and dormitory. This cloister court was sometimes called Paradise because it symbolized the heart of a garden wherein the brothers spent their lives. Often it contained a fountain, at which they washed before meals. Many of the cloister courts had a covered walk, with groined roof and arcades, as in some colleges at Oxford and Cambridge.

The chapter house, which was always set on the east side of the court, became the hub of home life. Every day, at about noon, after the service called Terce, the monks walked there in procession. When the abbot had taken his own place, the brethren bowed to him. Their salutation having been returned, all were seated. The abbot then preached a short homily on one of the rules of the order. Next were read the names of any brother, benefactor, or member of the fraternity who had died on that day of the year. If a monk had committed a slight breach of discipline, he confessed his fault, which the abbot remitted with a bow. Other business was then conducted.

The refectory usually had a row of pillars down the middle, supporting a groined roof. The degree to which our two ancient universities followed that monastic model was made very clear to me when, long ago, I first dined as an undergraduate at Oxford.

At the lower end of the Hall stood a timber screen, combating the draught from the door and also some unacademic badinage from the kitchen. At the upper end stood a dais and the dons' high table, as in a medieval monastery. Again, our Senior Common Room, to which the dons retired after dinner, took as its proto-type the frater house or brothers' room whither the monks retired to converse and to imbibe whatever strong drink their order allowed.

The dormitory was a spacious upper room whose pallets were arranged along the walls. There the prior or his deputy slept, with a light burning beside him, to maintain quietness. Unlike the laity, who in those years slept naked, the monks wore their daytime habits.

The *hospitium* or guest house was very different from the meditative cloister. There you would find noblemen, pedlars, prostitutes, minstrels, priests, housewives, jugglers, lawyers, knights, pilgrims, friars, beggars, soldiers; all sorts of people in every kind of condition from merriment to despair; the young and the old, the saintly and the criminal. Not everyone was able to understand the conversation in the *hospitium*, for during the early Middle Ages a Northumbrian shepherd and a Cornish fisherman each spoke a different language, to which a merchant from Essex added his own. Among those who could speak it, how-ever, Latin was Esperanto, so that a Swedish bishop talked with a Spanish friar while an Egyptian eremite nodded or dissented as the discourse unfolded. To the common people the *hospitium* must have been a source of wonderment. The fourteenth-century author of *Piers Plowman* was amazed when he first entered a Dominican friary:

> Halles full heigh, and houses ful noble,
> Chambres with chymneys, and chapels gaye.
> And kychenes for an high kynge....

The most important part of God's House was the church: 'Seek ye first the kingdom of heaven....' Many cathedrals were formerly the churches either of Benedictines or Augustinians. Bristol Cathedral was the church of regular canons; Ripon, of secular canons; Oxford, Gloucester and Peterborough, of Benedictine abbeys. The churches were nearly always cruciformed, with a

central tower. Only by looking at medieval paintings can we re-
create the warmth and splendour of a minster church; its candles,
incense, shrines. Piers Plowman was overawed by the carved and
coloured tombs:

> All it seemed saints y-sacred upon earth,
> And lovely ladies y-wrought lyen by their sides
> In many gay garments that were gold-beaten.

But the laity shared only a fraction of the worship and intercession that were the chief task of God's House, for medieval
Christendom knew nothing of once-a-week Protestantism. Every
day throughout the year the brethren met to worship and pray.
Excepting only the peasant, a pious monk was the most hard-
working man in England. His day began at about 1.30 a.m. when
he joined the rest of the community in procession from the
dormitory to the church, there to perform Nocturne or the night
service which, with private prayer and meditation, might last for
two hours. During his devotions the monk was allowed to wear
sheepskin boots as a protection against the chill of an unheated
church. At dawn came Matins and Lauds, followed at 6 a.m. by
Prime. Then the monk retired to doff his warm boots, to wash,
and to prepare for the first Mass and the Chapter meeting. Next
after that he began his allotted work as ploughman, shepherd,
nurse, cook, cobbler, tailor or scribe. From time to time he returned to take part in Sung Mass and the offices of Terce, Sext,
None. Then followed the principal meal of the day, taken in
silence while a brother read aloud from a religious manuscript.
More work was succeeded by the long office of Vespers, after
which the monk donned his sheepskin boots and then took a light
supper before proceeding to Compline, the last office of the day,
and thence to bed (in winter at 6.30, in summer at 8.15). St
Dunstan's *Regularis Concordia* decreed that each monastery
should contain one room heated by a fire; that during very cold
weather the monks be allowed to work inside, not among the
freezing cloisters; that prayers for the king be said throughout the
day; that the laity be admitted to the chief Mass on Sunday; and
that the bells peal at Christmas and on major feast days.

In mild weather an élite of scribes would take their quills and
parchment into the cloisters, to copy sacred or scholarly manu-

H

scripts. At Beaulieu Abbey in Hampshire you can see the skill with which the cloister windows were screened to create miniature studies. Every large monastery had its *scriptorium* or writing room, a lamp of English culture, burning despite civil war and foreign invasion. The scribes themselves were among the handful of Englishmen who could read and write. When the manuscripts of classical Greece and Rome were rediscovered, it was the monks who copied them, laboriously with frozen fingers and to flickering candles, day by day, night after night, year in and year out. Few men could now write so clearly, so gracefully, and through so many years of their life. This work of God's House transcends religious controversy, and becomes even more valuable when set against the fact that eight other nations had established printing presses before the first book in the English language was published at Bruges, about the year 1475. The name of the book was *Recuyell of the Historyes of Troye*, and it had been translated by William Caxton, who in 1476 set up the first English press, in a house bearing the sign of the Red Pole, within the precincts of Westminster Abbey. For at least another two centuries a printed book was a luxury which only the rich could afford to buy, or a poor scholar who had stinted himself of food and clothes in order to save enough money. Had the monks not preserved and copied such manuscripts as did exist; had they not written new chronicles and treatises and poems; then scholarship would have contracted and perhaps withered, and many great works would have been lost forever. Among those scribes was John Wessyngton or Washington, who served as Prior of Durham from 1416 to 1446. A member of his family moved south to Lancashire and thence became lord of the manor of Sulgrave in Northamptonshire, and ultimately the ancestor of George Washington, first President of the United States of America. John Wessyngton's family were entitled to bear arms: 'gules, two bars or in chief three mullets of the second.' Today those arms are enshrined as the stars and stripes of the U.S.A.

But God's House was more than a hive of copyists. Many monks were historians, linguists, botanists, painters, physicians, theologians, astronomers, jurists, mathematicians. Some were poets; Caedmon, for example, who entered a Benedictine house which the King of Northumbria had founded at Whitby, under the governance of his kinswoman, the Abbess Hild. Caedmon's biography—written by his contemporary, the Venerable Bede— states that on certain feast days the monks of Whitby were expected to sing a solo, accompanied by the harp. But Caedmon possessed (or imagined he possessed) so little either of music or of poetry that, whenever his own turn came, he fled from the hall. On one such night, feeling more than ever dismayed, he hid in the stables, and there found companionship, for it was his duty to tend the horses. Presently he lay down beside them, and slept on the straw. Even in translation Bede's narrative is memorable: 'While he slept, there stood by him in a dream a man who saluted and greeted him, calling on him by name: "Caedmon, sing me something." Then Caedmon answered and said: "I cannot sing anything, and therefore I came away from the feast and retired here, because I know not how to sing." Again he who spoke to him said: "Yet you could sing." Then said Caedmon: "What shall I sing?" He said: "Sing to me the beginning of things."' Now it may well be that the voice which Caedmon heard was his own, speaking from the depths of unconscious wisdom; yet the fact remains, Caedmon did not create the voice. When William Blake found himself in a comparable situation, he was content to describe his role as that of 'God's secretary' who merely copied the words as they came down from Heaven. Bede's narrative continues: 'On receiving this answer ["Sing to me the beginning of things"], Caedmon at once began to sing, in praise of God the Creator, verses and words which he had never heard, the order of which is as follows....' What did follow is the finest Christian poem in the Old English tongue: 'Now let us praise the guardian of the heavenly kingdom, the power of the Creator and the counsel of his mind, the works of the Father of glory; how He, the eternal Lord, originated every marvel. He, the holy Creator, first made the heaven as a roof for the children of earth....' The author of the *Book of Genesis* held a similar cosmogony; the verdict of modern physics is even more metaphorical, and remains a closed book to all who cannot translate the Graeco-Arabic symbolism in which it is written.

Bede himself was born *c.* 673 in County Durham. As a boy he entered the Benedictine monastery at Jarrow, where he spent the rest of a long life in teaching and writing. His seventy-nine works

—many of which were written in his own hand—include treatises on metre, spelling, astronomy, physics, music, arithmetic, history, metaphysics, medicine. His *History of the English Church and People* remains a standard work, culled from sparse sources that were scattered among monasteries throughout the kingdom. On Ascension Day in the year 735 Bede dictated the final words of his translation of the Bible into English. That same night he died. The manner of his going was described by Cuthbert, another monk with the gift of tongues: ' "It is time," Bede said, "if so it seem good to my Maker, that I should be set free from the flesh, and go to Him who, when I was not, fashioned me out of nothing." ' Such were the greatest monks of the greatest days of monasticism. It is reasonable to question the validity of their theology, but it is not reasonable to question the holiness of their lives, the zeal of their labours, and the debt which European civilization owes to their achievement.

The generality of monks were, in the nature of things, less eminent. If we acknowledge again that many of them grew lazy and immoral, still we are confronted by centuries of men who bred sheep, raised corn, copied manuscripts, tended the sick, fed the hungry, nursed the aged and—like Chaucer's monk—thought it no sin to go hunting:

> A manly man, to be an abbot able,
> Ful many a dainty horse had he in stable....

Some of the monks were unashamedly illiterate, like the lay brothers or *conversi*, chiefly of peasant stock, who dedicated their lives to serving God as farmhands, domestic servants and messengers. As a rule the *conversi* held their own simplified church services.

Throughout the Middle Ages a few men put a literal interpretation on the phrase 'God's House'. In other words, they had no house at all: 'the Son of Man hath not where to lay his head.' Even the most vagrant friar was nominally attached to a friary, but the truly homeless man took no thought at all for the morrow. Sometimes he found a night's lodging in the town; at other times he built a shack in the fields. Piers Plowman described such men as

> ... eremites that inhabit them by the highways,
> And in boroughs among brewers.

A notable eremite, Richard Rolle, who was born *c.* 1300 at Thornton-le-Dale in Yorkshire, cut short his career as an Oxford scholar in order to lead a hermit's life. When his sister heard the news, and saw his ragged clothes, she cried out: 'My brother is gone mad, my brother is gone mad!' But Rolle knew what he was about, and so did the Bishop, for reputable hermits received an episcopal licence to preach. Rolle's wanderings took him to many parts of Yorkshire. He ended his days at Hampole near Doncaster, cared for by Cistercian nuns whom he had so impressed that they campaigned—unsuccessfully—to have him canonized. Like all great mystics, Rolle kept his feet on the ground, as, for example, when he warned people against eating either too little food or too much. One of his mystical tracts begins with the words *Ego dormio et cor meum vigilat* (I sleep, and my heart wakes), a proposition which Wittgenstein approved: 'Essential to the mystical experience is the suspension, or obliteration, of the subject–object distinction....'

The general name for a religious house—whether of men or of women—was 'convent' or 'a coming together'. Nowadays a convent is assumed to be a community of nuns. The medieval Latin word for a monk was *nunnus*, whence the feminine *nunna*, usually applied to elderly women. In 1066 there were only nine sizeable English nunneries; in 1536 there were more than one hundred. Of the earliest nunneries, only Romsey Abbey remains (and of that, only the Abbey church). The first nunneries fulfilled some of the functions of a modern 'finishing school' for the daughters of the nobility. If the pupils did not marry, or if they became widows, many of them returned to their nunnery. Although such places helped the poor and the sick, they were primarily homes for gentlewomen. The more devoted nunneries appeared later. Some, like the Abbey of Lacock in Wiltshire, concentrated on philanthropy and corporate worship; others, like the Poor Clares, dedicated themselves chiefly to prayer and meditation. Most nunneries were smaller than most monasteries; their churches were simpler; their manual work was less arduous. Yet all performed the Divine Office by day and night, and were ruled either by an abbess or by a prioress.

One great nunnery—Lacock—survived the Reformation, at any rate sufficiently to remain recognizable. It was founded in the thirteenth century by Ela, Countess of Salisbury, for Augustinian canonesses whose chief task was to tend the sick, to educate girls, and to receive any family that was weathering a crisis. The Countess herself took the veil, and for seventeen years ruled as Abbess. Her lodgings—above the west range of the cloister buildings—befitted a noblewoman with great responsibilities. When she was about seventy years old the Abbess retired and served humbly as a nun. Lacock is an exception to the rule that monastic churches outlived monastic domestic quarters, for its own church was destroyed when a Tudor financier converted the abbey into a mansion. The cloister, however, was retained, as an open courtyard; the sacristy and the chapel, too, were retained. Although the eighteenth-century owners made some Palladian additions, the medieval nucleus survives as an example of God's House. Lacock Abbey passed to the Fox Talbot family, one of whom, William, became 'the father of English photography'. He was born there in 1800, and made his first negative through one of the oriel windows.

The Poor Clares, founded by St Clare of Assisi, were introduced to England in 1293 by Edmund, Earl of Lancaster, who established them near the Tower of London, in a quarter called the Minories (whence their other name, Minoresses). At about the same time a second convent was established at Waterbeach near Cambridge, and soon afterwards transferred to Denny, a few miles distant. When the religious houses were dissolved by Henry VIII, the last Abbess of Denny, Dame Elizabeth Throckmorton, retired with two nuns to her family home, Coughton Court, in Warwickshire, where the three women occupied one room, living their rule of cloistered prayer and meditation. Coughton Court has preserved its one-room convent and also the Dole Gate from Denny Abbey, carved with Dame Elizabeth's name. It is a heavy oak door, pierced by two wickets; the smaller was used for conversation; the larger, for passing dole or food to the poor.

During the reign of Henry VIII three facts put an end to monastic life in England: first, the antipathy of the English people toward any institution which reminded them of Italian interference in English affairs; second, the King's need to beget a lawful male heir, which led him to disown the Pope for refusing to annul his marriage with Catherine of Aragon; third, the wealth of the monasteries, which tempted plunderers in high places. Even before they had been dissolved, several monasteries were surveyed on behalf of the men who hoped to get them. Chief among the looters was Thomas Cromwell, a person of obscure origins, whom the Tudors created Earl of Essex. Having lived on his wits in Italy, Cromwell ingratiated himself with Wolsey, and in 1534 was appointed the King's chief secretary and Master of the Rolls. Some months later he became the King's Vicar-General in things spiritual, a subject with which he was by choice ill-acquainted. He immediately despatched a body of Visitors, several of whom were unsavoury characters, with orders to report (and, if necessary, to concoct) cases of immorality at religious houses. Within a year all the small monasteries were suppressed. The large ones followed soon after. The occupants lost both their home and their livelihood. Not a few lost their lives also, like the prior and senior brethren of the Charterhouse in London, who, because they refused to surrender their monastery, were hanged, drawn and quartered. Ten other Carthusians were chained upright in a cellar at Newgate prison, and there left to die of hunger or thirst. (Cromwell's agent, Thomas Bedyll, pronounced a pious *post mortem*: 'despatched by the hand of God'.) Such treatment was especially outrageous because the order had always maintained its austerity and zeal. Even the anti-clerical Lollards accepted the Carthusians' claim, *Nunquam reformata quia nunquam deformata* (never reformed because never deformed).

The beneficiaries of the dissolution were the rich men who waxed richer as receivers of stolen goods. Thus, in 1536 John Husey, agent to Lord Lisle, looked covetously at Waverley, England's premier Cistercian abbey. To the King he wrote: 'I am told that Waverley is a pretty thing.' The Abbot appealed to Cromwell: 'To the Right Hon. Master Secretary to the King.... Beseeching your good mastership for the love of Christ's passion to help in the preservation of this poor monastery that we your bedesmen may ... continue in the service of Almighty Jesus....' Both Abbot and agent were disappointed. Waverley went to Sir William Fitzwilliam K.G., Treasurer of the King's household. Lacock Abbey went to James Sharington, who had been jailed for dishonesty while serving as Vice-Treasurer of the Mint at Bristol. Despite a criminal record, Sharington was befriended by Queen Elizabeth, who not only stayed at Lacock but also knighted her host in his new library there. Cromwell himself chose St Pancras Priory at Lewes, the oldest Cluniac house in England. A gang of Italian workmen were imported, to strip the place of its valuables, to demolish the church and to convert part of the rest into a mansion. Within two months the new owner moved in, accompanied by his wife, who found the premises 'so commodious that she thinketh herself to be here right well settled'.

The dissolution of the monasteries was inevitable. Many of them had outlived their secular usefulness, and all represented a régime repugnant to the English people. One must regret, however, that a necessary act should have been performed so cynically and with such small regard for the victims, some of whom were doing good among those who most needed it. Above all, one must regret the apathy of our forefathers who watched unmoved while Time destroyed the masterpieces of master-masons. On the eve of the dissolution this kingdom was studded with God's Houses. They stretched from farthest north (a Cistercian nunnery at Berwick-on-Tweed) to farthest south (a college of secular canons at Buryan near Land's End). Not one of all that company now stands intact.

Throughout much of the seventeenth century every form of religious dissent was outlawed, partly because it had become a form of political dissent. Even when Roman Catholics were allowed to practise their rites, the anti-papal bias persisted. In 1800 the Commons passed Sir Henry Mildmay's Monastic Institutions Act, outlawing all religious houses and their schools. Mildmay, however, had lately sold one of his own residences as a Roman Catholic convent, which was one reason why the Lords rejected his Bill (another reason was a chivalrous speech by the Bishop of Rochester). In 1829 full rights of citizenship were restored to British Roman Catholics, so that they could once again hold public office, attend a university, and take a commission in the armed forces of the Crown. Nevertheless, the anti-Roman bias remained so bitter that Sir Robert Peel, who supported the Bill, lost his seat as member for Oxford University. It cannot be said that the Pope hastened to encourage his flock to indulge their rights. Not until 1895 did the Roman Church give general permission for British Roman Catholics to go up to Oxford or Cambridge Universities. Even today a Roman Catholic is not usually expected to enter an Anglican church during service-time. Many refuse to enter at any time at all.

The revival of monasticism in England began soon after 1850, when the Roman hierarchy was restored, with eight Vicars Apostolic and thirteen dioceses. The revival was not wholly Roman. A number of Anglicans—both lay and clerical—lived in monasteries or nunneries. At least one Roman order returned to its original house, the Carmelite Friary at Aylesford in Kent, which had been founded in 1245, and was partly intact when the brothers re-took possession in 1949.

It is important to remember that almost every medieval man not only worshipped God but also believed in Heaven and Hell. William Dunbar confessed that the Flesh is as brittle as the Devil is sly; therefore his hope of Heaven was haunted by a fear of Hell:

> Our pleasure here is all vain glory,
> This fals world is transitory,
> The flesh is bruckle, the Feynd is slee:
> *Timor mortis conturbat me.*

The twentieth century, by contrast, has little faith in Heaven, and none at all in Hell. So far from approving monasticism, the spirit of this age cannot even understand it. Nevertheless, some men still find virtue in prayer, meditation, hard work, and service to others. Their spokesman is St Patrick, who, having served awhile in God's earthly House, believed that he would dwell permanently in God's heavenly House:

> And so through all the length of days
> Thy goodness faileth never;
> Good Shepherd, may I sing thy praise
> Within thy house forever.

The Old Rectory / Great Hampden, Bucks

7 *The Priest's House*

YOU approach it via the narrow High Street at Alfriston in
Sussex, passing the base of a medieval market cross and
thence between an avenue of medieval houses. At one end
of the street a bridge crosses the River Cuckmere under the lee
of the Downs; at the other end a path reaches a hillock crowned by
the church of St Andrew, a noble sight, worthy of its sobriquet,
'The Cathedral of the Downs'. And within a few yards of the
church you see the Priest's House, the first English property ever
to be bought by the National Trust.

In 1896 the house was a pair of ruinous cottages that would
soon have collapsed had they not been rescued by Octavia Hill,
daughter of a Wisbech banker, who joined Canon Rawnsley as a
co-founder of the National Trust. Indeed, it was Miss Hill who
first proposed the Trust, as a body 'for accepting, holding, and
purchasing open spaces for the people in town and country'. In
1894 the newly-formed body received a Board of Trade licence as
a company not trading for profit. Forthwith it achieved its first
acquisition, four-and-a-half acres of cliff at Dinas Oleu in
Merionethshire, a gift from Mrs Fanny Talbot. Two years later it

bought the Priest's House at Alfriston for £10. Most of the credit belonged to Miss Hill, who fought hard to arouse public interest. Dinas Oleu had been a gift; but Alfriston, she wrote, 'is a *much* more difficult problem. . . . Still, into a safe state it must be got.' And so it was, for the cottages received a restoration grant from the National Trust.

The Priest's House at Alfriston is fifty feet long, and was built *c*. 1350. The interstices of its framework are filled with clay and chopped hay. The central hall, measuring twenty-three feet by seventeen, is open to the roof, and has tie beams and moulded king posts. As a rule, only the hall is accessible to the public, who therefore assume that the priests lived in one room. East of the hall, however, the house contains a storeroom and above that another room; westward of the hall, a kitchen and a buttery each have a fourteenth-century fireplace; above them is yet another chamber. Despite its age this venerable building is a relatively late specimen of a Priest's House, for when St Augustine and forty other missionaries reached England in 597 they were given a house (near the stable-gate at Canterbury) by Aethelbert, King of Kent, whose example many great landowners followed, so that priests received both a welcome and a residence. The early Saxon bishops sent from their household a number of itinerant priests who served the laity. As more and more churches arose, the priests went to live at one or two important centres within each diocese; and the churches at those centres were called minsters. Some, as at York, were large; others were very small, like St Gregory's Minster at the hamlet of Kirkdale near Kirkby Moorside in Yorkshire. Minsters, however, remained comparatively rare. Most of our Saxon churches were built by lords who themselves appointed and endowed the priest; whence the two indigenous features of the English Church, private patronage and the priest's freehold home.

Throughout the Middle Ages the average priest was as poor as his parishioners, and sometimes as ignorant. *Sicut populus, sic sacerdos* (The priest is a man of the people): those words from Isaiah were often quoted by the medieval Roman Church, and are still part of the practice of the modern Roman Church, for many a peasant hopes that his son will be accepted for the priesthood. St Cuthbert—Prior of Melrose and Bishop of Lindisfarne—

was once a shepherd boy in the Lammermuir Hills; Nicholas Breakspear, the only Englishman who ever became Pope, was the son of a Hertfordshire peasant; St Thomas Becket was the son of a London tradesman; Cardinal Wolsey, last of the great princes of the Roman Church in England, was the son of a Suffolk butcher. This recruitment from the lower orders of society was not due to an inherent excellence in the recruits themselves; it sprang from the law of supply and demand, because the upper classes regarded scholarship and contemplation somewhat as our grandfathers regarded the stage; that is, as an accomplishment best left to others.

Neither the priest nor his home can be rightly assessed without some knowledge of their history. The nations of medieval Christendom were organized to conform with Christ's maxim: 'Render therefore unto Caesar the things that are Caesar's; and unto God the things that are God's.' The organization was symbolized by the concept of the Two Swords; the Pope (representing God) and the Holy Roman Emperor (representing Caesar). Inevitably the Two Swords sometimes clashed, as when Becket defied Henry II; yet power politics never undermined the medieval role of religion. The rites of the Church touched every aspect of a man's life; his baptism, his marriage, his burial; work, warfare, play. At harvest time the priest blessed the reapers; at sowing time, the plough; in sickness, the sufferer. When a home was bedevilled he exorcised the evil spirit; when the land was parched he prayed for rain. Travellers, farmers, musicians, sailors, housewives, soldiers, doctors, farriers ... all had their patron saint, whose intercession they invoked. Nothing of importance was undertaken without the venturer commended himself and his enterprise to God. Even the writing of a letter opened and closed with an invocation: 'Son,' began Agnes Paston, 'I greet you well, with God's blessing and mine....' 'The Holy Trinity,' ended Margaret Paston, 'have you in his keeping.' Not without reason, therefore, was a priest called a parson (Latin *persona*, meaning a personage or important member of the parish). In spiritual matters he was *the* person in the parish; and in all other matters he ranked next after the lord of the manor. The peasants called him *persone*, and his home became the *personage*. The best type of priest, as described by Chaucer, was poor, pious, benevolent:

>   ... a povre Person of a toun
>   Yet riche he was of holy thoght and work.

And brave also, quick to defend his flock against covetous neighbours or an unjust lord,

>   What-so he were, of heigh or lowe estate.

Such was the role of a medieval parish priest.

We have noticed that at Alfriston the Priest's House contained several rooms and outbuildings. This was because all parish priests were required to receive travellers. Beggars and poor men paid nothing for their night's lodging; the rest paid a sum which seldom covered the cost of feeding them. Accommodation was further strained because retired priests were allowed to occupy their former parsonage, as in the Herefordshire parish of Weobley, where the retired priest in 1441 received a room on the ground floor and use of the kitchen. A fifteenth-century vicar of Gaynford in County Durham possessed seven brass pots, four grid irons, two carving knives, fifteen dishes, a frying pan and a toasting fork. Modern housewives may wonder how a bachelor managed to cope with his self-invited guests; but celibacy was rather a custom than a condition of the medieval Church in England. As late as the year 1276 John de Boulton, rector of West Rounton in Yorkshire, lawfully married a wife, Isabella. According to Gerald of Wales almost every English parish priest was married, and not a few kept concubines. Gerald, however, was a Welsh nationalist whose opinions of England must be taken *cum grano*. Whether married or single, most parish priests employed a lad to make their bed and to groom their horse. Very few of those medieval parsonages survive. Those that I have seen include the black-and-white house at Prestbury in Cheshire; the late medieval house at Gawsworth in the same county; several parsonages near the Scottish Border; the brick-and-timber Prebend's house at Thame in Oxfordshire; and a timbered house at West Hoathly in Sussex, which, although it never became a parsonage, was used until 1524 by tithe collectors from the Priory of St Pancras at Lewes (in 1972 the house was a museum of the Sussex Archaeological Society).

Who paid the medieval priest? He relied on tithes (Old English *teotha* or tenth). In 787 the English bishops decreed 'that all

take care to pay the tenth of all they possess, because that peculiarly belongs to God'. As with rates and taxes, so with tithes; few
men rejoice to pay them. Nevertheless, tithes were the Church's
chief source of revenue, augmented by cash gifts, grants of land
and fees for services rendered. In 1315 the Lateran Council drew
attention to gross inequalities of income: 'there are some regions
where the parish priests have for their sustentation only the
fourth of a fourth, to wit the sixteenth part of the tithes; whence
it cometh that in those regions scarce any parish priest can be
found who is even moderately well-educated.' More than 500
years later the tithe system was still a part of English country life,
as depicted in the *Diary* of a Victorian parson, Francis Kilvert:
'Today was the tithe audit and a tithe dinner to farmers, both
held at the Vicarage. About 50 tithe payers came, most of them
very small holders, some paying as little at 9*d*.' A good time was
had by all—except perhaps by the Vicar, who was partly out of
pocket because, having paid their dues in the front hall, the
villagers 'retired into the back hall and regaled themselves with
bread, cheese and beer, some of them eating and drinking the
value of the tithe they had paid'. If a priest happened to live near
a monastery, his housekeeping was sometimes lightened thereby,
as at Great Missenden in Buckinghamshire, where the vicar and
his lad were entitled to eat at the Abbey (and if the vicar's work
took him from home at dinnertime, the Abbot was required to
send food to the vicarage).

Vicarage and rectory; what is the difference between them? A
rector (Latin *rego* or I rule) governed the spiritual matters of his
parish. Unless he gravely misconducted himself, he held the freehold parsonage for life. Although the majority of parish priests
were rectors, the lay patrons were encouraged to present their
church to a monastery, which then became the rector, and employed a *vicarius* or substitute, of a kind that we would now call
curate, whose tenure depended on the approval of his employer.
The vicar ultimately received an ordinance—whence the word
'ordination'—granting him security of tenure and, in theory, a
stipend of one-third of the parish revenue. By the end of the
Middle Ages nearly thirty per cent of English rectories had become vicarages. Today both vicars and rectors enjoy freehold
rights over the parsonage, the church and the churchyard, which

lapse only when the incumbents die, retire or are deprived. Until the early years of the twentieth century a rector was responsible for the repair of the chancel; he still retains certain chancel privileges and obligations.

The Border counties devised an indigenous type of parsonage, the peel tower or fortified home, well-suited to priests who needed courage as well as conviction. In 1319, when Scottish raiders penetrated as far south as Mytton in Yorkshire, they were met by an army which included a contingent of priests, fighting in full canonicals, of whom 300 were killed. The battle of Mytton was ever after dubbed the Chapter of Mytton; and one can understand why the English Border ballads regarded the Scots as devils who could penetrate peel towers and bastel-houses:

> Nae bastles nor peels
> Are safe frae thae deils.

The vicar's peel at Corbridge in Northumberland had walls five feet thick, built of sandstone slabs which a thirteenth-century priest carted from the site of a Roman fort near Hadrian's Wall. The peel is nearly forty feet high and about twenty-seven feet long, and it remained a vicarage until the middle of the sixteenth century. By 1663 it had become 'antiently ye Lorde's gaole but is now ye place where ye Lorde's court is usually held'. The administration of justice must have been damp because 'ye roofe is much in decay'. The vicars of Corbridge washed themselves at the head of the stairs, using a basin whose contents were drained onto the heads of people passing below. The principal room contained a large hearth for cooking; a study on the upper floor contained a stone lectern or reading desk near the window. The peel had two entrances as a defence against being smoked-out by 'thae deils'.

At Elsdon, a remote village in the Northumbrian Cheviots, the rector's peel resembled a miniature castle on a knoll above the church. The blacksmith once told me that in his grandfather's day the rectory was still called 'the castle'; so hardly is a Borderer's memory of

> Old, unhappy, far-off things, and battles long ago.

Augustus Hare described Elsdon rectory as 'a dismal old castle built to fortify the rector in moss-trooping times'. One eighteenth-century rector prepared himself for sleep by stuffing three night-caps on his head and then winding a woollen stocking around his neck. Like many other Border parsonages, Elsdon rectory contained a basement for use as a cattle-pen during raids. The circular stone staircase led to a kitchen and the servants' quarters, thence to the rector's study and bed-sitter, and finally to a couple of attics. During the reign of George IV a kitchen, dining room, hall and various offices were added by Archdeacon Singleton, who converted the cattle-pen into a living room, the kitchen and servants' quarters into bedrooms, and the top storey into a library and a dressing room. He added also a new kitchen, dining room and other offices. In 1972 the old rectory was a layman's residence.

No peel tower now survives as a priest's home. The longest-lived was at Chatton in Northumberland, which remained the parsonage until 1834, when it became part of a new vicarage; twenty-six years later it was partly demolished to supply material for a newer vicarage. Another peel, at Alnham in the same county, collapsed during the seventeenth century and continued to decay until tne middle of the nineteenth, when it was restored and enlarged; in 1972 it served as part of a youth hostel. The rectors of Rothbury, another Northumbrian parish, lived in a peel tower at Whitton, just beyond the town. In 1679 the tower was restored by the rector; in 1934 it became part of an orphanage. The priest at Alwinton occupied a fortified house in 1541, but within a century it became an alehouse. The vicar's peel at Whittingham was converted as an almshouse in 1845. Ingram, a secluded hamlet near the foot of the Cheviot, had a vicar's peel until the sixteenth century, but in 1541 a census reported that 'for lacke of contynuall necessary rep'arns ys fallen into great decaye'. On several visits to Ingram I dibbled and delved, but failed to find the foundations.

The Border counties were not alone in possessing fortified priest's homes. Essex, for example, has more than a dozen moated parsonages. In the Staffordshire village of Swinford Regis the priest's home was moated until the middle of the eighteenth century, when it became a farm house, and the moat was filled-in. The priest's home at Pirbright in Surrey was still moated in 1941, though the water had been drained, the moat partly blocked, and the drawbridge replaced by an ordinary bridge. It seems probable that all of those moats were defences against civil war and local marauders.

When Henry VIII appointed himself Supreme Head of the English Church the majority of his subjects were content to regard the Pope as no more than a bishop of a foreign and hostile Church. Some priests adhered to Rome, and thereby lost their living. Although several Roman dogmas were discarded—papal jurisdiction and belief in purgatory—many Anglicans retained a High Church ritual and the belief in transubstantiation or the Real Presence. As with celibacy and marriage, so with ritual and dogma; by keeping 'the mean between the two extremes' the English Church recognized the influence of temperament and environment. Some Christians prefer a Quakerlike simplicity; others, the splendour of a High Mass. Like most of his flock, the average English priest steered and continues to steer a middle way between Anglo-Catholicism and Anglo-Calvinism. It may seem, therefore, that the Reformation scarcely affected the priest's domestic life. He still took his tithes, still obeyed his bishop, still occupied his house. Nevertheless, the Reformation did affect his domestic life, by changing his status. As we have seen, the Roman Catholic priest was a man of the people, not seldom half-illiterate, ruling solely by virtue of his office. The English priest, on the other hand, came to rule as much by his person as by his office. He was generally a graduate of Oxford or Cambridge, and by the middle of the eighteenth century was likely to be a kinsman or acquaintance of the squire. In short, the Reformation raised the priest's house until it ranked next after the manor, a place which it held until the early twentieth century.

This new or post-Reformation priest can be seen in the careers and homes of two poets, Robert Herrick and George Herbert. Herrick had been apprenticed to his uncle, Sir William Herrick, jeweller to King James I. At the age of twenty-six, as a graduate of Trinity Hall, Cambridge, he entered the priesthood, became chaplain to the Duke of Buckingham (with whom he saw brief military service), and in 1629 received from Charles I the living of Dean Prior on the edge of Dartmoor. A car-crammed highway now roars within a few feet of Herrick's church, but in his day the parish was so peaceful that it displeased the new parson from London:

I

> Dean-bourn, farewell; I never look to see
> Dean or thy warty incivility.

Worse was to follow:

> Before I went
> To banishment
> Into the loathed West;
> I co'd rehearse
> A Lyrick verse,
> And write it with the best.

As he grew older and wiser, Herrick ceased to hanker after the city, preferring his bachelor home and its capable housekeeper, Prudence Baldwin:

> We bless our Fortunes, when we see
> Our own beloved privacie.

Indeed, he so loved country life in Devonshire that he commended it to his brother, urging him to enjoy a similar Elysium:

> Thus let thy Rurall Sanctuary be
> *Elizium* to thy wife and thee....

The Cromwellians ejected Herrick because he refused to recognize their régime; but at the Restoration he returned to Dean Prior despite an earlier dislike of 'dull Devonshire'. So far from inhibiting his 'Lyrick verse', Devonshire enabled him to compose *Hesperides: or, the Works both Humane and Divine of Robert Herrick Esq*, in which he returned thanks for his house:

> Lord, thou hast given me a cell
> Wherein to dwell,
> A little house, whose humble Roof
> Is weather-proof....

In that 'little house' he no longer envied his London friends:

> Low is my porch, as is my Fate,
> Both void of state;
> Who thither come, and freely get
> Good works, or meat....

Like his medieval predecessors, the vicar of Dean Prior was largely self-sufficient:

> Thou mak'st my teeming Hen to lay
> Her egg each day:
> Besides my healthful Ewes to beare
> Me twins each yeare. ...

And when winter came he kept the priest's house snug:

> Some brittle sticks of Thorne or Briar
> Make me a fire,
> Close by whose living coale I sit,
> And glow like it.

Robert Herrick lived just soon enough to recapture a breath of the fresh airs of medieval English poetry, as in his epitaph to a faithful housekeeper:

> In this little Urne is laid
> Prewdence Baldwin (once my maid)
> From whose happy spark here let
> Spring the purple violet.

Herrick's contemporary, George Herbert, was born in 1593, either at or near to Montgomery Castle, the seat of his grandfather, Sir Henry Herbert, kinsman to those Herberts who became Earls of Pembroke. From Westminster School he went up to Trinity College, Cambridge, where his classical accomplishments won the coveted Public Oratorship. It seemed unlikely, however, that a gifted youth, with powerful connections, would chose to spend the rest of his life in a college. According to Izaak Walton, Herbert lived modishly, indulging 'a gentile humour for cloathes'. A word at Court would have procured a military or a diplomatic career. Herbert's friends were therefore astounded when he told them that he wished 'both to marry and to enter the Sacred Orders of Priesthood'. In the event, ordination preceded marriage. First, he became a deacon, but without any dramatic *volte face*, for (said Walton) the cleric had not yet 'chang'd his sword and silk Cloathes into a Canonical Coat'. Then he married a Wiltshire lady, daughter of Sir John Danvers. Finally, he sought the poor and sequestered parish of Fugglestone St Peter with Bemerton St Peter in Wiltshire. 'The Earl of Pembroke,' Walton explained, 'requested the King to bestow it upon his kinsman, Mr Herbert; and the King said, Most willingly to Mr Herbert, if it be worth his acceptance.'

On arriving at Bemerton the new vicar found that he must rebuild the priest's house, which had decayed because the previous incumbent lived away from his parish. Herbert's house still stands, albeit enlarged and marred by a Victorian vicar whose entourage included a wife, four daughters, two gardeners, two grooms, and ten indoor servants. Over the living room fireplace Herbert carved a greeting to his successors:

> If thou chance for to find
> A new house to thy mind
> And built without thy cost,
> Be good to the poor
> As God gives thee store
> And then my labour's not lost.

John Aubrey was correct in saying: 'Mr Herbert made a good garden and walks.' One of his mulberry trees was flourishing in 1970.

A married priest understands from experience the domestic joys and sorrows of his flock. Herbert's own book, *The Countrey Parson*, says: 'for salves, his wife seeks not the city, but prefers her garden and fields....' Mrs Herbert certainly acted as village doctor for the poor. Their married life became an exception proving the rule: 'there never was any opposition betwixt them' said Walton, 'unless it were a Contest which should most incline to a compliance with the others desires.' No children were born to them, but they consoled themselves by adopting three orphans, and together they practised Herbert's preaching, that a good priest must visit 'even the poorest Cottage, though he even creep into it, and though it smell never so lothsomly'.

Having established a home, and made friends with the parishioners, Herbert set about restoring his church, which was one of the smallest in Wiltshire. The task drained his resources. To his brother, Henry, he confessed himself 'more beggarly now than I have been these many years ... but difficulties are so far from cooling christians that they whet them'. Throughout his incumbency Herbert continued to write and revise the religious poems by which he is remembered. Like Sir Philip Sidney and Sir Thomas Browne, he felt no urge to publish, for most men of his time and class were content if their writings circulated in manuscript among friends. Shortly before he died, however, he handed his poems to a friend, directing him to burn them unless he believed that they might comfort 'any dejected poor soul'. The friend wisely passed the poems to Nicholas Ferrar, on whose advice they were published by the Cambridge University Press in 1633. Ferrar said of Herbert, that 'his faithful discharge was such, as to make him . . . a pattern for the age he lived in'. In *The Countrey Parson* he had depicted the ideal of the priest's house as a place which the shepherd shares with his flock, a refuge for any who is 'afflicted in mind, body, or estate'. Of the priest himself he said: 'Love is his business and aim.' At Bemerton Vicarage he fulfilled that ideal, and was buried in his own church, remembered by a small plaque on the chancel wall, bearing his initials: 'G.H.'

The eighteenth century regarded itself as an Age of Enlightenment, which is a disarming way of saying that it was sceptical. Not a few Anglican clergymen shared that scepticism. They set fox-hunting before man-fishing. They were too closely associated with the squire, either by birth or by marriage or by inclination. They left the care of their parish to an ill-paid curate; some, indeed, never visited their parish. Yet the eighteenth-century Church was redeemed by many faithful pastors in secluded places. If Goldsmith's *The Vicar of Wakefield* had been simply an idealized creation, the public would have laughed his novel out of print. But there is no need to rely on the testimony of fiction. A real-life vicar, James Woodforde, typified the best of his breed. Woodforde was the son of the Rector of Castle Cary in Wiltshire (also Vicar of Ansford). From Winchester he went up to New College, Oxford, and in 1764 received the curacy of Babcary, only a few miles from his father's parish. In 1771 he succeeded his father as Vicar of Ansford. In 1773 he resigned the living in order to become Sub-Warden of New College. In 1774 he was presented to the living of Weston Longeville in Norfolk, which he left in charge of a curate until 1776, when he moved to Weston Longeville Rectory, and served there until his death twenty-seven years later. Like his medieval predecessor, Parson Woodforde employed a lad to fetch and carry. On 6 April 1768, his diary stated: 'My new boy (George Hutchins) came home this morning.... He is a likely boy, and bears a good character.' The parson supplied him with 'a coat, a waistcoat and hat etc.' Again like the medieval priest, Woodforde cultivated his glebe: 'I have,' said his diary, 'been very busy all this day in planting my Peas and Beans and Radishes, and Spanish Onions in my garden at Babcary.' His labours were interrupted by a call for help: 'I was sent this afternoon to a Poor Woman that lives by the Church, to come and pray by her—which I did....' At Christmas in the year 1800 his Norfolk diary noted: 'I had at my house fifty-five [poor people]....' To each he gave the equivalent of fifty new pence, and to some an invitation to share his Christmas dinner: 'the following poor People, dined at my house, Eliz: Case, Thos. Atterton senr., Robt. Downing, Roger Sherwood and my clerk Willm. Large. Old Mary Heavers not being able to come I sent her some rost Beef and plumb Pudding and 0.1.0.' On that occasion the Rector exceeded Timothy's recipe: 'gave to those that dined at my House after Dinner some strong beer and when they went away, gave each of them 1 shilling.... The poor People went away about 5.o'clock happy and well pleased with their fare.' On St Valentine's Day the children knocked hopefully at the rectory door, and were not sent empty away: 'This being Valentines Day, I gave to the Children of my Parish that came to my House this morning ... a penny and I gave in all 53 of them....' The same entry revealed that Woodforde enjoyed plain and wholesome food: 'Dinner today Pork and Greens and Suet Pudding.' Later that year he mowed his glebe: 'Begun cutting my Clover being a fine Day.' Again we meet the medieval analogy: 'This being my Day for Tithe Audit the Farmers dined and spent the Afternoon and Evening till after 10 o'clock at Night at my House....' Despite their tithe-paying, the farmers enjoyed themselves: 'They were all pleased and went away in good Spirits.'

Woodforde employed what he described as a head maid, lower maid, man, farming man, and boy. They caused rather less trouble than most servants, and were certainly not responsible for the incidents which marred one of the rector's dinner parties: 'Mrs Howes,' he complained, 'found great fault with many things especially about stewing the Fish—she could not eat a bit of them with such sauce etc. Mrs Davy fell downstairs ... Miss Donne swallowed a Barley corn. Many accidents happened. . . .' Fortunately, however, 'none very bad . . .', and when the guests had departed, soon after nine o'clock, the rector was able to end the day on a gratified note: 'They all admired my plated candlesticks and snuffers. . . .' A good relationship with the manor house was more important then than it is now. Weston Longeville possessed a benevolent squire, and the rector was disturbed by the prospect of losing him: 'Mr Custance made us very uneasy by what he told us, which was, that they were going to leave Weston-House and reside at Bath in about a Month from this time, that their Children might be educated there. . . .'

Persons who wish to uncover the dark side of Augustan clerical life will find ample evidence; of the bright side also there is ample evidence, but—perhaps because it *is* bright—not everyone cares to uncover it. Let us therefore redress the balance by noting some of the ways in which Parson Woodforde fulfilled his good resolutions for the year 1783. On January 4: 'To poor old Joe Adcocks wife who very lately fell down and broke her Thigh— sent her by Will o.1.o.' On January 7: 'Gave Mr Priests Maid o.1.o.' On January 26: 'Sent old Mary Adcock at Noon—a hot roasted fowl, a fourpenny loaf and a Bottle of Beer.' On February 7: 'To a poor old Man with a Dulcimer gave o.o.6.' Those gifts may appear small, but the pound in those years was more sterling than it is now, and the rector's income not large. Moreover, the gifts occurred throughout the year, and were recorded by Woodforde as things there were a part of his daily life, things that Wordsworth called

> Those little, nameless, unremembered acts
> Of kindness and of love. . . .

Loving-kindness cannot be measured in terms of cash, but its cost to Woodforde can be so measured, for he still relied on tithes, and still suffered the inequalities of income which had existed during the Middle Ages. Indeed, Queen Anne was so dismayed by what she called the 'mean and insufficient maintenance belonging to the clergy', that in 1704 she used certain Crown revenues to create a relief fund, known as Queen Anne's Bounty. A census revealed that more than half of the livings in England were then worth less than £80 yearly, and that scores of priests had an income of less than £10 yearly. But the Church was so slow to act that in 1835 clerical incomes were still ill-adjusted. The richest bishop received £19,000; the poorest, £900. Some vicars and rectors received less than £100 yearly; most of the five thousand curates, less than £82. Those inequalities were reflected in the size of the priest's home. For example, the rectory at Settrington in Yorkshire contained twenty-one rooms, as did the vicarage at Mapledurham beside the Oxfordshire Thames. The rectory at Hathern in Leicestershire contained eighteen rooms; at Great Hampden in Buckinghamshire the rectory was a stately home; the rector of Asheldham in Essex owned (and was obliged to fence) forty acres of glebe. One vicar possessed an income of £3,000 yearly and a small home; another received a stipend which scarcely paid the rates of his sixteen-room house. Despite domestic difficulties, however, the eighteenth and nineteenth centuries achieved remarkable records for longevity. At Yalding in Kent the priest's house was occupied by the same family of incumbents from 1759 until 1889. At Shere in Surrey the parsons between 1658 and 1843 were all members of the Duncombe family. At Steeple Langford in Wiltshire the rectors from 1753 until 1899 were all members of the Hanbury family. At Rose Ash in Devon the Southcomb family served as rectors in unbroken succession for 250 years.

The domestic trials of a parson are vividly illustrated by the career of Charles Kingsley, sometime Regius Professor of History in the University of Cambridge, chaplain to Queen Victoria, and for thirty-one years rector of Eversley in Hampshire, where the rectory is a sixteenth-century house with three storeys and some eighteenth-century additions. Kingsley discovered that the previous rector had absconded, leaving the parsonage and church in disrepute and disrepair. The rectory, indeed, was so damp that the family were forced to rent a temporary house on higher ground. Kingsley met the heavy costs by overworking as writer, lecturer, tutor. Yet his house was at all times open to all comers; and, like George Herbert, he visited every one of his parishioners. Kegan Paul once accompanied him while he ministered to a fever-stricken cottager: 'The atmosphere of the little ground-floor bedroom was horrible, but before the Rector said a word he ran upstairs, and, to the great astonishment of the inhabitants of the cottage, bored, with a large auger he had brought with him, several holes above the bed's head for ventilation.' The same practical approach was made to the garden, which had become a wilderness. Kingsley's daughter, Rose, remembered the day when two guests—the Bishop of Durham and a future Archbishop of Canterbury—were co-opted to clear the brambles: 'What had been a wretched chicken yard outside the brick-floored room which my Father took for his study became the study-garden ("The quarter-deck", as they called it), up which and down which my Father paced bare-headed, composing sermon or novel, lecture or poem. . . .' Kingsley was 'a muscular Christian', hale and hardy. You can still see the Scots pines to which he lashed his summer hammock; and, in the study, the hooks which held his winter hammock. William Harrison, who served as curate, described the room: 'its brick floor covered with matting, its shelves of heavy old folios, with a fishing-rod, or landing-net, or insect-net leaning against them; on the table books, writing-materials, sermons, manuscripts, proofs, letters, reels, feathers, fishing-flies, clay-pipe, tobacco. . . .' In that study the rector wrote *Westward Ho!*, part of *The Water-Babies*, and the attack on Newman which was answered by *Apologia Pro Vita Sua*. With his own hands he built a play-hut for his children. Every form of wild life was accepted as tenants of the rectory garden (visitors received instructions not to disturb an especially fine array of glow-worms). Even the trees were dear to him. Shortly before he died, he noticed a large oak that had been felled: 'He stopped,' wrote his curate, 'and looked at it for a moment or so, and then, bursting into tears, exclaimed, "I have known that tree ever since I came into the parish." ' Kingsley was indeed a man of parts: poet, scholar, novelist, priest, radical Tory, sanitary engineer, fox-hunter, glow-worm protector, lover of trees. His house and garden were a place of pilgrimage for eminent visitors, for tramps, for cottagers, for all in need; and when, resting from multifarious labours, he gathered the family around him, he achieved his finest hours: 'I wonder,' he once asked, 'if there is so much laughter in any other home in England as in ours?'

Laughter: the word recalls another nineteenth-century parson, Sydney Smith, whom London society dubbed 'the wittiest man in England'. When Smith became rector of Foston-le-Clay in Yorkshire the parsonage was a derelict hovel. He therefore lived with his family at Heslington, a dozen miles away. In 1813, after seven years of commuting, he decided to build a new rectory at his own cost, for which purpose he hired an architect whose plans were so lavish that Smith gave him £25 and bid him be off, exclaiming: 'You build for glory, Sir, I for use.' The Smith family then began to build their own house, helped by a mason and a carpenter. They made the bricks—150,000 of them—and each was a dud. In order to fetch usable bricks from the nearest yard, Smith committed a second blunder, this time by purchasing four oxen to haul the cart. He named his ponderous quartet Tug, Lug, Haul and Crawl; and all of them failed to live up to their expectant names. Haul and Crawl lay down in the mud, more stubborn than mules; Tug and Lug did the same, but added insult to injury by fainting where they lay, and had to be revived with buckets of sal volatile. The burdensome beasts were then replaced by horses. On 17 March 1813, Smith sent a progress report to his brother: 'I am going on prosperously with my building, but am not yet out of sight of land.' After four months he sounded less optimistic: 'I am building a house without an architect, and educating a son without patience.' A year later he sighted his landfall: 'I shall be in my house by the 25th March, in spite of all the evils that are prophesied against me. I have had eleven fires burning night and day for these two months past....' At Christmas he expressed himself satisfied: 'I like my new house very much; it is very comfortable and after finishing it, I would not pay sixpence to alter it; but the expense of it will keep me a very poor man, a close prisoner here for my life, and render the education of my children a difficult exertion for me.' Smith spoke truly, for his stipend was only £600 yearly, and he had already borrowed £150 from Queen Anne's Bounty. Having settled in, he reported to Lady Holland: 'We live here in great seclusion but happily and comfortably. My life is cut up into little patches: I am schoolmaster farmer doctor parson justice etc. etc....' The farmer, alas, discovered that even the silliest sheep can be slippery. In a letter to *The Farmer's Magazine* he deplored the nimbleness of his Scotch flock: 'They crawled through hedges where I should have thought a rabbit could hardly have found admittance; and, when crawling would not do, they had recourse to leaping.'

When Lord Macaulay visited the house, twelve years later, he described it in a letter to his father: 'the very neatest, most commodious, and most appropriate rectory that I ever saw. All its decorations are in a peculiarly clerical style; grave, simple, and gothic. The bed-chambers are excellent, and excellently fitted up; the sitting-rooms handsome and the grounds sufficiently pretty.' One wonders why Macaulay described the rectory as 'gothic'; it is a plain Georgian house. Like Kingsley, Sydney Smith was a practical man. He devised an air tube to create enough draught to make his fire blaze merrily; a telescope, to keep an eye on his farmhands; and a loud-hailer, to rebuke, commend and generally supervise them.

Smith remained at Foston-le-Clay until 1827, when he became a Canon of Bristol and vicar of Halberton in Devon. His canonical residence, he told Lady Holland, was 'an extremely comfortable house—seventeen stables and room for four carriages'. In 1829 he accepted the living of Combe Florey in the Quantocks, and for a second time the rectory was so derelict that he had to rebuild it at his own cost and with the aid of twenty-eight workmen, not all of whom were helpful: 'Nothing,' he declared, 'is as vile as the artifices of this county.... A straight line in Somersetshire is that which includes the greatest possible distance between the extreme points.... Every day's absence from home costs me £10 in the villainy of carpenters and bricklayers; for as I am my own architect Clerk of the Works, you may easily imagine what is done when I am absent.' His chief foes were the climate and the thirst which it aroused in the workmen: 'What with the long torpor of the cider and the heated air of the West they all become boozy....' However, his impatience was rewarded: 'I continue to be delighted with my house and place.' His 'place', by the way, included sixty acres of glebe wherein he delighted to fool his fashionable London friends by fastening oranges onto shrubs, so that when the sophisticated Cockneys returned to Town they reported favourably on the West country: 'What a wonderful climate Somerset has! The Smiths actually grow oranges in December.' In one respect at least Smith resembled Herrick; having anathematized country life as 'a kind of healthy grave', he chose to live as a country parson.

Smith and Kingsley witnessed the high tide of pluralism, for not a few Victorian priests held more than one living, and some resided outside their parishes. Such apparent misconduct was frequently unavoidable because there were not enough habitable parsonages. Riding through Wiltshire in 1826, Cobbett noted: 'There are now no less than nine of the parishes, out of the twenty-nine, that have either no parsonage-houses, or have such as are in such a state that a parson will not, or cannot live in them.' Approaching Somerset, he detected a similar dearth; of twenty-seven parsonages, nearly one-third were 'such miserable dwellings as to be unfit for a parson to reside in'. Two parishes had no parsonage at all: 'there are sites: there are glebes: but the houses have been suffered to fall down and to be totally carried away.' In Worcestershire and along the Welsh Border the situation was even worse: 'more than one-half of the parishes have either no parsonage-houses at all, or have not one that a parson thinks fit for him to live in; and I venture to assert that one or other of these is the case in four parishes out of every five in Herefordshire.' George Eliot, a non-Christian, painted the portrait of a good Victorian parson, Rev. Tryan, in *Scenes from Clerical Life*: 'he gave himself no rest. Three sermons on Sunday, a night-school for young men on Tuesday, a cottage-lecture on Thursday, addresses to school-teachers, and catechizing of school-children, with pastoral visits, multiplying as his influence extended beyond his own district....' With a meagre stipend and a mean house, the parson spent much of his laborious life in one room: 'the man,' wrote George Eliot, 'who could live in such a room, unconstrained by poverty, must either have his vision fed from within by an intense passion, or he must have chosen that least attractive form of self-mortification which ... accepts the vulgar, the commonplace and the ugly, whenever the highest duty seems to lie among them.' Mr Tryan was a worthy successor of George Herbert, for he entered every cottage in his parish, even though 'it smell lothsomly'.

Many Victorian and Edwardian priests occupied homes that would nowadays be demolished as unsafe and unfit. In 1895 the walls of Maperton Rectory in Somerset were so damp that moss grew inside the bedrooms. Few parsonages possessed a bathroom until the twentieth century. During the 1920s the bathroom at Whatfield Rectory in Suffolk was a wooden partition in the hall.

Until the 1930s Radstock Rectory in Somerset lacked even a wash basin. In that same year the rector's wife at Beeston in Norfolk had to walk forty paces from the kitchen to the tap whenever she wished to fill a kettle. In 1950 the vicar of West Wickham in Kent occupied two small rooms, perched thirty feet high in the tower of the church of St Francis of Assissi. In 1951 the rector of St Mary's at Rye in Sussex was living in one room in the church wall. In 1955 the bathroom at Charlecombe Rectory in Somerset was an attic containing a twenty-gallon oildrum rigged above a paraffin stove; water had to be carried upstairs in buckets. By the 1970s the Church of England had set many of its priests' houses in order, partly because the decline in worship had closed many of its churches. Some of the vast Georgian and Victorian parsonages had long since been sold, whence the Old Rectories and Old Vicarages that are now a layman's residence; but it was not possible to replace every unsuitable house. The parson must do the best he can, as at Kirkby Lonsdale in Westmorland, where the many-roomed vicarage and some of its outbuildings have been converted into flats.

The priest's house waxes and wanes with the priest's function, and that rises and falls with the laity's willingness to accept it. Nobody can foresee what will happen to religion in general and to the Church of England in particular during the next hundred years. But one thing is certain; so far from being a personage in the parish, the parson has become a stranger to most of his parishioners. How many villagers now worship in their parish church? How many townsfolk can *name* their parish church? Nevertheless, the priest's house is still a haven and a meeting place; and the priest himself—more surely, perhaps, than at any other period in our history—may answer his critics as Dean Swift answered them: 'Those fine gentlemen who affect the humour of railing at the clergy, are, I think, bound in honour to turn parsons themselves, and shew us better examples.'

HMS Victory / Nelson's quarters

8 The Sea

LET us now praise famous men: Sir Walter Raleigh, Sir Francis Drake, Sir Richard Grenville, Sir John Hawkins, Sir Humphrey Gilbert: Martin Frobisher, John Oxenham, Stephen Borough: Captains Collingwood, Hardy, Marryat: Admirals Blake, Nelson, Hood, Jellicoe, Beatty, Cunningham, Mountbatten. Not without reason did a Frenchman, François de Chateaubriand, declare: 'The waves are a part of England.' The brine is in our blood, and on it innumerable Englishmen have made their home. To some of them the land seems less familiar than the sea; and when at last they are beached, their consolation is to gaze seaward with John Masefield:

> I must go down to the seas again, to the lonely sea and the sky,
> And all I ask is a tall ship and a star to steer her by.

Unlike the manor or the priest's house, ships as homes are relatively modern, for the Viking explorers were exceptions proving the rule that an early medieval ship was merely a vehicle—often an open boat—designed for short passages in fair weather. The evolution of ships as homes waited perforce on the evolution of design and building, which in turn waited on the explorers who discovered new trade routes. The long oar which steered the ship (steerboard or starboard) was replaced by rudders that were easier to handle, and less likely to be damaged. The bowsprit was hoisted inboard, to create a second mast. Medieval seamen used a magnetic needle or primitive compass, a device that was mentioned by an English monk, Alexander Neckham, in his treatise *De Utensilibus c.* 1180: 'They have also a needle,' he said, 'and it is turned and whirled round until the point of the needle looks north-east' (he meant 'north'). Needles, however, deviate. Columbus is commonly regarded as the first man to have observed that fact, but the early Portuguese explorers had anticipated Columbus, for they reported that their needle 'nor-easted and nor-wested'. Crude though they were, the fifteenth-century compass and chart enabled ships to make long voyages. By the beginning of the seventeenth century a considerable number of Englishmen were professional sailors whose calling kept them at sea for months at a time. Their vehicle had become their home.

The founders of English sea power were a father and son, Henry VII and Henry VIII. The former built the first dry dock in England; the latter, the largest ship, the *Great Harry*, of 1,500 tons. Together they created the Royal Navy insofar as they built their own ships instead of hiring them. Officers and men, however, did not receive permanent commissions and ratings. They remained merchant seamen who combined profit with patriotism by serving for a limited period, in return for the right to share such booty as they could capture without provoking a formal declaration of war. William Harrison set the Elizabethan maritime scene when he published *The Description of England*: 'The navy of England may be divided into three sorts, of which the one serveth for the wars, the other for burden, and the third for fishermen which get their living by fishing on the sea.' The Royal Navy took precedence: 'Certes there is no prince in Europe hath a more beautiful or gallant sort of ships than the Queen's majesty of England at this present, and those generally are of such exceeding force that two of them ... will not hesitate to encounter with three or four of those of other countries, and either bourge them or put them to flight, if they may not bring them home.' Harrison's was not an *ex parte* hallucination: 'the common report that strangers make of our ships amongst themselves is daily confirmed to be true, which is that for strength, assurance, nimbleness, and swiftness of sailing, there are no vessels in the world to be compared with ours.'

The domestic life of those ships would probably kill more of our own generation than they did of theirs. The only food preservatives were pickles and salt. Large ships might carry a cargo of livestock which was slaughtered *en route*; some carried cows and hens; but within a few days the crew were down to salt meat and weevil-biscuits. Thomas Nashe met several survivors of the Elizabethan voyages: 'Those that escape,' he wrote, 'tell of nothing but eating tallow and young blackamores, of five and five to a rat in every mess and the ship-boy to the tail, of stopping their noses when they drank stinking water that came out of the pump of the ship, and cutting a greasy buff jerkin in tripes and broiling it for their dinners.' Yet still the ships sailed with a full crew, leaving behind many who would have enlisted had there been a berth for them. In 1589 Richard Hakluyt's *Principall Navigations* improvised on 'the common report that strangers make of our ships'. The English seamen, he said: 'in searching the most opposite corners and quarters of the world, and to speake plainly, in compassing the vaste globe of the earth more than once, have excelled all the nations and peoples of the earth.' In October 1567 the Queen sent six ships with 408 seamen on a trading expedition to the Indies, under the command of Sir John Hawkins; among whose officers was a young man named Francis Drake. Before embarking, the entire company assembled in St Andrew's Church at Plymouth, to invoke a blessing on their enterprise; yet of all those hundreds of men, less than eighty ever saw England again. They fell to disease, storm, shipwreck, capture, enemy action. When Hawkins came to write the log of that enterprise, the memory of his shipmates and the directness of his speech achieved true eloquence: 'If all the miseries and troublesome affaires of this sorrowfull voyage should be perfectly and thoroughly written, there should neede a painfull man with his pen, and as great a time as he had that wrote the lives and deathes of the Martyrs.'

Despite the squalor of their home, the numbers of English sea-men continued to increase. Many of them carried their own stock of goods, which they sold profitably abroad, using the money to buy goods which they sold profitably in England. The coloniza-tion of America, the Anglo-Dutch wars, the growth of the New-foundland fishery; still the tide flowed, and still the ships re-mained dangerous and uncomfortable. Two centuries after the defeat of the Spanish Armada, Dr Johnson remarked to Boswell: 'A ship is worse than a jail. There is, in jail, better air, better company, better conveniency of every kind; and a ship has the additional disadvantage of being in danger.' When Captain Cook joined the Navy his first ship lost twenty-two men to illness dur-ing a four-week summer cruise in European waters; of her survi-vors, 130 went straight into hospital. When Captain Anson sailed around the world in 1740 only one in five of his crew returned alive; the ship's chaplain described many of the casualties as 'a decrepit detachment' of Army pensioners. Tobias George Smol-lett, who became a ship's surgeon, sailed in HMS *Cumberland* in 1740. Eight years later he recounted some of his impressions in *The Adventures of Roderick Random*: 'I was much less surprised that people should die on board than that any sick person should recover. Here I saw about fifty miserable distempered wretches, suspended in rows, so huddled upon one another that not more than fourteen inches space was allotted for each ... deprived of the light of day as well as of fresh air, breathing nothing but a noisome atmosphere of the morbid steams from their own excre-ment and diseased bodies, devoured with vermin hatched in the filth that surrounded them. ...' Why were conditions in the Royal Navy so conspicuously harsher than those in merchant ships? The answer is provided by England's persistent refusal to defend her-self efficiently until the battle has begun. Poor pay and bad food were the price of that pacifism, and because few men were willing to pay it, many had to be 'pressed' or dragged on board, forming a very hard core of criminals who acknowledged only one law; ruth-less discipline. What a paradox, that with such unpromising material England ruled the waves.

Officers fared more privately than ratings, but not a great deal more comfortably. To regard them as tyrannical aristocrats is to contradict the truth. The foremost naval historian of our time,

K

Dr J. A. Williamson, has emphasized that the majority of Nelson's officers 'were good sound men, many of them from the professional middle class rather than from the land-owning families who officered the army. They had to be severe in an age when all punishment tended to be corporal, but they did their best for their men, not conniving at the evils under which they suffered, but remonstrating, though with little effect, against the poisonous beer, the putrid meat, the maggoty biscuit, which the scamps ashore were allowed to pass off upon the fleet.' Merchants made fortunes, the shopkeepers grew rich, by depriving the Royal Navy of its fair share of wholesome food. Nevertheless, had conditions been so bad as some people suppose, the Service would have disappeared, denuded of men as they deserted whenever they stepped ashore. The backbone of the Fleet were merchant seamen who enlisted in the hope of promotion; men like James Cook, who joined as an able-seaman, became a petty officer in less than four weeks, and ended as a Captain. Every aspect of an eighteenth-century Englishman's home at sea is illustrated in the career of Vice-Admiral Viscount Nelson, Duke of Brontë, sixth of twelve children of the rector of Burnham Thorpe in Norfolk, where the twenty-first of October was observed as a rubric. On that day, in the year 1759, Mrs Nelson's brother, Captain Maurice Suckling, had engaged a superior French force in the West Indies. During the battle the Captain used the sword of his great-uncle, Captain Galfridus Walpole (an example of 'naval families' serving generation after generation). When Nelson was nine years old he happened to read a copy of the local newspaper, which announced that Captain Suckling had received command of HMS *Raisonnable*, a ship of sixty-four guns. The child at once sent a signal to his father, who was then at Bath: 'I should like to go with my uncle Maurice to sea.' Uncle acknowledged that signal: 'What has poor Horatio done, who is so weak, that he above all the rest should be sent to rough it out at sea. But let him come; and the first time we go into action, a cannonball may knock off his head, and provide for him at once.' On New Year's Day, 1771, being then twelve years and three months old, Horatio Nelson was rated as midshipman in the *Raisonnable* (a rank which Captain Suckling afterwards changed to 'Captain's servant'). The boy's new home, the Gun Room or living quarters of junior midshipmen, was very different

from the spacious comfort of Burnham Thorpe. John Masefield's
Sea Life in Nelson's Time describes the Gun Room: 'It was
generally below the water, in the after cockpit, in a dingy den,
lit partly by a lantern, and partly by a thick glass scuttle, crusted
with filth, let into the ship's side. From deck to deck it measured
perhaps 5 feet 6 inches, so that its inhabitants had to uncover as
they entered.... Twelve feet square was reckoned fairly large for
a berth.... The atmosphere so far below water and the upper air
was foul and noisome. The bilges reeked beneath the orlop in
continual pestilential stench, unlike any other smell in the world.
Near the berth, as a sort of pendant to the bilges, was the purser's
storeroom where the rancid butter and putrid cheese were served
out once or twice a week....' The furniture was a table which the
surgeons used for amputations; the table cloth served as handker-
chief and dish cloth. The Gun Room was lit by tallow dips,
known as 'purser's glims', stuck into beer bottles. As there were no
chairs, the 'young gentlemen' sat on their sea chests. The only
servant was a ship's boy. They shared this dark dungeon with the
Captain's clerk, the mates and the junior surgeons, not all of whom
were fit company. Punishment and humiliation became the daily
lot of midshipmen, on the principle that to obey is the best
method of learning to command. A first-rate ship carried twenty-
four midshipmen; a third-rate, only twelve. Until their fifteenth
birthday the midshipmen were dubbed 'youngsters'. In a sixth-
rate ship they received less than £2 each month, out of which they
had to pay £5 per voyage to the schoolmaster who instructed
them. At sea they worked alongside the ratings, sharing the most
arduous tasks in the most dangerous situations. Many Captains
expected their 'youngsters' to beat the men in the race to reef the
topgallant during a storm. If the Lieutenant caught them loung-
ing with their hands in their pockets, he sent them aloft, sometimes for twenty-four hours. Neither in conversation nor in writing did Nelson ever complain about his harsh apprenticeship in
the Gun Room. Many years later, however, when he was Com-
mander-in-Chief in the Mediterranean, he gave a dinner party to
celebrate the anniversary of his victory at the Battle of Cape St
Vincent; on his right, as the youngest officer present, sat Mr
Midshipman Parsons, who, forty years afterwards, in *Nelsonian
Reminiscences, Leaves from Memory's Log*, recalled that the

Admiral had asked him at what age he became a midshipman; to which he replied: 'Eleven years, my lord.' Nelson muttered: 'Much too young.'

When Nelson received his first command he secured relatively comfortable quarters, but at the cost of companionship, for a Captain lived alone. Only so could he elicit the unquestioning obedience on which the lives of the crew and the outcome of the battle might depend. He took no part in the working of the ship, nor did he stand watch, unless during a crisis. He lived alone in his cabin, guarded day and night by a red-coated sentry with drawn sword. Sometimes he eased the isolation by inviting one or two officers to dine with him. When he appeared on deck the Lieutenants moved to the lee side, as a mark of respect. No man presumed to address him except about the day's work. Seamen uncovered before answering his question. Whenever he came on board he was piped by the boatswain; a Marine sentry stood to attention; all hands uncovered. The Captain then saluted the quarter-deck, and went aft to his cabin, usually without any sign of recognition to the assembly. As Masefield remarked, the ratings 'liked to sail with a smart and strict seaman who knew his duty, and made his men do theirs. They disliked slack captains.... When a mild and forgiving captain came aboard a ship, either on a visit or to command her, there was little interest displayed. But when a "rogue" or a "taut hand" came alongside, there was a rush to the ports, to see the man.' Sailors used to say that 'every ship was a separate navy'. Certainly the Captain was monarch of all he surveyed, with power of life and death; power also to dress the gig's crew as he pleased (one Scottish peer arrayed them in kilts, bonnets, and jackets adorned with a worsted thistle).

On his last command Nelson occupied quarters under those of his Captain, Thomas Hardy, below the poop in HMS *Victory*. They consisted of a state room, dining cabin, sleeping cabin, and a cubby for his steward. The stateroom (known to the Service as 'the great cabin') was fifteen feet long, lit by nine sash windows in the stern; there the Admiral worked with his secretaries. Two doors led from the state room to the dining cabin, thirty-five feet wide, from which Nelson ordered a stairway to be built so that he could reach the quarter-deck quickly. The dining cabin led to a lobby containing a kitchen and pantry, and thence to the sleeping cabin, which measured twelve feet by twenty. The floors or deck of the Admiral's quarters were covered with black-and-white check canvas; the furniture, though of fine quality and workmanship, was for use rather than for display. Like many great men of action, Nelson could sleep between his labours. The *Victory*'s chaplain, Rev. Alexander John Scott, remembered that the state room contained two black leather armchairs, lashed together, which Nelson used as a couch.

In two short lines Robert Bridges etched the statue of Nelson in Trafalgar Square:

> ... riding the sky
> With one arm and one eye.

Nelson, in fact, had been crippled by enemy gunfire. The stump of his arm caused continual pain; the useless eye blinked under a green shade. For years he was an invalid, wracked by private stress and the task of defending England with a fleet that was short of ships. Yet he started his day's work at six in the morning. Forty-five minutes later he took a breakfast of tea, hot rolls, toast, cold meat. About seven hours of each day were spent on deck; another seven, with secretaries and captains. Dinner at three o'clock was announced by a roll of drums and the tune of 'The Roast Beef of Old England'. The meal itself was simple—three courses only— followed by dessert, wine, liqueurs. The *Victory*'s surgeon, Sir William Beatty, observed that Nelson ate sparingly, preferring the wing of a fowl and a small plate of macaroni. He seldom drank more than two glasses of wine, each diluted with Bristol water. An hour's pacing on the quarter-deck followed, while the band played. At seven o'clock he relaxed among his officers: 'he was,' said his surgeon, 'at all times as free from stiffness and pomp as a regard to proper dignity will permit....' At eight o'clock a steward appeared with rummers of punch, and cake or biscuits, after which the officers withdrew, and work was resumed.

When Nelson last saw his seafaring home, at a little before eleven o'clock on the morning of 21 October 1805, it was almost empty of furniture, everything having been stowed in the hold, because the French fleet was in sight, and its leading ships almost within range. Nelson had gone below in order to prepare for what he knew would be his finest—and perhaps his last—hour. In his pocket book he made a brief entry: 'May the Great God, whom I worship, grant to my Country, and for the benefit of Europe in general, a great and glorious Victory; and may no misconduct in anyone tarnish it; and may humanity after Victory be the predominant feature in the British Fleet. For myself, individually, I commit my life to Him who made me, and may His blessing light upon my endeavours for serving my Country faithfully. To Him I resign myself and the just cause which is entrusted to me to defend. Amen.' The last person to see Nelson in his quarters was the Signal Lieutenant, John Pasco, who found him on his knees, praying. Shortly afterwards, Nelson ordered Pasco to make the most famous signal in English history: 'England expects that every man will do his duty.' Two hours later, Nelson was dead, shot through the spine by a sniper. He had forbidden the surgeons to attend him until they finished with the seamen who had preceded him. His last words were: 'Thank God, I have done my duty.'

Several English kings, and the husband and the eldest son of Queen Elizabeth II, made their home in the Gun Room. The first king, William IV, endured the same hardships as Nelson had done, though he was already sixteen when the joined the *Prince George*, patrolling home waters against a surprise attack by the French or Spanish fleets. The newcomer set aside his rank of HRH Prince William Henry, son of George III, and became Mr Midshipman Guelph, eating the same food, sharing the same duties, as his shipmates. Within a few months the king-to-be transferred to the Mediterranean fleet. Off Cape St Vincent he was recognized by the defeated Spanish Admiral, Don Juan de Langara, who exclaimed: 'England deserves to rule the waves if her Princes are sent to rough it in the Gun Room.'

The future King George V and his elder brother, the Duke of Clarence, joined the Navy on the same day, 5 June 1877, despite the Queen's regal and maternal doubts: 'the very rough sort of life which boys are exposed to on board ship is the very thing not calculated to make a refined and amiable Prince.' Unlike Elizabeth I, Victoria was not 'mere English', for she added a second argument against sea service: 'Will a nautical education not engender and encourage national prejudices and make them think that their own Country is superior to any other?' In the end, however, the Queen concurred, and the two children were allowed to share one small cabin, though in all other ways they lived as their messmates. Looking back on those ordeals, George V confessed to Sir Owen Morshead: 'It never did me any good to be a Prince, I can tell you, and many was the time I wished I hadn't been. It was a pretty rough place and, so far from making any allowances for our disadvantages, the other boys made a point of taking it out of us on the grounds that they'd never be able to do it later on. There was a lot of fighting among the cadets and the rule was that if challenged you had to accept. So they used to make me go up and challenge the bigger boys—I was awfully small then—and I'd get a hiding time and again.... We were only given a shilling a week pocket money.' When the Prince joined the *Bacchante* as a midshipman, his commanding officer, Captain Lord Charles Scott, was ordered to treat him 'in all respects as other midshipmen on board, with the exception of keeping Night Watch, from which he is to be excused under medical advice, as well as employment on boat service in tempestuous weather'. The Prince's log confirmed that the Captain obeyed both the spirit and the letter of those orders: 'April 26 1881. At sea, Cape to Australia. Got up at 6.0 o'clock and had drill.... I had breakfast about 8.0. Went to school with Mr Lawless from 9.30 to 11.45. Had dinner at 12.0. Did some French with Mr Sceales. At 1.45 we went aloft with the ordinary seamen and boys and exercised shifting topsail. Then we did rifle and cutlass drill. Kept the 4 to 6 watch. After quarters, we exercised shifting topsail.... Tea at 6.30. Then after tea I wrote some log up. Went to bed at 9.30.' Commander Hillyard, who served as a midshipman with the Prince, gave a BBC broadcast about their daily life: 'Weeks and weeks at sea,' he remembered, 'sometimes very monotonous weeks, living on food that was more than monotonous, and also exceedingly nasty. Mostly salt pork and ship's biscuit. There were no comforts in those days. No such thing as electrical freezing plant. So fresh vegetables, fruit and fresh provisions lasted a very, very short time. Yet in all those years I never remember Prince George losing his temper.'

When the Prince became King George V he sent his eldest son to endure a similar régime as cadet at Osborne. Although the son had been baptized Edward Albert Christian George Andrew

Patrick David, a truly German-British litany, the father called him David, as in his diary for 18 February 1907: 'David went up before a Committee and was examined to see if the Admiralty would give him a nomination for the Navy. I am glad to say that he did remarkably well....' The cadet's own memoirs confessed that, at twelve years of age, he felt very homesick: 'Despite my most determined efforts to uphold what I guessed must be the traditions of the British Navy, I left Marlborough House with tears drenching my new blue uniform.' His new home was a group of damp buildings near Queen Victoria's stables: 'The structure of the dormitories in which we slept had deteriorated so much by the time I joined that we could kick holes in the outer walls without hurting our feet....' The senior cadets at once decided 'that Cadet Prince Edward would look much better with his fair hair dyed red. So one evening, before "quarters" [evening parade], I was cornered by my betters and made to stand at attention while one of them poured a bottle of red ink over my head.' On balance, however, the future King Edward VIII approved his new home: 'my life at Osborne was no different from that of any other British naval cadet, which, by contrast with the pampering that goes on in some schools today in the name of progressive education, was a fairly Spartan business.'

The Prince's younger brother, who became George VI, followed his father's example, and chose the Navy as his career; followed, too, the example of William IV by discarding rank, to become Mr Midshipman Johnson, without privilege or exemption. He stood watch, commanded a picket-boat, laboured in the hold of a collier, and supped on bread and cheese and onions. Not the least of the boy's achievements was to deliver safely a boat-load of drunken 'liberty-men'. In HMS *Collingwood* he fought at the Battle of Jutland, though he was in the sick bay when Action Stations sounded, and might have stayed there had he chosen. Instead, he went at once to his station in a gun turret, where he survived the ordeal of being straddled by an enemy salvo, and was afterwards mentioned in despatches. With almost biblical brevity the King told Admiral Sir John Jellicoe: 'I am pleased with my son.'

No type of ship has a monopoly of homeliness, yet the smaller is usually the homelier. For a short time I served in the very smallest ships, mere cabin-cruisers, armed with a single outdated gun. Thereafter I lived for several years in a converted lifeboat, learning by experience that life therein is either shipshape or chaotic. There can be no middle course. If the householder is not always neat, he becomes forever slovenly; and his disorder can breed disaster, for at sea the crisis may leap from calm waters and a clear sky. If fire-extinguishers need to be extricated from a jungle of rope, or if the anchor lies fouled in its own chain, then the time lost in righting those wrongs is irrevocable, and the damage perhaps irremediable. With one glance a seaman sizes another's home: unwashed plates, a leaking dinghy, a loose rope-end, petrol in the bilges, rickety pump-handle, fenders adrift; by their neatness shall ye know them. 'Pusser' or Purser was the naval rating's name for whatever is well-polished, well-painted, well-stowed, well-lashed. Even when he is ashore, a sailor uses his vernacular. Paul Dombey's friend, Captain Cuttle, had but one phrase for drawing attention to something: 'Stand by!' The Senior Service is also the Silent Service, the home of men who waste nothing, not even their words. Said Captain Cuttle: 'I never wanted two or three words in my life that I didn't know where to lay my hands on them ... it comes of not wasting language as some do.' The language of the sea says what it means, and says so more effectively than any other language, by using the proper quantity of correct words. The floor is 'the deck'; windows are 'portlights'; a ventilator is 'a louvre'; the kitchen is 'the galley'; a needlework basket is 'the fetch-log'; brasswork is 'brightwork'. Landsmen tend to sound vague: 'You'll find it somewhere in one of those cupboards.' A seaman comes close to the mark: 'Starboard locker in the lazarette.' Joseph Conrad, himself a master-mariner, summed it up: 'To take a liberty with a technical language is a crime against clearness, precision, and beauty of perfected speech.'

A house may be alive with the memory of former occupants, but its fabric is motionless and without life. A ship, by contrast, lives and has her being in motion. She speaks in her own tone of voice, as when she crushes a wave, or is hurt by the wind, or tugs at the chain. She indulges moods, being sometimes sluggish, sometimes volatile; one day submissive, the next day wayward. The best description of a ship as a home appears in Conrad's *The*

Rescue, which tells of a man who commands his own brig: 'He felt her live in every motion, in every roll, in every sway of her tapering masts.... To him she was always precious—like old love; always desirable—like a strange woman; always tender—like a mother; always faithful—like the favourite daughter of a man's heart.... He was aware that his little vessel could give him something not to be had from anybody or anything in the world; something specially his own.... To him she was unique and dear; this brig of three hundred and fourteen tons register—a kingdom!'

The background to a landsman's home is more varied than the sea, yet less profound in the austerity of its wisdom. Hilaire Belloc, who loved his own seagoing home, believed with Euripides that the waves wash away the ills of men: 'Truth,' he wrote, 'is one of the great gifts of the sea. You cannot persuade yourself nor listen to the persuasion of another that the wind is not blowing when it is, or that a cabin with half a foot of water in it is dry, or that a dragging anchor holds. Everywhere the sea is a teacher of truth....' And he ended with a sailor's benediction: 'The sea is the consolation of this our day, as it has been the consolation of the centuries. There, on the sea, is a man nearest to his own making, and in communion with that from which he came, and to which he will return.'

Many sailors who are still on active service have witnessed the transformation of an Englishman's seagoing home. Instead of pacing an open bridge, rinsed and rasped by wind and water, a naval officer now sits in a centrally heated room. Instead of seeking the sun with a sextant, he steers more or less mechanically, and may, if necessary, discover his position by making a signal. The ships themselves have been reduced in number and size, cut, as it were, to fit the role of a second-rate power. So be it: most of the domestic changes are for the better; and if events should by mischance take a turn for the worse, Thomas Campbell's *Naval Ode* will evoke a right response from

> Ye Mariners of England
> That guard our native seas,
> Whose flag has braved, a thousand years,
> The battle and the breeze....

Houses / Lavenham / Suffolk

---

9 *The Town House*

T HE best parts of my childhood and early youth were spent
at a rambling old country house. Later, as a young man,
I had sometimes to make rare and reluctant visits to
London. Whenever it was possible, I escaped before nightfall;
when that was impossible, I stayed at a house belonging to my
father, which was built about 1770, on the edge of what is still
called Highgate Village, no great distance from the West End,
and only a short way from green fields at Barnet. The house
itself made no claim to be grand. It had been designed for a man
of modestly comfortable means, who maintained a carriage, a
coachman, and two or three domestic servants. The stables and
coach-house, adjoining the main building, were converted into a
drawing-room whose parquet floor and French windows opened
to a paved garden. The dining-room, which served as a second
sitting room, contained the overflow from my father's library; and
its French windows led to a miniature terrace, sheltered by a

Georgian portico, and thence into the garden. A windowed cellar, underneath the kitchen, became a store room and scullery.

The main stairway from the hall led to a bathroom and to a small bedroom which my father used as his dressing room, whence a passage reached my mother's dressing room and after that her bedroom, bow-windowed and beautifully proportioned. A back stairway climbed sinuously to two servants' bedrooms on the third floor. The rear of the house was flanked by a private cul-de-sac which in those years resembled a country lane. Except on the topmost storey, the rooms were lofty and spaciously windowed. The whole house was agreeable to look at and comfortable to live in. On returning to it after visiting a modern house, we became aware of its character, and of the modern house's lack of character. Partly, no doubt, the difference could be explained in terms of age, for whereas an old house possesses a long pedigree, the new one does not.

The character of a house, however, is conditioned by something more tangible than the ghosts of its former occupants. The character of many late eighteenth-century houses owed much to the Georgians' importation of Scandinavian soft timber which could be worked more easily than oak. In any event, few timber-frame houses were built after the seventeenth century, so that oak lost something of its ancient eminence. The Georgians devised, too, a system of joists that could support very heavy weights. Since soft woods lack an oak tree's durability, some of the early Georgian houses were unduly vulnerable to damp, a flaw which the next generation overcame by discovering that a solution of lead oxide will protect timber. Their discovery fostered the paint industry, whose first factories were built beside the lower Thames. The earliest lead oxides caused wood to turn white, whence the Georgians' apparent fondness for white paint. The Georgians introduced bow windows also, and developed the double-pitch roof which gave such relatively good head-room to the top floor of our Highgate house. The double-pitch roof had been perfected by a Frenchman, Mansard, who died in 1666; architects still call it a mansard roof. Finally, our own house contained chair rails, three feet above the floor, with which the Georgians protected their plastered walls against the products of Chippendale, Hepplewhite and Sheraton. But already we are proceeding too fast, for the distinction between a town house and a country seat is comparatively modern.

Celts spoke of a *dun*, by which they meant a fortified place; Saxons spoke of a *tun*, by which they meant a plot of enclosed land; and both were using a word that can be traced to the Greek *zaun*, meaning a hedge or enclosure. Since land was seldom enclosed unless one or more families dwelt thereon, the *tun* came to mean, first, a sizeable settlement, and, later, any settlement larger than a village. To a citizen of Imperial Rome the first English towns would have seemed crude and small. Even at the end of the Middle Ages the population of England was smaller than the present population of Greater Manchester. In Shakespeare's time the City of London was bounded by green fields, some of whose names are still used (Lincoln's Inn Fields). When Victoria became Queen, Kensington was a village, separated from the West End by pastures and orchards. One of my grandmothers remembered Highgate when it really was a village, approached via a steep hill where cattle grazed.

Medieval Londoners were keenly aware that the prevailing wind wafted the stench of privies toward the East End, wherefore a well-to-do citizen built his home in or near the West End. Even after London had become the largest city in the kingdom, it retained a quasi-rustic intimacy, especially when polite society indulged one of its seasonal emigrations to the country: 'I find,' wrote Samuel Pepys, 'all the town almost going out of town.' A century later, London was already Cobbett's 'great wen' or cancerous tumour. Nevertheless—and incredible though it now seems—a vestige of Pepysian intimacy lingered until the 1920s, when *Punch* published a cartoon showing Bond Street during the season of fashionable rustication; despite a throng of sightseers and tradesmen, one colonel, recognizing a crony among the crowd, exclaims: 'Not a soul in Town, eh.' But again we have anticipated events.

A particular account of the evolution of the town house would need to interrupt itself by incessant qualifications. A general account, on the other hand, is justified in remarking that the average town house differed from a country house only by being nearer to its neighbours. Nor did the urban way of life differ greatly from the rural, for industry had not yet arisen, nor the present chasm between agriculture and industry, nor the present habit of regarding large towns as the only centres of civilization. True, a medieval king held court in London, yet his subjects were countrymen. A Northumbrian earl and a Cornish baron spoke each his own dialect, and if either of them did venture as far as London, they certainly needed a phrasebook for foreigners. The early medieval towns were appanages of a fief, and each guarded its own privileges. At nightfall the gates were locked; throughout the day a watch was kept for any stranger who might deprive the citizens of their employment or of their municipal monopolies. As late as 1580, when Queen Elizabeth I recognized Gloucester as a port, the Bristol merchants protested so strongly that within two years she annulled Gloucester's right to collect harbour dues.

Unlike the countryside, which retains many medieval homes, our large towns are predominantly Victorian and post-Victorian, partly because trade compelled them to expand and modernize themselves by demolition, and partly because many were ravaged by fire. The classic example is the Great Fire of London, which Pepys described in his diary: 'Some of our maids sitting up late last night to get things ready against our feast-day, Jane called us up about three in the morning, to tell us of a great fire they saw....' Within an hour or so, Jane reported 'that above 300 houses have been burned down ... and that it is now burning all Fish Street, by London Bridge'. Pepys then went to investigate the cause of the disaster: 'So down, with my heart full of trouble, to the Lieutenant of the Tower, who tells me that it begun this morning in the King's baker's house in Pudding Lane....' Later that day he met the Lord Mayor, who was running around 'like a man spent, with a handkercher about his neck. To the King's messenger he cried, like a fainting woman, "Lord! What can I do? I am spent: people will not obey me. I have been pulling down houses; but the fire overtakes us faster than we can do it."' From her Chancery Lane mansion Lady Hobart scribbled a letter to Sir Ralph Verney down in Buckinghamshire: 'O dear Sir Raph—I am sory to be the mesinger of so dismall news, for por London is almost burnt down.... i am all most out of my wits, we have packed up all our goods and cannot get a cart for money, thay give 5 or 10 pound for carts.' When it was all over, Sir Ralph received an account from a surveyor who said that the fire had raged for four days, consuming 373 acres within the City, and 64 acres beyond; 89 churches and chapels were destroyed, with more than 13,000 houses. So, in a hundred hours, fire destroyed much of the work of a thousand years. Yet in 1709—nearly half a century after the fire—London still contained so many timber homes that the government ordered all window-frames to be set back at least six inches from the wall, lest fire spread from room to room, and house to house, and street to street.

London, then, arose like a phoenix from the ashes of affliction. Many other towns arose less painfully, on the crest of their own prosperity, like Bewdley in Worcestershire, which rebuilt itself in order to meet an expanding Tudor market. As we have already noted, John Leland saw the new town in all its glory: 'att rising of the sunne the whole town glittereth, being all of new building, as it were of gold.' Despite fire and rebuilding, a few towns have preserved enough old houses to create an impression of what they looked like at the end of the Middle Ages. Perhaps the most impressive example is Chester, the Roman *castra* or military base, which became a Norman bastion against North Wales. Britain has nothing to excel the timbered shops and merchants' homes flanking both sides of Eastgate Street, Bridge Street and Watergate Street. The buildings are in two tiers, the one at ground level, the other set back a little, so that its overhanging storeys form a covered promenade. Their topmost rooms were occupied by traders. Shrewsbury, a middling-size town, has preserved the gateway to Roger de Montgomery's castle. Some of the upper storeys in narrow streets are so close to their neighbours across the way that it is possible to shake hands above the cobbles. The sixteenth-century merchants' homes—like Ireland's and Owen's mansion—were large replicas of medieval houses. Much of Shrewsbury is industrial and therefore ugly, unlike the Sussex town of Rye, which, although it was once larger and more important than Shrewsbury, remains small and relatively unspoiled. Rye was one of a large number of medieval Channel harbours which associated under the name of Cinque Ports. Dominated by a hilltop church, the streets descend to the quay, step by step echoing wherever they are cobbled, all the while offering a kaleidoscope of English architecture; thirteenth-century friary, fourteenth-century town gate, fifteenth-century Mermaid Inn, many sixteenth and seventeenth-century residences, and the eighteenth-century Lamb House (once the home of Henry James, the novelist). Lavenham in Suffolk is another small medieval town, dominated by a church which the merchants and farmers built, with encouragement and cash from the lord of the manor, John de Vere, Earl of Oxford. The richly carved Guildhall, built in 1592 by merchants of the Guild of Corpus Christi, was the town's commercial centre or Bourse (so-called after the Bruges banking family, De Bourze). Some of the houses are nearly 600 years old; many are 400 years old. Bolton Street, for example, was named after John Bolton, who died in 1440. Shilling Street was named after John Schylling, who died in 1476. Shilling Old Grange was the home of Miss Taylor, who composed a famous verse:

> Twinkle, twinkle, little star!
> How I wonder what you are!
> Up above the world so high,
> Like a diamond in the sky!

Only a painter could do justice to the houses at Lavenham: their crazy contours, switchbacking over the timbers that support them; the weathered complexion of those timbers, tanned by the centuries; doors that make you duck; dormers that wink like a retina among eaves; oak-plank floors, smooth as a shaving mirror; nooks, crevices, corners, crannies. Again it is necessary to remember the filth and the plagues; the diseases that could now be cured by a chemist; the stench from privies and conduits (water-closets had been invented by Sir John Harington in 1596, but were still absent from many English homes at the beginning of the twentieth century). Nevertheless, those sombre facts cannot dim the colourful individuality of medieval houses, none of which was a replica of the rest. Builders had not the time, nor householders the wish, to make every rafter and all windows appear identical. A rope and a pulley raised those homes; and bare hands hauled at the rope.

Not even the wealthiest medieval townsman possessed much furniture. Sofas, settees and couches were unknown. Clocks were rarities until the Lantern type appeared during the reign of James I. Mirrors were an extravagance (Anne Boleyn admired herself in a small circle of burnished steel). The average bed was a homemade thing, standing a few inches above the floor. Paupers and many servants slept on straw. Chairs remained a status symbol, whence the importance of Mr Chairman when he presided over those who either sat on benches or stood beside his chair.

The gulf between town life and country life is, we agreed, relatively modern; but by the middle of the seventeenth century a *distinction* between them had arisen, which would have puzzled the early Tudors. The distinction is revealed in the career of Samuel Pepys, a man of humble origins, who in 1660 was appointed a Commissioner of the Admiralty Board, through the influence of his patron, the Earl of Sandwich: 'I shall,' the diarist prophesied, 'in a little time come to be a man much taken notice of in the world.' That prophecy was fulfilled. Having acquired a London house next to his office in Seething Lane, Pepys built a passage between the two: 'At the Navy Office I got leave to have a door made me into the leads.' It was important for him to maintain appearances: 'I find that I must go handsomely whatever the cost....' In 1669 he bought a carriage and horses, and a set of silver dishes to impress his guests: 'I did make them all gaze to see themselves served so nobly in plate....' Even a man of moderate means ate what would now be considered immoderate meals. After dining at home with his wife, Pepys recorded their menu: 'We had a fricasee of rabbits, and chickens, a leg of mutton boiled, three carps in a dish, a great dish of a side of lamb, a dish of roasted pigeons, a dish of four lobsters, three tarts, a lamprey pie, a dish of cloves, good wine of several sorts, and all things mighty noble to my great content.' An indigestible postscript followed: 'My ordinary housekeeping comes to £7 a month, which is a great deal.' Tea was a luxury, and the King himself accepted the East India Company's gift of eighteen ounces. When Pepys first took a cup he recorded the fact: 'I did send for a cup of tee (or China drink) of which I had never drunk before....' Another London novelty was skating, which had been introduced by cavaliers who shared the King's exile in Holland: 'over the Parke, where I first in my life, it being a great frost, did see people sliding with skeates, which is a very pretty art....' In Pepys's day it was still possible for a cultivated man to become master of several arts, not least of the art of music. The Tudors had set the

L

fashion, led by Henry VIII, whose manuscript song-book contains some of his own songs:

> O my hart and O my hart!
> My hart it is so sore,
> Sens I must nedys from my love depart
> And I know no cause wherefore.

Pepys himself bought an organ and after that a recorder 'which I do intend to learn to play on, the sound of it being, of all sounds in the world, most pleasing to me'. He held musical soirées at his house, where he and the guests were both audience and performers. The cost, however, continued to alarm him: 'I have for this last half year been a very great spendthrift in all manner of respects, that I am afraid to cost up my accounts. . . .' The remedy was desperate: 'I have newly taken a solemn oath about abstaining from plays and wine. . . .' When his assets reached the sum of £1,849, Pepys uttered a *Te Deum*: 'The Lord make me ever thankful to his holy name. . . .' Yet he was something more than an Occasional Conformist, as is shown by one of the earliest references to his town house: 'Home, and at night had a chapter [of the Bible] read; and I read prayers out of the Common Prayer Book, the first time I ever read prayers in this house. So to bed.'

As his stock rose, Pepys enhanced his home, draping the rooms with 'green serge hangings and gilt leather which is very handsome'. New fireplaces followed, and large mantelshelves. Pewter pots decorated the hall and staircase. Finally, the house received an extra storey, though not until Pepys had discovered that the British workmen exceeded both their estimate and their welcome: 'Looking after my workmen whose laziness do much trouble me.' His furniture was more plentiful and more comfortable than any that Queen Elizabeth had known. Hitherto even the nobility had sat on hard wood, cushioned by padded breeches; but when their breeches became unfashionable, the padding was transferred from the buttocks to the chair itself. In prosperous households an oak chest was giving way to the chest of drawers: 'This morning into the city to buy several things as I have lately done for my house. Among other things, a fair chest of drawers. . . .' When Pepys was obliged to stay at home, having

taken 'a dose of physick', he spent most of the time on a commode
or Chaucer's *chaise percée*, which answered to several other
names: close-stool, close-chair, night-stool, night-table, necessary.
Pepys's father would have been satisfied with any timepiece that
neither lost nor gained above an hour a day; but English clock-
making was encouraged by Charles II, a cultivated and scientific
man, who sponsored the founding of the Royal Society. Indeed,
clock-making became so fashionable that Sir Christopher Wren
drew some designs for Thomas Tompion. Pepys may have owned
one of the new eight-day spring-driven clocks. He certainly possessed a watch: 'I cannot forbear carrying my watch in my hand,
in the coach, all this afternoon, and seeing what o'clock it is one
hundred times, and am apt to think with myself, how could I be
so long without one. . . .' Another domestic innovation was shellac
or the resin secreted by an insect, *coccus lacca*, which formed the
basis of lacquer. At the end of the Stuart dynasty John Stalker
and George Parker published their *Treatise of Japanning and
Varnishing*. We know that Pepys owned a sideboard or carving-
table, and also one of the new barometers. His contemporary,
Robert Boyle, F.R.S, was the first Englishman to fit a barometer
with a plate which showed both the state of the weather and the
height of the quicksilver. The earliest portable barometer was
invented in 1688 by an English clock-maker, Daniel Quare.

Pepys, a childless man, described his London household affec-
tionately: 'My family is my wife . . . her woman, Mercer, a pretty,
modest, quiet maid; her chambermaid Besse, her cook-maid Jane,
the little girl Susan, and my boy, which I had about half a year,
Tom Edward, which I took from the King's Chapel; and as pretty
and loving quiet a family I have as any man in England.' It was
not always so, for Tom Edward's predecessor had proved troublesome: 'I reckoned all his faults, and whipped him soundly.' The
punishment pained the master more than the servant: 'the rods
was so small that I fear they did not much hurt to him, but only
to my arm, which I am already, within a quarter of an houre, not
able to stir almost.' Being master in his own house, Pepys sometimes clashed with its mistress, as, for example, when he stipu-
lated that her new gown must *not* be laced: 'she flounced away in
a manner I never saw her, nor which I could ever endure. So I
away to the office, though she had dressed herself to go to see my

Lady Sandwich. She by and by in a rage follows me, and tells me in a spiteful manner like a vixen and with a look full of rancour that she would go buy a new one and lace it and make me pay for it, and then let me burn it if I would ... and so went away in a fury. ...' In that fury Mrs Pepys pursued her husband to his office, but was met with guile: 'I made her stay, being busy with another, half an houre. ...' The lady soon came to heel: 'we were presently friends.' On no account was Mrs Pepys allowed to use cosmetics, a vanity that was becoming fashionable among London women. Pepys shared the opinion of his fellow-diarist, John Evelyn, who complained because 'the women begin to paint themselves, formerly a most ignominious thing and used only by prostitutes'.

Pepys was neither the first nor the last man whose chimney smoked: 'This day my wife showed me bills printed wherein her father, with Sir John Collidon and Sir Edward Ford, have got a patent for curing smoking chimneys. I wish they may do good thereof.' Like many practical householders, Pepys was not always satisfied with the advice which he received: 'bought a little book, "Counsell to Builders" ... not worth a farthing.' The weather played perennial tricks: 'When I wake, I find a very great thaw, and my house overflown with it, which vexed me.' The neighbours, too, were much as many of them have always been: 'My Lady Batten did send to speak with me, and told me very civilly that she did not desire, nor hoped I did, that anything should pass between us but what was civil, though there was not the neighbourliness between her and my wife that was fit to be, and so complained of my maid's mocking her.' Domestic alarms were sometimes false: 'This morning, about two or three o'clock, knocked up in our back yard, and rising to the window, being moonshine, I found it was the constable and his watch, who had found our back yard door open, and so come in to see what the matter was. So I desired them to shut the door, and bid them goodnight.' If only for safety's sake, most people remained indoors after dark. In London a watchman walked the streets, calling the time of day: 'I staid up till the bell-man came by with his bell just under my window as I was writing this very line, and cried, "Past one of the clock, and a cold, frosty, windy morning." ' When Pepys left his town house after dark he either carried a candle-lantern or was escorted by a link-boy with a blazing brand. Even in his day, however, Londoners were not left wholly in the dark. In 1559 an Act of Common Council had ordered that, from the first of October until the first of March, every householder should 'cause a substantial lanthorn and a candle of eight in the pound to be hang'd without their doors'. In 1694 a certain Edward Heming received licence to place lights at the door of every tenth house, from six p.m. until midnight, between Michaelmas and Lady Day, and to charge six shillings annually to each householder *en route*. Heming wished to experiment with the new oil lamps, but was prevented when the Tallow Chandlers protested to the Lord Mayor against an innovation 'so pernicious to the publick good. . . .' Tallow, said the tallowers, 'will be cheaper to the inhabitants than any sort of lamp'. Meagre though they were, the lights deterred some of the marauders, and London was slightly less unruly than it had been during the Middle Ages when—according to Stow's *Survey of the Cities of London and Westminster*—'it was then a common practice in the city that a hundred or more in a company, young or old, would make nightly invasions upon the houses of the wealthy, with the intent to rob them; and if they found any man stirring in the city that were not of their crew, they would presently murder him, insomuch that when night was come no man durst adventure to walk in the streets.' Candles were the common means of indoor lighting. When one of Pepys's clerks was ordered to refute an accusation of extravagant lighting at the Navy Board, he discovered that the Board had bought 96,840 candles for use during 2,441 working days. Twenty-five candles were allowed each night in the Treasurer's ticket office; eighteen in the Controller's office; and one apiece for messengers. The Board emphasized that none of its offices 'was shut up till nine o'clock, at night, and some continually staying till twelve, and past that hour sometimes'.

Pepys lived long enough to witness the change from basically medieval to relatively modern town houses; a change wrought by the first speculative builders, chief of whom was a Cromwellian, named Praise-God Barebones, who leased from the Duke of Bedford a large estate in north London, which he divided into building plots. Needing to erect as many houses as possible, Barebones crammed them into a terrace formation. Each house had four storeys, each storey had two rooms. This early example of mass-produced pre-fabrication was foreseen in Sir Thomas More's *Utopia*: 'He who knows one of the cities, will know them all, so exactly alike are they....' Barebones himself built in brick, which had ceased to be a luxury in the south and west of England because the prospectors were discovering many areas of brick earth. When James VI of Scotland became James I of England he was dismayed by the wooden appearance of his new capital, so unlike the stone city of Edinburgh. Partly in order to reduce the risk of fire, he decreed that all new houses in London must be faced with brick. He would, he boasted, change the city's appearance from 'stykkes to brykkes'.

When Pepys's father developed a painful illness, the son brought him to London, where he was cured: 'I long to have him in town.' The phrase 'in town' proves that London had already become something more than a political and commercial capital; it was *the* town, the summit of the ladder of endeavour, the nursery of Grub Street, Harley Street, Bloomsbury, Theatreland. Playgoing, indeed, was part of town life dinner at 2 p.m., followed by the theatre at 4 p.m.) Pepys himself went regularly, except during intervals of economy. He admired especially Jonson's *The Alchemist*, and was bewitched by the music for Massinger's *The Virgin Martyr*: 'I could not believe,' he wrote, 'that ever any musick hath the real command over the soul of man as this did upon me....' The behaviour of the audience was not always genteel: 'a lady spat backward upon me by mistake, not seeing me.' Pepys, however, would gladly have turned the other cheek: 'seeing her to be a very pretty lady, I was not troubled at all.' On a later occasion he *was* troubled 'to be seen by four of our office clerkes, which sat in the half-crowne box, and I in the 1s.od.' Hitherto it had been held immodest for women to appear on the stage, but the Restoration drama gave Pepys a surprise: 'To the Theatre ... and here the first time ever I saw women come upon the stage.' No Londoner needed to travel in search of diversion, for all classes could share the mid-day promenade down the Mall, where the King sometimes displayed his skill at the game of pell-mell, watched by noblemen, milkmaids, lawyers, beggars, tradesmen, apprentices, soldiers, diplomats and orange-girls. The inner or true City was still the home of peers, gentry and merchants, some of whose thoroughfares have kept the names—though not much else—by which Pepys knew them: Strand, Holborn, Chancery Lane, Haymarket, Gray's Inn Road, Gracechurch Street, Bishopsgate, Cornhill.

The Great Fire, the shortage of building sites, the rise of property developers ... all those things paved a way to the summit of urban elegance, which was reached during the second half of the eighteenth century, when town houses reflected a new vogue in design and materials. Chimney stacks—once so conspicuous—became a plain rectangle; the main doorway predominated, flanked with columns, crowned by cornice and frieze. The best example is Bath, the most beautiful city in Britain, whose chief creator, Ralph Allen, was born in 1694 at St Columb Major in Cornwall, where his grandfather kept a shop, and became postmaster. At the age of nineteen Allen was appointed deputy postmaster in Bath; the postal service being then farmed out to private enterprise. Allen's own enterprise was such that—to shorten a long story—he acquired and improved the postal service of a large part of the southern half of England and Wales. But he never degenerated into a business tycoon. Having become rich, he felt no urge to grow richer; on the contrary, he gave much of his wealth to charity. Despite the laborious postal work, he resolved to exploit the local freestone, 'to show' (as he put it) 'what the Bath stone would do in Town'. He began by purchasing a quarry above the River Avon, near the site which he chose for his own town house, Prior Park. Allen reduced the wages of his workmen, thereby reducing the cost of his products, thereby increasing his turn-over and with it the income of his workmen. Their mutual reward was a contract to supply and erect stone for St Bartholomew's Hospital in London. With the help of an architect, John Wood, he proceeded to create the finest streets and terraces in Bath. Writing in 1743, Dr Oliver—inventor of Bath Oliver biscuits—confirmed Allen's achievement: 'Bath, I find, alters and improves every year, and whatever is new built is spatious and rich in Pediments, Pillars, Porticos.' Allen and Wood created *inter alia* Queen Square, Wood Street, Duke Street, Terrace Walk, North and South Parades, Chandos Buildings, The Circus; an achievement which Sir John Summerson described as 'something unique in the urbanism of Europe'. Ralph

Allen was honoured while he lived. Pope and Fielding were among his friends; the latter protraying him as Squire Allworthy, the ideal of a self-made man: 'Neither Mr Allworthy's House, nor his Heart, were shut against any Part of Mankind, but they were both more particularly open to Men of Merit.... For though he had missed the advantages of a learned Education, yet being blest with vast natural Abilities, he had so well profited by a vigorous though late Applications to Letters, and by much Conversation with Men of Eminence in this Way, that he was himself a very competent Judge in most kinds of Literature.'

Bath, of course, stood in a freestone region; its homes were rather High Renaissance than true Georgian. The typical Georgian town house was a product of red brick walling, white-painted cornices, and bay windows. In very large houses the medieval great hall became an entrance hall to the ground floor rooms, backed by a stately staircase. Known in France as a *salon*, the new type of hall served as a reception room, the place where guests at an important social occasion were greeted and entertained. Smaller urban houses made do with a withdrawingroom on the first floor, which became the principal reception room. Only the rich medieval householder had possessed a room for his exclusive use; lesser households lived *en famille*, sleeping on straw or pallets, as in a dormitory. François Villon thought it luxurious to sleep alone behind closed doors; and as late as 1660 the King of England dressed in public, dined in public and did much of his work in public. Georgian householders, by contrast, learned to value privacy. Theirs were the first English homes to be designed as a series of private rooms.

Design for privacy was enhanced by design for beauty. The Georgian house answered as it were to a roll-call of fame, the like of which had never been heard before, and has remained silent ever after. Robert Adam, for instance, spent four years studying architecture in Italy and then worked on Syon House for the Duke of Northumberland. Adam maintained that an architect must supervise all the domestic fittings. His own designs for furniture set a vogue which Sir John Soane approved: 'The light and elegant ornaments ... of Mr Adam, imitated from the Ancient Works in the Baths and Villas of the Romans, were soon applied in designs for chairs, tables, carpets and in every other species of furniture.' Thomas Chippendale, senior, born in 1718, was a son of the village carpenter at Otley in Yorkshire. In 1754 he published *The Gentleman and Cabinet Maker's Director*, which claimed that its designs could be copied by any craftsman. We now know that Chippendale was rather the head of a prosperous firm of decorators than a man who spent much time making furniture. His son, Thomas Chippendale, went bankrupt in 1804, but afterwards owned shops in St Martin's Lane and in Haymarket. During the 1960s a set of eight of his chairs was sold for £8,500. George Hepplewhite was a Lancashire apprentice who opened a shop in Cripplegate. Two years after he had died, his widow published his book, *The Cabinet-Maker and Upholsterers' Guide*, containing 300 of his drawings, together with a preface which proves that he did not invent the so-called Hepplewhite chair-back. Thomas Sheraton, who migrated from Stockton to London in 1790, published a *Drawing Book* of furniture, and specialized in mechanical gadgets, such as disappearing shelves and intricately-devised writing-tables. Robert Gillow, founder of a furniture shop at Lancaster in 1695, was succeeded by his son and grandsons, who expanded the business by shipping their products to a shop in London's Oxford Street. The military chest of drawers and the Davenport desk were probably designed by Gillow.

Georgian architecture poses a question: why did the ponderous oak carving of the seventeenth century give way to the slender mahogany carving of the eighteenth century? The change in timber was made possible by the expansion of empire, which itself advanced the practice of navigation and ship building. We must recognize, too, the improvement in machinery, and the invention of lacquer, veneer, japanning. Yet the question remains: why were those devices employed so deftly that their products still delight the eye? It is possible that the preoccupation with physical comfort was a result of the decline in religious faith, or at any rate in religious fervour. Most people agree that the summit of church architecture was reached during the Middle Ages; that its decline can be seen in the flamboyant style of the sixteenth century; and that, instead of building to the glory of God, men thereafter lavished their skill and resources on secular architecture, as symbolized by Chatsworth, Hatfield, Syon, Compton

Wynyates, Audley End, Hampton Court. If, in an attempt to discover the root of the matter, we analyse the decline in religious fervour, we still find no adequate answer; only a jig-saw of facts and theories which, though they clarify the course of human evolution, cast no light at all upon the mystery of taste. One thing, however, is certain; the Georgians were as brutal as the Carolines, and more cynical than the Tudors. It is difficult to detect any way in which the artistry of Sheraton reflected a mellowing in the spirit of the English people; difficult indeed, yet not impossible, for it was a Georgian Lord Chancellor who declared that in England a runaway Negro slave became a free man; it was a Georgian Tory who did most to outlaw slavery from the British Empire; it was a Georgian Tory who ordered the Royal Navy to seek and destroy any slave ship which it could find throughout the world, regardless of her nationality and of the risk of war; it was a Georgian Tory who persuaded Parliament to improve conditions in factories, mines, shops.

The mystery, then, abides, and the paradox multiplies; for the Georgian sanitation was as unhygienic as the Tudor. Only the richest families enjoyed the luxury of piped water. In London the streets were an open sewer. Yet in Rome the oldest monument *is* a sewer, *Cloaca Maxima*, which the ancients built so soundly that, after nearly 3,000 years of continuous use, it still serves their city. The inhabitants of Ur, who died before Rome was born, possessed nothing so handsome as a Chippendale chair, yet, unlike Chippendale, they were accustomed to piped water, brick-lined drains and flushable interior lavatories. Louis XIV was amazed when the new earth closets were installed at the Palace of Versailles; so, too, was a Chinese visitor to Georgian Bath when he learned that toilet paper, a commonplace among his own people, was almost unknown in England. William Cobbett, who lived until 1835, could feel agreeably surprised on entering a town that did not stink: 'Huntingdon I like exceedingly.... It is one of those clean, unstenched, unconfined places that tend to lengthen life and make it happy.'

The last phase of the Georgian era, commonly called the Regency, witnessed the beginning of the end of English domestic architecture. In its most ornate form the style was used by John Nash, who designed Cumberland Terrace near Regent's Park.

Smaller Regency homes were elegant and simple. Chimney pots became even less obtrusive; windows lost something of their ornamentation, but none of their light; brick façades were covered by gleaming stucco:

> But is not Nash, too, a very great master
> —He found us all brick, and left us all plaster.

Many of the provincial towns contained houses as beautiful as any in London, and homelier because fewer (Plato's ideal city was so compact that its assembled citizens could be addressed by one speaker). The smaller the town, the greater its awareness of civic pride. Newcastle-upon-Tyne, for example, was largely rebuilt by three Regency men; Richard Grainger, John Dobson, John Clayton. Few northern towns had anything so stately as Grey Street, dominated by the domes of the Central Exchange, graced by the portico of the Theatre Royal, flanked by the tall-windowed homes of shopkeepers, merchants, and professional men. In 1964 the *Observer* declared that 'houses should be being built for a use expectancy of not more than thirty years'. What a prospect for home life! How different from the small Regency houses in Newcastle's Greenfield Place, which were built 'for a use expectancy' of several centuries, and by their plain comeliness shame the horrors which the *Observer* wished to multiply.

The invention of powered machinery enabled Regency craftsmen to exercise new skills on new materials such as rosewood, calamander, bronzed cast-iron. Although some of their domestic fittings were exotic—Grecian, Oriental, Egyptian—each was restrained by that mysterious influence which we call taste. Regency décor seldom lapsed into the vulgarity of Victoriana. Alas, cheap metal furniture was already on the market, and with it the 'bronze' candelabra that were made of stained cast-iron. Of London's 214 Regency churches, 174 contained cast-iron columns. Nonconformist Liberal manufacturers hawked a portable font at fourteen shillings, and a set of Communion plate at £3 19s (trade mark, 'Britannia Metal'). Pugin declared war on the Philistines: 'The improprieties and absurdities committed in the mass of paltry churches is a disgrace to the age.'

A foreigner once told Defoe that 'England was not like other countries, but it was all a planted garden'. London contained only half-a-million people, yet was fifteen times larger than its nearest rivals, Norwich and Bristol. Manchester's population was 7,000; Liverpool's, less than that of some modern villages. At the beginning of the nineteenth century nearly eighty per cent of the people lived in the country; but by the middle of that century the population had doubled, and more than half of it lived in towns. In 1844 Samuel Laing wrote an essay, *National Distress, Its Causes and Remedies*, which described the town houses of the late Industrial Revolution: 'One third of the workers are plunged in extreme misery, and hovering on the verge of actual starvation; another third or more ... under circumstances very prejudicial to health, morality, and domestic comfort—viz, by the labour of young children, girls, and mothers of families in crowded factories....' Ten years later George Godwin, editor of *The Builder*, visited a London home: 'The room is little more than 7 feet long by 6 feet wide.... The roof and part of the wall are mildewed with damp; through parts of the roof the sky is distinctly visible. The room is occupied by a married couple of about 22 or 23 years of age, and a little girl about 2 years old.' After another ten years Dr Edward Smith published his *Practical Dietary for Families, Schools, and the Labouring Classes*: 'In very poor families,' he reported, 'the children are fed at breakfast and supper chiefly on bread, bread and treacle, or bread and butter, with so-called tea; whilst at dinner they have the same food, or boiled potatoes or cabbage, smeared over with a little fat from the bacon in which it was boiled....' William Cobbett did not live to see the worst excesses of industrialized life, but what he had seen appalled him: 'Talk of serfs!' he cried. 'Did feudal times ever see any of them, so debased, so absolutely slaves, as the poor creatures who are compelled to work fourteen hours a day, in a heat of eighty-four degrees....' Small wonder that in 1885 the average working class family spent one-quarter of its wages on alcohol. By the end of the century several industrialists were providing meals at less than cost price. J. E. Budgett Meakin's *Model Factories and Villages* stated that at some canteens the workers could buy a plate of roast beef and two vegetables for fourpence.

So much for the dark aspect of the homes of the Victorian

urban proletariat; but in that darkness a light was shone by Prince Albert, President of the Society for Improving the Conditions of the Labouring Classes, who designed a new type of town house, and displayed it at the Great Exhibition in 1851. A guide-book stated: 'His Royal Highness had this building raised at his own account, with a desire of conveying much practical information calculated to promote much-needed improvement of the dwellings of the working classes, and also of stimulating visitors to the Exhibition, whose position and circumstances may enable them to carry out similar undertakings, and thus ... permanently to benefit those who are greatly dependent on others for their home and family comfort.' The Prince's design showed a two-storey block of flats to hold four families. Each living room—measuring 120 square feet—contained 'a closet on one side of the fireplace, to which warm air may be introduced from the back of the range....' The scullery was fitted with a sink, draining board, and covered shute to convey ashes to a bin under the stairs. Each home had three bedrooms, of which the largest contained an airing cupboard. The water closet with Staffordshire glazed basin was served by a 160-gallon cistern on the roof. Floors were a blend of Portland cement and Staffordshire tiles; the walls, of hollow brick; the roof, treated with metallic lava as a protection against changes of temperature. Each five-roomed home cost £110, and could be rented for about £9 a year. The Prince's good example encouraged many sorts of people to make many kinds of improvement. Thus, John Ruskin gave a sum of money to Octavia Hill so that she could buy three overcrowded lodging houses in the worst part of Marylebone. Miss Hill detested idleness as heartily as she despised sentimentality. Having therefore ejected persistent prostitutes, incurable criminals, and all who believed that society owed them an income, she set the rest to scrub their filthy premises. That done, she established a common room for recreation, and charged each inmate a rent which, although it was nominal, enabled the venture to plough back a profit of five per cent. In *Homes of the London Poor* she announced real progress: 'That a consciousness of corporate life is developed ... is shown by the not infrequent use of the expression "one of us".'

Even the eighteenth-century magnates had been slow to improve their sanitary arrangements, relying rather on a retinue of servants who carried chamber pots to the cesspit. Not until the second half of the nineteenth century did the English working class town house begin to acquire a water-closet, an amenity which Sir John Harington had invented during the second half of the sixteenth century. The WC has eliminated so many plagues and added so greatly to personal cleanliness, that it deserves some notice. Harington, a godson of Queen Elizabeth I, inherited a mansion at Kelston in Somerset, but his flair for persiflage commended him to London and the Court, where he over-reached himself by lampooning the memory of the Queen's favourite, the Earl of Leicester, for which he was banished to Kelston: 'The merry poet, my godson,' declared the Queen, 'must not come to Greenwich till he hath grown sober.' At Kelston the exile invented the water-closet. Lytton Strachey, who wrote an article on the subject, believed that Harington devised a WC 'because he had been made to suffer agonies by the sanitary arrangements in the houses of the great'. It seems more likely that Harington's agonies were caused by the cottages at Kelston, for many great houses had already improved their drainage. In 1565, over thirty years before Harington's invention, Sir William Petre built five stool-houses or lavatories at Ingatestone Hall in Essex (which still belongs to the Petre family). The lavatories were flushed by 'very clear sweet water' into 'divers vaults and gutters of brick, very large, under the ground, round about the whole situation of the house, conveying the waters from every office'. Many years later Harington described his own WC in a flippant treatise, *The Metamorphosis of Ajax*. The Queen was neither amused by the treatise nor impressed by the invention, for only one royal water-closet was installed, at Richmond Palace. During the 1950s, more than three centuries after Harrington's death, thousands of Englishmen's homes still lacked a water-closet.

In *The Complete Servant*, which was written for the benefit of mid-Victorian householders, Samuel and Sarah Adams reckoned that the middle and upper classes spent a quarter of their income on domestic help. A man with £5,000 a year could afford to employ twenty-four servants (eleven females, thirteen males). Widows or spinsters with only £100 were advised to employ a girl at five guineas per annum. In those years potatoes cost one-halfpenny a pound; milk cost one penny a pint; beef cost four-pence a pound; coal cost ten shillings a ton. In 1861 Mrs Beeton's *Book of Household Management* suggested that a family with a weekly income of £20 would employ a cook, a boots and two housemaids. When the income was only £10 weekly the family must make do with a cook and a maid. Richard Church's auto-biography, *Over the Bridge*, shows that at the beginning of the twentieth century there was even a London postman who kept a maid.

'Be it never so humble, there's no place like home.' Those words stand firm against ridicule. While Hitler was bombing the Port of London I came to know several East End families whose homes were as mean as any in England. The whole environment, it seemed, was barricaded against beauty—against the sky itself—by factories, warehouses, wharves. Not one family in a hundred owned their home, yet ninety-nine in a hundred tended it as though it were a palace. Women in black shawls whitewashed the front doorstep. They rinsed and mangled soot-sodden curtains. They polished the brass. They black-leaded the grate. I have seen whole streets of those houses in flames. I have seen an old woman sitting beside what appeared to be a brazier on a bomb site, but was in fact her own hearth ... all that remained of the house where she was born and had lived for eighty years. Slum-clearance has almost finished its overdue task, but the twentieth century will not live to see the end of every squalid environment, for there are many dreary streets in the industrial regions of Eng-land. You will find them at Hull, drenched by the smell of fish, marooned among wasteland. You will find them at Bristol, Norwich, Swindon, Stratford-upon-Avon, Oxford, Exeter; there are few towns where you will not find them. Yet those streets are lit with the same love of home which held that old woman to her hearth. You do not need to tell such people about architecture. They would neither understand nor thank you for a homily on good taste. To them a home is any four walls on which they have tacked Grandpa's medals, Mum's wedding photograph, and another of Self and Friend eating fish-and-chips. Though they are debilitated by television; though they fly to Majorca; though they lease-lend a new car every few years; still they love the same old house, the same old street, the same old shops. They have discovered the secret of homemaking, which is another way of saying that they are good husbands and wives, good fathers and mothers, good sons and daughters, for unless they *are* those things, their home is simply a private collection of bric-à-brac.

Hill Top Farm / Sawrey, Lancashire

10 *The Farmhouse*

THE word 'farm' is derived from the Latin *firma*, meaning a fixed payment. The word 'farmhold' first appeared in 1449, denoting an agricultural holding; 'farming' appeared in 1599, denoting the work of one who cultivated the land, either as its owner or as a tenant; 'farmeress' appeared in 1672, and was followed two years later by 'farmerly', denoting the skill of a farmer. One tends to assume that the farmstead traces its ancestry back to the Middle Ages and beyond, yet it is a relatively modern feature of the scene. The word 'farmhouse' did not appear until 1598. 'Farmyard' waited until 1748, and 'farmstead' until 1807. Where, then, did the medieval farmer live? If 'farmer' is used in its current sense, meaning one who lives and works on a farm, either as owner or as tenant, then we may say that the medieval farmer did not live anywhere, because he did not exist. To jurists the farmer or *firmarius* was neither a labourer nor a landlord; he was a bailiff. The owner of the farm, the lord of the manor, resided at his castle or in the manor house. The farmhands occupied a *cot* nearby. Toward the end of the Middle Ages, however, when feudal obligations were supplanted by hired labour,

M

the more enterprising type of farmhand was able to rent a holding, and sometimes to buy it. Such were the ancestors of the
modern farmer, and most of them lived away from their holding,
either in a village or in a town, because the average medieval
holding was too small and too scattered to justify a house and
out-buildings.

Chaucer's *firmarius* or bailiff was a farmerly man, responsible
for maintaining

> His lordes sheep, his meet, his dayereye,
> His swyn, his hors, and his pultrye.

A well-trusted bailiff would keep his master acquainted with the
latest news, like John Russe, agent to John Paston of Norfolk,
who in 1462 sent an urgent despatch to London: 'Please your
worshipful mastership to weet, here [at Yarmouth] is a ship of
Hythe which saith ... that the fleet of ships of this land met with
sixty sail of Spaniards, Bretons, and Frenchmen, and there took of
them fifty....' Chaucer's ploughman was a good neighbour, willing to help any other poor man or 'povre wight' with his threshing and ditching and digging:

> He wolde thresshe, and ther-to dyke and delve,
> For Cristes sake, for every povre wight,
> Withouten hyre, if it lay in his might.

Only by an informed act of imagination can we picture England as it was during the Middle Ages. North of Nottinghamshire
the land grew wilder, its villages fewer. Most parts of the Border
counties remained a wilderness of forest and fell. In what is now a
densely populated area between Coventry in Warwickshire and
Alvechurch in Worcestershire, the compilers of the Domesday
Book discovered a twenty-mile belt of uninhabited wasteland.
The little town of Henley-in-Arden did not exist, the nearest
settlement being the village of Wootton Wawen, which contained
forty-five peasant families and one priest. The greater part of the
Kentish and Sussex Weald was dense woodland, void of human
habitation. The Fens, too, were unpeopled, except for a few
island sites, like Ely, and a narrow coastal strip. So late as the
seventeenth century the Chilterns' hilltops were shunned as im-
penetrable forest, inhabited only by a few robbers and other

criminals, against whom the Stewards of the Chiltern Hundreds waged perennial war. When at last the robbers were ousted, the Stewardship became a Crown sinecure, and was granted temporarily to Members of Parliament who wished to retire; a convenient arrangement because Members cannot ordinarily retire unless they forfeit their seat by accepting an office of profit under the Crown.

In such a cold and uncultivated countryside an important item of farm life was the tunic or smock-frock, which survived in modified form until the nineteenth century, having evolved from the ancient Egyptian apron. The Greeks called it *chiton*; the Romans, *tunica*; the English, *cote*. It was a knee-length and sleeved garment, made of two straight pieces of material which the womenfolk spun and wove at home, from coarse wool, or hemp, or linen. For centuries the smocks were dyed blue, the poor man's colour. As footwear, a medieval peasant wore square-toed ankle boots, fastened by a leather thong. The *galoche* or Gaulish shoe, forerunner of the patten, was known to Chaucer, who says of a man: 'He were worthy to remake his galoche.' Pattens and clogs outlived many fashions. In 1742 Robert Walpole wrote: 'I remember at the playhouse they used to call for Mrs Oldfield's chair, Mrs Barry's clogs, and Mrs Bracegirdle's pattens.' Gaiters were an English innovation, mentioned by a tenth-century document. In the north of England they are called cockers (Latin *coccus* or boot).

Medieval peasant women worked in the fields. Queen Mary's fourteenth-century *Psalter* shows them wearing a knee-length smock, over which is draped a loose and sleeveless kirtle or gown, reaching to the ankle. The sumptuary laws compelled all people to dress according to their class, so that everyone's status was immediately recognizable. The nobility wore tuppence coloured; the common people, penny plain. To ourselves, however, 'plain' would appear dazzling, for the farmhand's clothes were gaily dyed. Thirteenth-century paintings show that the smocks were red, pink, blue, mauve, brown. The yeoman's daughter in *The Roxburghe Ballads* rated herself as fine as any lady:

> I think myself as good as thou
> That gay apparell weare.

> My coat is made of comely gray
> And though I keep my father's sheep
> A garland of the fairest flowers
> Shall shield me from the sun.

She scorned the fashionable gee-gaws:

> I care not for the fan or mask,
> A homely hat is all I ask
> Which will my face protect
> When we together milking go
> With pail upon our heads.

During the second half of the fourteenth century the Black Death and an ensuing lack of manpower wrought profound changes in the pattern of rural life. The landowners turned more and more to sheep, which could be tended by a few shepherds. Sir Thomas More, Lord High Chancellor of England, lived long enough to see those flocks run amok: 'Your shepe,' he declared, 'that were wont to be so meke and tame, and so smal eaters, now, as I hear say, be become so great devowrers and so wylde, that they eate up, and swallow downe the very men themselfs. They consume, they destroye, and devoure whole fields, howses, cities. . . .' This was the era which saw the rise of the yeoman or 'young man', meaning a servant. 'The King,' wrote Sir Thomas Malory, 'called upon his knights, esquires, yeomen and pages.' To the Tudors a yeoman was a tenant-farmer. Bishop Latimer felt proud of his yeomanry: 'My father,' he acknowledged, 'was a Yoman, and had no landes of his own, onlye he had a farme.' Latimer's definition was revised by William Cobbett during the nineteenth century: 'Those only who rent,' he insisted, 'are, properly speaking, called farmers. Those who till their own land are yeomen.' Today the word is used to denote any farmer who ranks below the gentry.

The earliest Tudor yeomen built splendid homes for themselves, though not always of the sort which we would now call farmhouses. Instead of living in isolation among their fields, they occupied houses in the nearest village or town; partly for companionship, partly for protection. England abounds in such houses. You see them *par excellence* at Lavenham in Suffolk; timbered, colour-washed, crazily unsymmetrical. Each storey was built separately, and each floor projected over the lower storey (whence the word 'jetty'). Floor joists were laid across the narrow way of the house, while jetties traversed the long side. The medieval great hall became the kitchen, the hub of a farmer's domesticity. Sometimes it was partitioned to form either a parlour or a dairy; always it contained a log-burning hearth and an array of cooking utensils, for the farmer's wife fed both her family and the labourers. The former sat furthest from the draughty door, at a gate-leg table near the fire; the latter jostled and joked at a trestle table. All baking was done in an oven behind the fire, fitted with a cast-iron door. At night the housewife filled her oven with hot wood-ash or smouldering heather. In the morning she raked it out, and inserted the puddings and loaves. Such were the farm kitchens which Shakespeare knew; cool in summer, snug in winter

> When icicles hang by the wall,
> And Dick the Shepherd blows his nail,
> And Tom bears logs into the hall,
> And milk comes frozen home in pail
> ... While greasy Joan doth keel the pot.

The farm labourers—or hinds, as they are still called in Westmorland—continued to sleep in attics or barns; but the yeoman and his wife had their own bedroom, or 'chamber of estate', whose social prestige was later transferred to the 'state room' of a ship.

The frames for a yeoman's house were made and assembled at the saw pit, to ensure accuracy, and were then dismantled and transported to the site. Joists were identified by means of Roman numbers because Arabic numerals were not used in England until the sixteenth century. The men who cut the timbers seldom built the house. That was done by the owner himself, helped by neighbours and friends. Having finished their task, they held a feast. In 1972 a few village carpenters still hoisted a Union Jack on the ridge timber to crown their efforts. Building within the London area was controlled by the Tudor sovereigns, who strove to maintain a green belt around their capital. Elsewhere a man was free to build where he could. Even in London, however, a new house was allowable if the owner could begin and finish it between dusk and dawn. Many of those Tudor farmers'

M2

homes were founded on the wool trade, as an old jingle acknowledged:

> I thank my God
> And ever shall
> It was the sheep
> That paid for all.

Sheep, however, were not ubiquitous, nor the ports from which
their fleece could reach the Continent. That is why the most comfortable of the early Tudor homes were confined chiefly to the
Home Counties, East Anglia, Sussex and Hampshire. In stone
country, by contrast, the best houses were built near to a quarry,
unless they belonged to men who could afford to transport the
stone over a considerable distance.

If you could obtain the deeds of every farmhouse in England,
you would find that nearly all of them were built after the
Restoration. Of that majority, most were built by landowners
for tenants, many of whom were arable farmers because the wool
trade had waned, the population had increased, and cottage
crafts were being killed by urban factories. Thus, the Gloucestershire town of Northleach was for centuries a capital of the Cotswold wool trade which, when it declined, caused one of the
townsmen, William Dutton, to build six almshouses and to be-
queath and endow his own home, hoping that they would be used
to revive the trade or 'any other such trade as may keep the
people from idleness'. Although the Lord Chancellor still sits on a
woolsack, the contents of his cushion no longer symbolize the
wealth of the kingdom. Farmers, in short, were compelled to
adjust themselves to a decline in sheep farming which continued
far beyond the seventeenth century. In 1850 Gloucestershire
farmers sold 5,000 Cotswold sheep; in 1860 the number fell to
4,000; in 1972 only one flock of true Cotswold or Lion sheep remained, reared by a Mr Garne of Aldsworth. Many farms in the
county relied on raising barley for brewers. There were, of course,
exceptions, especially in remote regions. In his introduction to
county reports for the Board of Agriculture, which appeared in
1818, William Marshall cited the lack of cultivation on the
Northumbrian Cheviots: 'The produce, at present, is grass—a
continued sheet of greensward—from base to summit. . . .

Formerly, many or most of the lower grounds, where any degree of flatness would admit the plow, have evidently been cultivated; probably at a time when these borders were fuller of people than they are at present; when a very few large sheep farmers (each perhaps holding a parish of several thousand acres in extent) and their shepherds, are the only inhabitants; and, even to supply these few, the arable crops, that are at present grown, are insufficient.'

With the seventeenth century we come at last to the farmhouse somewhat as it exists today; not in a village nor in a town, but standing apart, perhaps several miles from the nearest neighbour. The common fields remain, but the cottagers' strips of land have become less scattered, and are no longer held solely by service on the lord's estate. The new houses vary according to local geology. In the far north they are of stone; darkly dour on the gritstone belts of Derbyshire and Lancashire; less dour in the Yorkshire dales; warmly rubicund along the red sandstone country near Appleby in Westmorland and near Carlisle in Cumberland. In south Devon the farmhouses are often of thatch above cob; in the Chilterns, of brick-and-flint; in the Kentish and Sussex wealds, of redbrick; and wherever wood was plentiful, or stone scarce, they are heavily timbered, as in Cheshire, Herefordshire, Shropshire, Warwickshire. Many of them were built by old-established farming families; others, by merchants and professional men who, having retired, wished to cultivate their land. Of the latter sort, few are more beautiful than Bateman's in Sussex, the last and best-loved home of Rudyard Kipling, who was born at Bombay, in 1865, son of the Professor of Architectural Sculpture at Bombay University. Having been educated at the United Services College, Westward Ho!, North Devon, Kipling became a sub-editor on the Lahore *Civil and Military Gazette*; an experience which enabled him, at the age of twenty-three, to publish *Plain Tales from the Hills*, a youthful *tour-de-force* wherewith he established his reputation as a story-teller. Before he was thirty-five he had sailed around the world, cruised with the Fleet, married a wife, lost a daughter, and published *The Light that Failed, The Jungle Book, Captains Courageous, Stalky and Co.* In 1902 he took his wife on a house-hunting tour through Sussex. They travelled in an ancient hired car (Kipling described it as a 'heart-breaking locomobile') and at once approved the village of Burwash, which stands on a hill, dominated by the Norman church, and flanked by handsome old houses. Just beyond the village the 'locomobile' turned into Bateman's Lane ('an enlarged rabbit hole' Kîpling called it). Although the lane has been widened a little, it remains steeply secluded, and from it you see what the Kiplings saw: first, a bevy of Caroline chimney-stacks against a skyline of hills; then a series of tiled roofs and the tip of an oast house; and finally Bateman's itself, set among gardens, surrounded by fields, watered with a stream. It was, said Kipling, a case of love at first sight. 'That's her!' his wife exclaimed. 'The only She!' Second thoughts confirmed the foresight of first impressions: 'We went through every room and found no shadow of ancient regrets, stifled memories, nor any menace....'

Bateman's—a large house of Wealden stone—was built in 1634 to the specifications of a Sussex iron-master whose name has been lost. After several changes of owner the house was bought by a Victorian farmer who seems not to have cared for it, because in 1870 the property had become derelict. Happily, it was acquired by an architect, named Macmeiken, who set the place in order. Kipling himself purchased the adjoining fields, to create an estate of 300 acres which, on the death of his widow in 1937, passed to the National Trust. In 1972 the house looked much as it had done in 1634, except for some minor alterations during the seventeenth and nineteenth centuries, and the addition of an oast house westward from the main buildings. Some people, Kipling observed, can tell a lie and get away with it, but their home, 'which is their temple, cannot say anything save the truth of those who have lived in it'. Bateman's certainly tells the truth about Kipling, a much-travelled collector of antiques, who, despite his international fame, chose to lead the life of a country landowner. He planted the yew trees which now flank the garden gate. He designed the present pattern of paths and yew hedges. He paved the pond so that his children might swim and boat there. He made a cemetery for the family cats and dogs, each with its own headstone. He flooded the banks of the stream with daffodils, narcissi and yellow arum flowers. With his own hands he engraved the sundial: 'It is later than you think.' On the archway of the three-storeyed porch he and his family carved their initials.

The iron bell-pull came from the home of Kipling's uncle, one of the Burne-Jones family, with whom he had spent many childhood hours; he hoped that 'other children might feel happy when they pulled it'.

Bateman's has a typical seventeenth-century oak-panelled hall, containing two seventeenth-century clocks, one of them Dutch, the other Cromwellian. The hall furniture is chiefly oak, set-off by some Indian brasses and an Indo-Chinese chest. Here the family took tea, which was served on a Benares tray, a wedding gift from one of Kipling's sisters. The dining room walls are covered by Cordova painted leather, another acquisition of the Kiplings during their travels. The seats of the Chippendale chairs were designed and worked in *petit-point* by the Royal School of Needlework. The drawing-room, too, reflects its itinerant host, notably in some prayer mats from Central Asia, and several Chinese water colours. Kipling's Christian name is explained by a painting of Rudyard Lake in Staffordshire, where his parents had first met each other. The west bedroom contains an Elizabethan canopy bed and several sketches which Sir Edward Burne-Jones painted for the Kipling children.

Kipling's study is a large upper room with cavernous hearth, magpie ceiling, oak-planked floor; on three sides lined ceiling-high by books, not academic books, but rather the tools of an artist's craft and the lanterns of his leisure. His desk is a seventeenth-century chestnut writing table, at which he sat in an eighteenth-century walnut chair. The writing table carries a dozen of his pipe cleaners, a block of his favourite writing paper ('large off-white sheets', he called them), and an assortment of pens, knives, clips. In *Something of Myself*, which he wrote at Bateman's, Kipling compiled a catalogue of the objects on his writing table: 'I always kept certain gadgets on my work table which was ten feet long from North to South and badly congested. One was a long, lacquered, canoe-shaped pen-tray, full of brushes and dead "fountains"; a wooden box held clips and bands; another, a tin one, pins; yet another, a bottle-slider, kept all manner of unneeded essentials from emery-paper to small screwdrivers; a paper weight, said to have been Warren Hastings', a tiny, weighted fur-seal and a leather crocodile sat on some papers; an inky foot-rule and a Father of Penwipers which a much-loved housemaid of ours presented yearly, made up the main-guard of these little fetishes.... Left and right of the table were (and still are) two big globes, on one of which a great airman had once outlined in white those air-routes to the East and Australia which were well in use before my death.' The most conspicuous object is 'an outsize office pewter ink-pot, on which I would gouge the names of the tales and books I wrote out of it'.

Kipling was thirty-seven years old when he settled down at Bateman's, and for another thirty-four years he lived there. Yet during that long half-lifetime he produced only six books of short stories, together with some poems and miscellaneous prose. However, it would be wrong to imagine that he ran to seed at Bateman's, or was content to play the squire. Perhaps because he was older he wrote less swiftly, and revised more carefully: 'In an auspicious hour,' he advised, 'read your final draft and consider faithfully every paragraph, sentence and word, blacking out where necessary. Let it lie by to drain as long as possible. At the end of that time, re-read and you should find that it will bear a second shortening. Finally, read it aloud at leisure.' But Kipling never practised what Thomas Hardy (in a tilt at Henry James) called 'eternal proof-reading'. Kipling's motto was: 'Maybe a shade more brushwork will then indicate or impose itself. If not, praise Allah and let it go....' The books which he did write at Bateman's include *Puck of Pook's Hill*, a tapestry of England in general and of Sussex in particular. The tale concerns two children who encounter Puck, the Timeless Spirit of England, and are introduced by him to Celts, Romans, Normans, and the heirs and successors thereof ... smugglers, yeomen, squires, farmhands, parsons. 'The children were at the Theatre, acting to Three Cows as much as they could remember of *A Midsummer Night's Dream*. Their father had made a small play out of the big Shakespeare one, and they had rehearsed it with him and their mother till they could say it by heart.' That is how the book opens. It is also how Kipling opened it to himself: 'One summer morning in the early 1900s,' his daughter remembered, 'we children and my father acted scenes from *A Midsummer Night's Dream*. Our stage was an old grass-grown quarry, and there my brother as Puck, myself as Titania, and my father as Bottom rehearsed and acted happily.' Meanwhile, alone in the meadow beyond Bateman's, the two children are visited by Puck, that ever-young Ancient of Days, to whom the centuries seem as a twinkling of the eye. He comes, he says, 'from one of the oldest hills in Old England ... Pook's Hill—Puck's Hill ... it's as plain as the nose on my face!' It was plain to Kipling also, whenever he gazed westward from Bateman's. Under its spell, he put into the mouth of a Norman conqueror some words from his own heart, for he, too, had come from afar, and was bewitched by what he found:

> I followed the Duke ere I was a lover;
> To take from England fief and fee;
> But now the game is the other way over
> ... But now England hath taken me.

Even the millpond at Bateman's is remembered when Puck asks:

> See you our little mill that clacks
> So busy by the brook?
> She has ground her corn and paid her tax
> Ever since Domesday Book.

Some people caricature Kipling as a drum-beating jingoist who wished the sun never to set on the sahibs' ill-gotten gains. If, however, you read what Kipling wrote about the Empire, and not simply what other men wrote about Kipling, you will discover the truth of the matter. Kipling had sailed around the world. He had seen the roads, hospitals, schools, universities and courts wherewith England had weaned most of the natives from their custom of killing and sometimes eating the other tribe. He neither desired nor expected the Empire to last forever; but he did hope that it would last until the majority of its peoples had learned to live at peace with themselves and their neighbours. Meanwhile, at his new home in an old farmhouse, he took root and was content:

> Each to his choice, and I rejoice
> The lot has fallen to me
> In a fair ground—in a fair ground—
> Yea, Sussex by the sea!

By the time we reach the Georgian rural scene, we discover decay alongside renascence. On the one hand, many farmers were ruined by the enclosure of commons and by the Napoleonic blockade; others, who prospered, forsook their old home in the village, and built a new one, nearer to their fields. In both design and décor the Georgian farmhouse was more comfortable than any which the Tudors had known, for this was the era of 'country Chippendale'. Servants still sat on benches, it is true, but the farmer ceased to be 'chairman' or occupant of a household luxury. Walnut became *démodé* during the reign of George I, partly because a tempest of 1703 had destroyed many walnut trees, partly because a disease decimated them in the colonial plantations. A well-to-do yeoman of the 1770s would have a mahogany chair in his parlour, no doubt with a 'Chippendale' back, derived from the earlier Dutch design. If he lived in beech country he would acquire some Windsor chairs or perhaps get the carpenter to make them from his yews. A Midland yeoman would display the new 'Brummagem Ware' of Birmingham metal utensils. His father's bracket clock may have been fitted with an anchor escapement and a heavy pendulum. If his wife followed the fashion in top-heavy coiffures, the height of her mirror would need to be greater than its width. If the yeoman was wise he retained his grandfather's oak refectory table, and left the new half-octagon-enders to the manor house, where they were soon supplanted by 'pillar-and-claw' tables.

Although a Georgian farmhouse looks relatively modern, a Georgian landscape would now seem comparatively archaic. True, the village had already adopted its present pattern of church, green, inn, manor and cottages; but beyond his village a Georgian farmer saw few indeed of those neat hedges and patterned fields which to us appear timeless. His daily walk took him past the open field, which may have been a mile long and half-a-mile wide, and was still criss-crossed by scattered smallholdings that were difficult to reach and difficult to cultivate. A balance must therefore be achieved between sympathy for cottagers whose commons were enclosed by the squire, and sympathy for the beasts that were expected to grub a living therefrom. In 1822 *The Farmer's Magazine* stated: 'It is painful to observe the very wretched appearance of the animals, who have no other dependence but upon the pasture of these commons, and who, in most instances, bear a greater resemblance to living skeletons, than any thing else.' The magazine spoke for the yeomanry and gentry, arguing that enclosure was inevitable if English agriculture were to supply the needs of an increasing urban proletariat. Nevertheless, the method of enclosure was so harsh that many of its advocates pitied the small-holder and cottager: 'by nineteen out of twenty Enclosure Bills,' said Arthur Young, 'the poor are injured and most grossly.' For example, the tenants of Sir James Graham, lord of the Yorkshire manor of Netherby, were forbidden to keep sheep lest their flocks should damage the enclosing hedgerows. Farmers at Felstead in Essex faced a crippling outlay of time and money: 'The several new fences,' they were told, 'hereby directed to be made by the several proprietors in their respective allotments shall consist of ditches $4\frac{1}{2}$ feet wide at the top and 3 feet deep and of banks adjoining such ditches and formed of earth taken from the same; and that the banks of such fences shall be planted with white thorn layer in a proper manner and that half-hurdles or thorns shall be set on the summit of such banks and shall there remain, or if taken away or spoiled, shall be from time to time renewed during the space of 7 years next ensuing.' A Lincolnshire Enclosure Act of 1767 imposed a fine (in modern currency) of £500 on anyone who wilfully damaged a fence; for a third offence he might be transported.

Not every Georgian yeoman needed to build a new home when he left his old one. If he were rich he might buy a manor house. That is why some farms seem to have descended the social ladder. A typical example can be found at Parham in Suffolk, where the sixteenth-century moated farmhouse was built as a private residence by Sir Christopher Willoughby. During the seventeenth century it became the seat of Lord Willoughby of Eresby and Parham, whereafter it was bought by a yeoman, John Tovell, a member of whose household befriended George Crabbe, the poet, who was then apprenticed to a physician at Woodbridge. Many years later Crabbe and his son visited the farmhouse; and when the son came to write the father's biography, he recalled the aura of lineage: 'On entering the house, there was nothing at first sight to remind one of the farm—a spacious hall paved with blue and white marble—and at one extremity a very handsome drawing-room, and at the other a fine old staircase of black oak, polished till it was as slippery as ice. . . .'

Whether he occupied an old house, or built a new one, the go-ahead Georgian yeoman rode on the crest of a wave. Under George II he had been content to eat bacon that was cured by his wife and to wear clothes that were spun by his daughter. He drank home-brewed ale from a brown jug, and although he dined at his own gate-leg table by the fire, he did so in the presence of the unmarried labourers who lodged with him. William Howitt's *The Rural Life of England* looked wistfully on the kindlier aspects of Georgian farm life: 'At night,' he wrote, 'the farmer takes his seat on the settle, under the old wide chimney—his wife has her work-table set near—the "wenches" darning their stockings, or making a cap for Sunday, and the men sitting on the other side of the hearth, with their shoes off.' Having scanned last week's local newspaper, the farmer turns to business: 'He now enjoys of all things, to talk over his labours and plans with the men—they canvass the best method of doing this and that—lay out the course of tomorrow—what land is to be broken up. . . .' Some historians are reluctant to admit that many farmers were kindly and generous men, who, according to the standard of the age, gave their labourers a decent life. Under George IV the go-ahead yeoman's wave had reared so high that William Cobbett, himself a yeoman's son, detected the pride which precedes a fall: 'The English farmer has, of late years, become a totally different character. A fox-hunting horse; polished boots; a spanking trot to market; a "get out of the way or by G-d I'll ride you over" to every poor devil upon the road; wine at his dinner; a servant (and sometimes a *livery*) to wait at his table; a painted lady for wife; sons aping the young squires and lords; a house crammed with sofas, pianos, and all sorts of fooleries.' The yeoman no longer dined among his men; instead, he moved the gate-leg table into a parlour. As a result, Cobbett complained, the farmhouse was 'too neat for a dirty-shoed carter to be allowed to come into it'.

When at last the wave crashed, it destroyed a large number of farmers. Lord Ernle's *English Farming, Past and Present* described the effects of the Napoleonic wars: 'Bankers pressed for their advance, landlords for their rents, tax collectors for their taxes, tradesmen for their bills. ... Farmhouses were full of sheriffs' officers. Many large farmers lost everything, and became applicants for pauper allowances.' And not only the farmers, for in their downfall they carried with them farriers, saddlers, carpenters, masons, wheelwrights. Vast areas of England ran to seed. In the Isle of Ely nineteen farms remained empty for years; in Norfolk the bankrupt yeomen offered land worth a million guineas, and not one acre of it found a buyer; the Duke of Bedford advertised in vain for tenants to occupy his farms. Cobbett witnessed the exodus: 'When I was in Norfolk, there were four hundred persons, generally young men, labourers, carpenters, wheelwrights, millwrights, smiths and bricklayers ... going to Quebec, in timber-ships.' Displaced farmers felt thankful if they could raise a steerage passage in search of work as farm labourers among the colonies: 'From Boston,' Cobbett reported, 'two great barge loads had just gone off by canal, to Liverpool, most of them farmers. ...' But why worry? asked the City. The profit from our manufactured exports would purchase food from nations enabling them thereby to purchase even more of our manufactured exports.

By the middle of the nineteenth century, life at the farmhouse had become less penurious, but agriculture never regained its role as national breadwinner. Factories, not farms, empowered Lord Palmerston to deliver his famous *Civis Romanus sum*: 'a British subject, in whatever land he may be, shall feel confident that the watchful eye and the strong arm of England will protect him against injustice and wrong.' Exports ruled the waves. In 1842 their value was £47 million; in 1870 it was nearly £200 million, or more than the combined exports of Germany and Italy and France, and four times larger than America's. Between 1851 and 1871 the mileage of English railways was doubled. Yet English farming continued to go downhill. Between 1850 and 1899 the acreage of cultivated land was almost halved. During the 1870s nearly seventy per cent of British corn came from abroad.

The foremost historian of late-Victorian farm life was Richard Jefferies, son of a Wiltshire yeoman. Some people dismiss him as an amateur naturalist who lapsed into mysticism: 'The great sun burning with light; the strong, dear earth; the warm sky; the pure air ... all filled me with a rapture, an ecstasy, an inflatus.' It is true indeed that Jefferies possessed a poetic vision of reality; true, also, that a lack of education sometimes impaired his style, and often confused his thought; yet no man has achieved a keener insight into the life of the farmhouse. Jefferies worked as a labourer in his father's fields, and as a reporter on country newspapers. He could lay a hedge, plough a meadow, make a bid, assess a crop. Edward Thomas rightly said of him, that he was able with equal skill to 'describe visible things and states of mind'. In an essay called *The Old House at Coate*, Jefferies recreated his birthplace, Coate Farm, which was then a hamlet, though now a suburb of Swindon. The farm itself—a seventeenth-century stone building—contains a small museum with some of his manuscripts and personal belongings. The essay introduces us to Jefferies's father, an intelligent and self-educated man, whom the son had already depicted as Mr Iden of *Amaryllis at the Fair*. In a confidential letter to his publisher, Jefferies described Mr Iden as 'a great reader, with a considerable library of the best authors, and above all the keenest observation of nature and natural phenomena. I remember he discovered Donati's comet then a speck in the northern sky one evening before any announcement of it had appeared in the newspapers.' The astronomer was also a botanist: 'The other day (at the age of 70) he walked 20 miles (being still athletic) to see a herb which he had not previously seen growing.' In another book, *Wild Life in a Southern County*, Jefferies again described his father: 'of all other men the farmer is the most deeply attached to the labour by which he lives, and loves the earth on which he walks.... He will not leave it unless he is suffering severely.'

Despite its seclusion, Coate Farm was never lonely: 'Lost as the hamlet was, it was not separated, or divided ... wagons with corn and hay and straw, or returning with coal; carts; traps; conveyances of every kind; steam-ploughing engines; gipsies' vans, horsemen; men on foot; someone and something was always drifting by.' The farmer's wife was a practical woman: 'The mistress of the household still bakes bread in the oven now and then. She makes all kinds of preserves, and wines too—cowslip, elderberry, ginger....' She was also an artistic woman: 'The farm parlour is always full of flowers—the mantelpiece and grate in spring quite hidden by fresh green boughs of horsechestnut in bloom, or with lilac, bluebells or wild hyacinths....' Her husband's artistry preferred rather to be reminded of winter pleasures: 'On the walls are a couple of old hunting pictures ... bright scarlet coats, bright white horses....' Winter or summer, the yeoman carried a fellow-traveller: 'No matter whether he strolls to the arable field, or down the meadow, or across the footpath to a neighbour's house, the inevitable double-barrel gun accompanies him.' Like every other farmhouse, Coate contained several skeletons: 'Up in the lumber-room are carved oaken bedsteads of unknown age; linen-presses of black oak with carved pommels, and a drawer at the side for the lavender-bags; a rusty rapier ... a flintlock pistol....' But Jefferies was something more than a painter of pictures; he could spear the eddies of current affairs: 'agriculture generally is shaken to pieces ... imports of foreign foods of all sorts, from frozen flour to frozen mutton ... continue to increase in quantity....' England, the richest and most powerful kingdom in the world, could not feed herself.

Every prosperous Georgian squire had been proud of his estate. He either improved his old cottages and farms, or built new ones of local material in the latest style. The Victorians, too, built in the latest style, but not always of local material, which is why England contains so many cottages and farmhouses which clash with their setting and the venerable neighbours. An exception was provided by a family of Midland industrialists, named Knight, who in 1818 bought a large part of Exmoor from the Crown, Sir Francis Bampfylde, Sir Thomas Acland, and Sir Arthur Chichester (a forebear of the present Sir Francis Chichester). The Knights, however, loved neither the land nor its people. On the contrary, Sir Frederick Knight, who divided his time between Worcestershire and London, wished to 'develop' Exmoor as a mining area, served by roads, railways and the port of Porlock Weir, which was to become a second Barry Docks. Fortunately, his wishes were never fulfilled. It is therefore charitable to remember the Knights by their better deeds, including several farmsteads that are household names on Exmoor: Cloven Rocks, Driver, Duredon, Horsen, Pinkery, Warren, Wintershead. Each was built of local material, except for the roof, whose slates came from Wales via Lynmouth. Each stood like a stockade against the climate and a treeless skyline, forming a rectangle of barns, stables, shippons, byres; with the house itself abutting outward from one wall; the whole sheltered by a windbreak of newly-planted sycamore or beech. The Knights acquired their Exmoor estates before Georgian architecture had given way to Victorian jerrybuilding; a fact that is proven by the simple dignity of their farmhouses.

Victorian, Regency, Georgian, Jacobean, Tudor; all of those labels fulfil a useful purpose, but only if each is seen to overlap the others. When Thomas Hardy described Gabriel Oak, the shepherd of *Far from the Madding Crowd*, he very likely drew on his own recollections of a man whose father had buried the silver spoon against a Napoleonic invasion. Yet that same description would have fitted a Tudor shepherd as neatly as it fits a modern hill farmer: 'He wore a low-crowned felt hat, spread out at the base by tight jamming upon the head for security in high winds, and a coat like Dr Johnson's; his lower extremities being encased in ordinary leather leggings and boots emphatically large, affording to each foot a roomy apartment so constructed that any wearer might stand in a river all day long and know nothing of damp....' Farmer Oak's timelessness was measured by his own timekeeper: 'a watch as to shape and intention, and a small clock as to size. This instrument being several years older than Mr Oak's grandfather, had a peculiarity of going either too fast or not at all. The smaller of its hands, too, occasionally slipped round the pivot, and thus, though the minutes were told with precision, nobody could be quite certain of the hour....' Oak himself personified private enterprise: 'It was,' said Hardy, 'only lately that people had begun to call Gabriel "Farmer" Oak. During the twelve-month preceding this time he had been enabled by sustained efforts of industry and chronic good spirits to lease the small sheep-farm of which Norcombe Hill was a portion, and stock it with two hundred sheep. Previously he had been bailiff for a short time, and earlier still a shepherd only....' Some English farmhouses still contain the same sort of books whereby Shepherd Oak graduated as Farmer Oak: '*The Young Man's Best Companion, The Farrier's Sure Guide, The Veterinary Surgeon, Paradise Lost, The Pilgrim's Progress, Robinson Crusoe*, Ash's *Dictionary*, and Walkingame's *Arithmetic* ... though a limited series, it was one from which he had acquired more sound information by diligent perusal than many a man of opportunities has done from a furlong of laden shelves.' Oak, in fact, was a gallant exception to the gospel which Mammon had already begun to preach, that bigger is better, and biggest is best. Francis Kilvert deplored such 'efficiency': 'I passed by the ruined sheds which sadly, regretfully, mark the site of the ancient small homestead of Watling Street. The dwelling house has entirely disappeared and the scene of so many joys and sorrows, hopes and fears, is now waste, silent and desolate, and overgrown with nettles and weeds. What a pity that these ancient humble farms should be destroyed and thrown into the great farms, thereby taking away all the poor man's prizes and chances of his rising in the world.'

In 1792 the Hon. John Byng made this entry in his diary: 'a man must be born and bred a country gentleman or a country labourer; for a citizen and an artisan, will never make one, or the other.' That generalization is partly valid. At the approach of winter a modern townsman shudders whenever he thinks of his country cousins. Nevertheless, good farming has been achieved by people who were neither country labourers nor country gentlemen. A notable example was Beatrix Potter, daughter of a London barrister whose private income was so comfortable that he never bestirred himself to practise law. Between the ages of fourteen and thirty Beatrix Potter kept a diary, in which, on 13 April 1885, she remarked: 'I wish we had a settled home!' The Potters did have a settled home (in Kensington), but during the summer they leased Wray Castle, a Victorian mansion at Windermere; and it was there that Beatrix Potter wished for a settled home in Lakeland. One other quotation must suffice to cut a long story short. In 1893 Miss Potter wrote to a friend's child: 'My dear Noel, I don't know what to write to you, so I shall tell you a story about four little rabbits, whose names were Flopsy, Mopsy, Cottontail and Peter.' So was conceived *The Tale of Peter Rabbit*, a classic that has been translated into French, German, Spanish, Welsh, and several other languages despite the author's failure to find any publisher who would accept it. In 1900, therefore, she printed it at her own expense (and her second book also—*The Tailor of Gloucester*—for the same reason). Not long afterwards she accepted a proposal of marriage from a man who died before the wedding. The harvest of her grief was a stream of books whose titles are household names, and whose royalties enabled her to buy 'a settled home' at Hill Top Farm, a seventeenth-century house, at Sawrey in Lancashire, only a few miles from Windermere and Coniston Water. Ultimately she acquired more farmland in the district, the conveyancing for which was done by a local solicitor, William Heelis, who proposed and was accepted by the fifty-year-old celebrity after she had rejected her parents' protest that a country solicitor was beneath her. From that time onward Beatrix Potter became Mrs Heelis: even the letters to her publisher were signed 'Beatrix Heelis'; and whenever an admirer referred to her as 'Miss Potter', Mrs Heelis looked displeased, and sometimes sounded so.

Although the couple moved to a more convenient house nearby, Mrs Heelis not only continued to farm but also set farming before writing. In 1916 an earnest lady wrote to Hill Top, offering her services as a land girl. In reply Mrs Heelis described the domestic life of a world-famous author: 'We live very quietly in a cottage separate from the old farmhouse; I have one young servant here. . . . My husband helps with the hay. . . . I have poultry, orchard, flowers, gardens, vegetables.' Her home, she explained, 'is a lovely old house, in fact the furniture and old oak is so good I can only have a careful occupier'. She enjoyed good conversation, but was too big for small talk: 'I don't go out much, haven't time; and the little town seems nothing but gossip and cards.' Even so, the author was not wholly submerged beneath the farmer, for she ended her reply with a postscript: 'Your letter is very earnest: I wonder if you have a sense of humour?' Helped by her bailiff, John Cannon, she raised Herdwicks, a breed of sheep that can nibble a living from thin soil at high altitudes in a cold climate. Only a Lakelander who remembers the 1930s can fully understand the magnitude of the compliment that was paid when the Herdwick Association—perhaps the most masculine club in Britain—chose Mrs Heelis as its president.

Hill Top Farm and many acres of Lakeland were bequeathed by Mrs Heelis to the National Trust. The farmhouse contains a family Bible, inscribed with names and dates which explain why

Beatrix Potter chose to settle in that part of England. Her maternal forebears, the Cromptons, came from Lancashire. Their surnames had a northern timbre (Gawthorp, Hutton, Hayhurst); their Christian names rang with the resonance of rural dissent (Adam, Abraham, Samuel). Mrs Heelis was indeed in the land of her fathers: 'I am descended,' she told an American reader, 'from generations of Lancashire yeomen and weavers.....' And elsewhere she wrote: 'To me no tongue can be as musical as Lancashire.'

I used to spend a part of each year in Westmorland, at no great distance from Hill Top, and there I met several people who had known Beatrix Potter: 'She were a gurt walker,' one said. 'Thought nowt on't weather. And nowt on't clothes neither. I've seen th'owd girl wi' a bit o' sack for a shawl agin't blizzard.' 'Aye,' said another, 'and I'll tell thee summat else. If thee were a tramp, and knocked on't door o' Hill Top, the servant had orders to gie thee a sup o' tea and a silver coin. And didn't the tramps know it!' In the land of the Herdwicks, the land of her fathers, Beatrix Potter is still overshadowed by Mrs Heelis: 'Books? Aye, she wrote books all right. But we thought more on't when she took to 'Erdwicks. She were a gurt one wi' sheep, were owd Mrs 'Eelis.' This self-taught farmer died at the age of seventy-seven on 22 December 1943. Almost her last conscious act was to send a hogmanay greeting to the shepherd who for sixteen years had come down from Scotland to help at lambing time: 'Dear Joe Moscrop.... Still some strength in me. I write a line to shake you by the hand, our friendship has been entirely pleasant. I am very ill with bronchitis. With best wishes for the New Year....' The last things she saw on earth were her husband and, behind him, through the window, her fells: 'Sorrows of yesterday,' she once wrote, 'and today and tomorrow ... the vastness of the fells covers' all with a mantle of peace.'

We may regret that Beatrix Potter did not write about farms, but one cannot do everything. If she *had* written about them, it is probable that she would not have written about rabbits. Her contemporary, Miss Flora Thompson, did write about farms (which may explain why she did not write about rabbits). Her portrait of country life, *Lark Rise to Candleford*, neither dilutes what was evil nor exaggerates what was good. Commenting on the rarity of illness among farmfolk, she added: 'The healthy open-air life and the abundance of coarse but wholesome food must have been largely responsible for that; but the lack of imagi-nation may also have played a part. Such people at that time did not look for or expect illness, and there were not so many patent medicine advertisements then as now to teach them to search for symptoms of minor ailments. . . .' Nature is more amazing than what we call the marvels of science: 'Toothbrushes were not in general use; few could afford to buy such luxuries; but the women took a pride in their strong white teeth and cleaned them with a scrap of clean, wet rag, dipped in salt.' Nearly every Vic-torian and Edwardian farmhouse employed domestic help: ' "Everybody who was anybody" as they used to say, kept a maid in those days—stud grooms' wives, village schoolmasters' wives, and, of course, inn-keepers' and shop-keepers' wives. Even the wives of carpenters and masons paid a girl sixpence to clean knives and boots and take out the children on Saturday.' The farmer and his men could, if they wished, read good books. True, they had no mobile libraries, but they did have public libraries and many more village literary institutes than exist today: 'Modern writers,' said Flora Thompson, 'who speak of the book-lessness of the poor at that time must mean books as possessions; there were always books to borrow.' Although the farmer and his men continued to be sacrificed on the altar of manufactured goods, they remained loyal to their calling while it supported them. Like Richard Jefferies, Miss Thompson emphasized the conflict: 'there was nothing wrong with their work, as work, the men agreed. It was a man's life, and they laughed scornfully at the occupations of some who looked down upon them; but the wages were ridiculously low and the farm labourer was so looked down on and slighted that the day was soon to come when a country boy leaving school would look for any other way of earn-ing a living than on the land.'

Modern farmhouses suffer much noise. Aircraft boom and roar overhead; cars create a continual cacophony; tractors, blow-lamps and power-saws increase the din. One sound, however, has almost vanished from the English scene, though Miss Thompson was born to its gaiety: 'Most of the men sang or whistled as they dug or hoed. There was a good deal of outdoor singing in those years.

Workmen sang at their jobs; men with horses and carts sang as they went from door to door; the baker, the miller's man, and the fish-hawker sang; even the doctor and the parson on their rounds hummed a tune. People were poorer and had not the comforts, amusements, or knowledge we have today; but they were happier. Which seems to suggest that happiness depends more upon state of mind—and body, perhaps—than upon circumstances and events.' When Thoreau was living quietly in the country a neighbour enquired what he thought of the trans-Atlantic cable that would soon enable men to speak with one another across vast distances. Thoreau was unimpressed. 'Surely,' his neighbour persisted, 'the new invention is an important thing?' Thoreau replied: 'The important thing is, not *whether* men speak, but what they say.' The modern English farmhouse must endure many kinds of evil communications. 'No man,' said Donne, 'is an island.' Even the remotest English farm is now a continent—a world of continents—and must therefore bear the burden of Atlas, starting with a breakfast bulletin, and ending with the late night summary. Only by a miraculous balance between receptivity and immunity can the farmer keep abreast of events without being swamped by them, or numbed into a coma of couldn't-care-less. It is therefore good that England should be steadied by a national network of havens which are too busy ever to brood on the storm that broke yesterday, and may—or may not—recur tomorrow. The farmhouse retains whatever was best in the past; it adopts whatever is best in the present; and then it combines them in a way which enhances both. The mud-filled yard becomes a concrete pavement; electric light outshines oil lamps; earth closets pull the plug; and the hip-bath is a water-trough. Yet logs still blaze in a cavernous hearth; rafters still shine like ebony; flagstones still cool the kitchen in summer; cocks still rouse the house in winter.

Of all our English homes, the farmer's is the slowest to accept change; and having accepted it, is the least disturbed. 'One generation passeth away,' says the Bible, 'and another generation cometh, but the earth abideth forever.' Seedtime and harvest, milking and mowing, hedging and ditching, dipping and shearing: though he ploughs by tractor, and motors to market, a farmer still quizzes the sky, still wakes betimes, and is asleep before the townsfolk have returned from the cinema. Virgil summed it up, two thousand years ago. Town life, he said, is always in a hurry, but the farmer walks with the seasons: *O fortunatos agricolas*, O happy husbandmen!

Cley-next-the Sea / Windmill, Norfolk

11 A Mixed bag

UNLIKE the French, who have no word for 'home', the
English improvise on that theme, more variously than any
other nation. From our Anglo-Saxon ancestors we inherit
'homely', 'homecoming', 'homestead', 'homeward'. The phrase
'home-bred' was first recorded in 1587; 'homespun', in 1590;
'homekeeping', in 1591; 'homeward-bound', in 1602; 'homeless', in
1615; 'homeland', in 1670; 'homesick', in 1795; 'homelike', in 1817.
For centuries the boys of Winchester College have greeted the end
of term with a song, *Dulce domum* or *Sweet home*. In our own day
Hilaire Belloc gave thanks whenever he returned to his house:

> Here am I homeward from my wandering,
> Here am I homeward and my heart is healed.

The Englishman's modern home is more comfortable and more
hygienic than ever before. It is also uglier than ever before; more
expensive than ever before; more crammed with ersatz or
counterfeit material, from imitation leather to plastic wood. It

N

wears the faceless identity of the mid-twentieth century. It is the outward and visible sign of an inward and spiritual void. And it begins to disintegrate before the owner has paid the first year's mortgage.

Confronted by shoddy material and bad workmanship, some people have chosen to live in a building that was raised when good workmanship and sound material were taken for granted; as, for example, at Limington village school in Somerset, which was built in 1834, and in 1972 was sold for £1,500 to an elderly couple who converted it into a home with three bedrooms, two living rooms, a bathroom and a sun loggia. In that same year and county, the church of St James at East Cranmore was sold on condition that the owner neither opened nor disturbed the churchyard tomb of the Pagets of Cranmore Hall. At Christmas Common in the Oxfordshire Chilterns a dissenting chapel has for decades been a cottage. Railway stations, too, feel the pinch of Progress. During the 1960s a station on the line between Aylesbury and Princes Risborough in Buckinghamshire was converted into a cottage. A few years later, in Westmorland, I watched the conversion of Ravenstonedale Station, and very attractive it looked, with Ladies and Gentlemen adjacent, and the platform as a rock garden.

At Gazeley in Suffolk the old brick mill became a private house in 1947. During the 1930s Mr Peter Scott, the painter-naturalist, occupied a lighthouse beside the River Nene where it enters the Wash. A famous golfer, Mr Henry Longhurst, made his home in a Sussex windmill; and another wise man did the same at Turville in Buckinghamshire. During the 1920s there was a rush to buy old railway coaches and to convert them as bungalows (one of them can still be seen in the Buckinghamshire village of Prestwood). They made snug homes, at a time when conveniences were less modern than they are now.

Some householders pay only a nominal rent for their home, like the Dukes of Wellington, who, on the anniversary of the Battle of Waterloo, present to the Sovereign a miniature tricolour as quitrent for the mansion of Stratfield Saye near Reading in Berkshire, which the nation gave to the first Duke of Wellington when he defeated Napoleon. The Duke of Marlborough was granted Blenheim Palace on a quit-rent of a white silk flag, decorated with three fleurs-de-lys, to be submitted every year on August 13, the anniversary of the Battle of Blenheim. Wyfold Court, near Henley-on-Thames in Oxfordshire, was granted on condition that the owner and his heirs or successors handed a red rose to the Sovereign whenever he or she passed by (which they very seldom did).

Families whose windows rattle during a gale may console themselves by sharing the annoyance with Lord Clive, who in 1772 rebuilt Vanbrugh's mansion of Claremont near Esher in Surrey. It is unlikely, however, that any modern family will share Lord Clive's remedy, which was to wedge the windows with guineas (his housemaids then pocketed the wedges, and prayed for another gale). When Lord Alfred Paget stayed at Claremont he confronted another sort of annoyance, for the guinea-glad housemaids kept a fireguard permanently in front of every hearth. 'Whenever he came into his room,' said Kilvert, 'the fire-guard was sure to be on. He tried to hide it in every corner of the room, but the housemaid always found it and put it on again. One day Lord Alfred was found on his knees to the great surprise of one of his friends who came in suddenly, for it was not a posture which was familiar to Lord Alfred. But it was discovered that he was striving to put away the fire-guard into his portmanteau and so effectually hide it from the careful search of the housemaid.'

The baptism of an Englishman's home is relatively new and in many places already obsolescent. 'Shangri-la' and 'The Laurels' are being replaced by '1999 the Housing Estate' and 'Block E Wing 8 Flat 13'. A good deal of ingenuity went to the naming of houses. A man who lived in Hat Street named his house Tophat; another, who suffered at the hands of incompetent builders, named his house ODTAA which being translated meant One Damned Thing After Another. Some names commemorate a merger, as when a Mr Pink, having married a Miss Lily, set up as publican near Loosley Row in Buckinghamshire, and called his tavern The Pink and Lily (Rupert Brooke used to stay there). One or two people have identified their premises pictorially, like the Bedfordshire blacksmith at Biggleswade, who in 1840 made and erected a weathervane showing one of the new steam threshing machines whose repair was a source of profit to him (a replica of the vane may be seen in Bedford Modern School Museum).

The owner of a garage at Patcham in Sussex erected a weather-vane showing a policeman halting a speeding motorist. In 1929 the winner of several Stock Exchange walking races from London to Brighton was presented with a vane showing the stride of a long distance walker. Oxburgh Hall, for five centuries the Norfolk seat of the Bedingfield family, has a vane (c. 1660) showing the arms of the Pastons; Lady Bedingfield at that time being the former Margaret Paston.

'An Englishman's home is his castle'; the saying is old indeed. Four centuries ago it was known to Sir Edward Coke, the jurist, who declared: 'A man's house is his castle.' Sir Edward did not imply that the Law had no right to enter a man's house, but rather that the Law favoured the privacy of a man's house; a point which John Ray's *Compleat Collection of English Proverbs* emphasized in 1670: 'This is a kind of Law Proverb, "*Jura publica favent privata domus*".' When the Law did *not* favour the privacy of his house, one Victorian Englishman—Lord Harborough—defended himself by means of artillery. The attack had been launched by a clique of financiers who believed that everyone (themselves especially) would become richer if a railway from Leicester to Peterborough were to invade Lord Harborough's estate of Stapleford Park. The financiers' Parliamentary friends therefore passed a Bill authorizing the invasion; whereupon Lord Harborough armed and mustered his servants, and drove off the invaders. When the police arrived they received an equally warm reception. Indeed, such hard knocks were exchanged that the financiers demanded that the Army be sent to overawe the peer, who replied by displaying a brass cannon which had been brought from his yacht. After more blood and blows, the Government surrendered, and the Midland Railway withdrew and was compelled to build a detour until, forty years later, a less resolute and more mercenary occupant of Stapleford Park was paid to allow the trains to pass closer to his house. The number of strangers who may now legally enter an Englishman's home is so numerous that only a lawyer can count them. Meter-readers, weed-inspectors, sanitary inspectors, Post Office engineers, final demanders, income taxers, excisemen ... the list is legion; and no doubt the country would become disordered without them.

Why does a house or a piece of land need to be formally 'conveyed' from seller to buyer? The simplest answer is also the most obvious ... in order that the buyer may prove his title or ownership. Until relatively recent times the purchase of a freehold was both intricate and costly, being based on the medieval Common Law which conveyed land by means of *feoffment* (that is, the gift of a *fief* or freehold), followed by what the lawyers call delivery of possession. In 1875 the Land Transfer Act de-feudalized the procedure by entering the sale in an official register, by examining the relevant deeds, and, if the deeds were valid, by granting a land certificate to the new owner. Later statutes, such as the Law of Property Act 1922, further simplified the conveyance and lessened its cost.

At the beginning of the twentieth century most Englishmen did not own the house they occupied; by the end of the century most of them *will* own the house they occupy. The credit for that change belongs to—and, in another sense, was largely supplied by—the building societies, an English invention, first recorded *c.* 1775 when a group of Birmingham people paid a small monthly sum to a society which not only purchased land but also built houses. When every subscriber had moved into his new home, the society dissolved itself, whence the name 'terminating building society' as opposed to the later 'permanent building society' which merely borrowed and lent money, without acquiring land or erecting houses. In 1836 the first Building Societies Act put every such society on a footing with the Friendly Societies, binding all members to obey its rules, and vesting the society's property with trustees. The Building Societies Act of 1874 remains the basis of present practice whereby societies become corporate bodies with full legal powers, rather like a limited company. By the middle of the twentieth century it was apparent that home-ownership had ceased to be a privilege of the few. In 1919, for example, the total assets of all British building societies were £77 million; in 1939 they were £773 million. One hopes that our building societies will continue to prosper, for the man who owns a bit of England can feel as proud as the tycoons who own large chunks of it. Such a man enriches and refreshes himself by indulging (to quote Abraham Cowley again) 'that pleasantest of human industry, the improvement of something which we call our own'. And if he has children or grandchildren to succeed him, then his foresight will be doubly rewarded by knowing, as Wordsworth knew, that 'what we have loved, others will love'.

A home, we agreed, includes the family and the fittings in a house, and the people and the places round about. All those attributes have changed ceaselessly down the centuries, yet remained recognizable because they symbolized a way of life and a code of conduct which scarcely changed at all. Moreover, a home may withstand the loss of several attributes, for death and poverty and new environment do not necessarily change the way of life; but when the way itself is changed, then the home changes also, even though its fittings and family remain the same. That is what happened during the second half of the twentieth century. Within a single generation the effects of transport and communication, which hitherto had touched only a minority, swamped the entire nation. At the beginning of the century many Englishmen were still what Gilbert White described as 'stationary men', living and working in a relatively small area. Their fathers could remember John Smeaton, architect of the third Eddystone lighthouse, who was born and died at Austhorpe Lodge near Leeds in Yorkshire; and for nearly seventy years lived there, returning whenever he had fulfilled an engineering project. Francis Kilvert died less than a century ago, yet his diary mentioned villagers whose notion of geography was as restricted as their experience of travel: 'There is a general belief among Clyro and Langley people that I cannot travel from Radnorshire to Wiltshire without going over the sea.' In the village of my boyhood the majority of elderly cottagers had never been to London; of those who had, not a few vowed never to go there again. When I assured a census official that I had occupied the same house for thirty-three years he stared as though I were Methuselah. The Industrial Revolution banished millions of Englishmen from their native soil, forcing them to set root in bricks and mortar. The Technological Revolution now uproots them every few years. But such rootlessness is incompatible with home life, which requires long residence. Five years are not enough; ten hardly suffice; twenty achieve both a *de facto* and a *de jure* allegiance.

As for a code of conduct, we must remember that until the middle of the twentieth century most Englishmen assumed that their marriage would be lifelong. Despite manifold defects and hypocrisies, there was a kind of permanence about family life. Men and women repaired it, as they repaired the fabric of their house. Today, by contrast, many people leave home when the first crack appears, so that their children regard the dissolution as a legitimate escape from the hard road toward personal maturity. Some women have abdicated their position of prime importance as mothers and home-makers. They believe that the rearing of happy and therefore healthy children is not, after all, a whole-time occupation, but simply a hobby to be combined with more liberating activities, such as work in an office or a factory. Men, too, have changed their domestic way of life. All sorts and conditions of them now use their home as a dormitory which they never see by daylight during the working days of winter. Their summer evenings and spring weekends are taken up by a race to the sea or to the nearest car-crammed countryside. The long winter nights are shared in communal solitude gaping at television. The record-holding commuter in 1972 was a Mr Ernest Lawrence, who travelled 1,220 miles each week between his house at Swanage and his office at London. He left home at 5.55 a.m., and returned at 9.10 p.m. In other words, his waking home-life lasted for about half an hour each day.

This new way of technological life has made man's future less foreseeable than ever before. It may ultimately obliterate his future. Nevertheless, the human race is resilient, and a small part of it not wholly devoid of common sense. For a time, no doubt, our great-grandchildren will spend their six non-working days in dashing about the face of the earth; but when they have nearly killed themselves and everyone else in cars and aircraft they may decide to learn to walk. If they do so decide, they may once again pass the greater part of their lives in the same home; travelling indeed, for the enrichment of those lives, yet returning with affection to what Fynes Moryson called 'the same walls, the same faces, the same orchards, pastures and objects of the eye'. So, in the end, England may recover the wisdom of Kipling:

> God gives to men all earth to love,
> But, since man's heart is small,
> Ordains for each, one spot shall prove
> Beloved over all.

Poetry is a prerogative of the few; but love belongs to all. When each encompasses the other, both embrace mankind. Perhaps it is fitting that the most beautiful description of English domesticity was conceived by a woman, Dorothy Wordsworth: 'It calls home the heart to quietness.'

Index